T0327271

"Doug O'Donnell is becoming one of the most edifying pastors of our time. I heartily recommend this wise and winsome set of comments on a biblical book beloved by many Christians through the ages but sorely neglected in the present. May God use this commentary to renew the courage of pastors in preaching the Song of Solomon once again."

Douglas A. Sweeney, Professor of Church History and the History of Christian Thought, Director of the Jonathan Edwards Center, Trinity Evangelical Divinity School

"The wisest man this side of the incarnate Christ, inspired by the Holy Spirit, on a topic that always grabs attention, in poetry, in the Bible—could it get any better than the Song of Songs? You won't want to miss Doug O'Donnell's exposition of the most sublime song."

Jim Hamilton, Assistant Professor of Biblical Studies, The Southern Baptist Theological Seminary; author, *God's Glory in Salvation through Judgment*

"Song of Solomon is a delicate portion of Scripture, and Christians in our sex-crazed culture desperately need a biblical perspective on love and intimacy. Doug O'Donnell is a thoughtful, knowledgeable, reliable guide to this seldom-preached book. O'Donnell is himself a poet and scholar, sensitive to both the art and academic rigors of Solomon's Song. He hits the mark of being exegetically accurate, thoroughly canonical, and boldly Christological."

James A. Johnston, Senior Pastor, Tulsa Bible Church, Tulsa, Oklahoma

"These days the Song of Solomon is often treated on the one hand as merely a manual of practical teaching about sex and relationships that says nothing about Christ or, on the other hand, as a picture of the relationship between Christ and the church that says nothing to the marriages of ordinary men and women. Doug O'Donnell has given us a masterful exposition that unfolds the book's very real wisdom for human relationships in a way that constantly and without allegory points us to the gospel. Highly recommended!"

Iain Duguid, Professor of Old Testament, Grove City College; author, *Numbers* (Preaching the Word)

"It is a rare commentary that stirs the emotions. But then it makes sense that a commentary that ably presents the Song of Solomon would lead the reader not only to think deeply, but also to feel deeply and to worship whole-heartedly. O'Donnell's insights are fresh, clear, and personal, equipping readers to communicate the love of Christ for his bride from this ancient book in a compelling way."

Nancy Guthrie, author, Seeing Jesus in the Old Testament Bible study series

"Our culture treats sex as an idol and the church often treats it as a taboo, rarely talking about it. This situation is a formula for disaster. We need more preaching and teaching in our churches, and the Song of Songs is an essential biblical resource that God has given us to lead us toward a godly theology and holy practice of sexuality. Doug O'Donnell has given us a profound, rich, and witty reflection on the Song that will encourage depth of understanding and motivation for right thinking and behavior. I recommend this book enthusiastically for everyone, but particularly for those who preach and teach the book in a church context."

> **Tremper Longman III,** Robert H. Gundry Professor of Biblical Studies, Westmont College

"Doug O'Donnell unfolds the Song of Solomon with personal and pastoral delight—and with attention to the poetic text and the biblical context. Into his exposition are woven warm-hearted exhortations, rich literary allusions, and a great deal of wit. This volume helps us celebrate the Bible's celebration of married love."

> **Kathleen B. Nielson,** Director of Women's Initiatives, The Gospel Coalition; author and speaker, *Living Word Bible studies*

"Simply brilliant! This is the book on the Song of Solomon I've been waiting for—funny, moving, powerful, provocative, rigorously faithful to the text, and utterly Christ-centered. Doug O'Donnell explains and applies this trickiest of books in a way which is always fresh, responsible, and captivating. As you read, you will be delighted and deeply challenged, and you will gasp at the incredible intimacy which God gives to his people, both in marriage and in knowing him forever. I know of no more helpful work on the Song of Solomon."

> **J. Gary Millar,** Principal, Queensland Theological College; author, *Now Choose Life*

"How absolutely refreshing, challenging, and affirming is Pastor O'Donnell's in-depth study of this love song—this Middle Eastern, centuries-old, wedding song celebrating the truly free love between a man and a woman in marriage. It is God's provision to sustain loving marriages and renew loveless ones. This Song was written to give wisdom to the unmarried to wait and to give the married the wisdom to warm up to each other again and again. Pastor O'Donnell lays down his own soul and writes in places, not only expositorily but also experientially, and the reader gasps. Here is a man who is as tender and as bold as the author of the Song of Songs. So with testimony and Biblical insight we are wonderfully led to the gospel, to God-breathed love that changes everything."

> **Wendell Hawley,** Pastor emeritus, College Church, Wheaton, Illinois; author, *A Pastor Prays for His People*

"Douglas O'Donnell has a special gift in integrating careful exegesis, poetic sensitivity, theological reflection, and relevant application, all seasoned with vivid language and winsome humor. His commentary on the Song of Solomon opens up the richness of this delightful book, which unfortunately is too little preached and too little understood today."

> **Daniel J. Estes,** Distinguished Professor of Old Testament, Cedarville University

THE SONG OF SOLOMON

PREACHING THE WORD
Edited by R. Kent Hughes

(((PREACHING *the* WORD)))

THE SONG OF SOLOMON

An INVITATION *to* INTIMACY

DOUGLAS SEAN O'DONNELL

R. Kent Hughes
Series Editor

:: CROSSWAY®

WHEATON, ILLINOIS

Song of Solomon

Copyright © 2012 by Douglas Sean O'Donnell

Published by Crossway
    1300 Crescent Street
    Wheaton, Illinois 60187

Cover illustration: Jon McGrath, Simplicated Studio

Cover image: Adam Greene, illustrator

First printing 2012

Printed in China

Unless otherwise indicated, Scripture quotations are from the ESV® Bible (*The Holy Bible, English Standard Version*®), copyright © 2001 by Crossway. Used by permission. All rights reserved.

Scripture quotations marked KJV are from the *King James Version* of the Bible.

Scripture quotations marked MESSAGE are from *The Message*. Copyright © by Eugene H. Peterson 1993, 1994, 1995, 1996, 2000, 2001, 2002. Used by permission of NavPress Publishing Group.

Scripture references marked NEB are from *The New English Bible* © The Delegates of the Oxford University Press and The Syndics of the Cambridge University Press, 1961, 1970.

Scripture references marked NIV are taken from The Holy Bible, New International Version®, NIV®. Copyright © 1973, 1978, 1984, 2011 by Biblica, Inc.™ Used by permission. All rights reserved worldwide.

All emphases in Scripture quotations have been added by the author.

ISBN-13: 978-1-4335-2338-0
ISBN-10: 1-4335-2338-8
PDF ISBN: 978-1-4335-2346-5
Mobipocket ISBN: 978-1 -4335-2347-2
ePub ISBN: 978-1-4335-2348-9

Library of Congress Cataloging-in-Publication Data

O'Donnell, Douglas Sean, 1972-
    The Song of Solomon : an invitation to intimacy / Douglas Sean O'Donnell.
       p. cm.— (Preaching the Word)
    Includes bibliographical references and index.
    ISBN 978-1-4335-2338-0 (hc)
    1. Bible. O.T. Song of Solomon—Criticism, interpretation, etc. 2. Intimacy (Psychology)—Religious aspects—Christianity. 3. Love—Religious aspects—Christianity. I. Title.
BS1485.6.L66O36   2012
223'.907—dc23   2011049813

Crossway is a publishing ministry of Good News Publishers.

RRDS		34	33	32	31	30	29	28	27	26	25	24
16	15	14	13	12	11	10	9	8	7	6	5	4

To
Emily
my sister, my bride, my friend

Who is that coming up from the wilderness,
leaning on her beloved?

Under the apple tree I awakened you.
There your mother was in labor with you;
there she who bore you was in labor.

Set me as a seal upon your heart,
as a seal upon your arm,
for love is strong as death,
jealousy is fierce as the grave.
Its flashes are flashes of fire,
the very flame of the Lord.
Many waters cannot quench love,
neither can floods drown it.
If a man offered for love
all the wealth of his house,
he would be utterly despised.

SONG OF SOLOMON 8:5–7

Contents

A Word to Those Who
Preach the Word

There are times when I am preaching that I have especially sensed the plea-sure of God. I usually become aware of it through the unnatural silence. The ever-present coughing ceases, and the pews stop creaking, bringing an almost physical quiet to the sanctuary—through which my words sail like arrows. I experience a heightened eloquence, so that the cadence and volume of my voice intensify the truth I am preaching.

There is nothing quite like it—the Holy Spirit filling one's sails, the sense of his pleasure, and the awareness that something is happening among one's hearers. This experience is, of course, not unique, for thousands of preachers have similar experiences, even greater ones.

What has happened when this takes place? How do we account for this sense of his smile? The answer for me has come from the ancient rhetorical categories of *logos*, *ethos*, and *pathos*.

The first reason for his smile is the *logos*—in terms of preaching, God's Word. This means that as we stand before God's people to proclaim his Word, we have done our homework. We have exegeted the passage, mined the significance of its words in their context, and applied sound hermeneutical principles in interpreting the text so that we understand what its words meant to its hearers. And it means that we have labored long until we can express in a sentence what the theme of the text is—so that our outline springs from the text. Then our preparation will be such that as we preach, we will not be preaching our own thoughts about God's Word, but God's actual Word, his *logos*. This is fundamental to pleasing him in preaching.

The second element in knowing God's smile in preaching is *ethos*—what you are as a person. There is a danger endemic to preaching, which is having your hands and heart cauterized by holy things. Phillips Brooks illustrated it by the analogy of a train conductor who comes to believe that he has been to the places he announces because of his long and loud heralding of them. And that is why Brooks insisted that preaching must be "the bringing of truth through personality." Though we can never perfectly embody the truth we preach, we must be subject to it, long for it, and make it as much a part of our ethos as possible. As the Puritan William Ames said, "Next to the Scriptures, nothing makes a sermon more to pierce, than when it comes out of the inward affection of the heart without any affectation." When a preacher's *ethos* backs up his *logos*, there will be the pleasure of God.

Last, there is *pathos*—personal passion and conviction. David Hume, the Scottish philosopher and skeptic, was once challenged as he was seen going to hear George Whitefield preach: "I thought you do not believe in the gospel." Hume replied, "I don't, but he does." Just so! When a preacher believes what he preaches, there will be passion. And this belief and requisite passion will know the smile of God.

The pleasure of God is a matter of *logos* (the Word), *ethos* (what you are), and *pathos* (your passion). As you preach the Word may you experience his smile—the Holy Spirit in your sails!

R. Kent Hughes

Preface

When Kent Hughes asked me to write this commentary, I had mixed feelings. I was, of course, very honored. What an honor to be a part of the Preaching the Word series, and what an honor to be trusted with this tricky text and its touchy themes. But I was also humbled. For how does one preach through a book in which every section raises structural questions, every phrase has philological complexities, and every verse contains metaphors that leap like seven young stags in seven different directions (metaphorically speaking, of course)? And how does one show the bones of a text (poetic structure, parallelisms, etc.), yet leave enough flesh for the text to remain warm and stay alive? At times I wished I'd been assigned a more scientific commentary, where I could dissect, to the best of my ability, each exegetical issue; other times I wished I'd been given a brush and paint (God knows I can't paint, but if I could) and had been asked to capture the essence of each beautiful scene. But in the end I have done all I could do. Lord willing, I have mixed science with art adequately enough for you to hear something of each individual note without losing the cadence, tune, and voice of Solomon's greatest song.

The extensive endnotes were necessary, I felt, both to explain more fully how and why I reached my conclusions and to acknowledge the scholars whose shoulders I gratefully and gleefully climbed upon to complete this work. Obviously the men cited most often are those I deemed most helpful. Buy their work. Support their labors.

I would be remiss if I did not thank Emily Gerdts for her proofreading and formatting of the manuscript and Matt Newkirk for his careful and skillful editing of it. I also thank New Covenant Church for eagerly receiving the Word of God opened and taught each week. These sermons were a joy to preach to you!

Lastly but firstly, I acknowledge my dear wife, Emily. This book is not dedicated to you out of necessity (who else does a married man dedicate a commentary on the Song of Solomon to but his wife?), but out of sincere and deep love. I am both honored and humbled to be your husband.

Douglas O'Donnell
St. Valentine's Day, 2011

1

Understandest Thou What Thou Readest?

THE SONG OF SOLOMON 1:1

The Song of Songs, which is Solomon's.

1:1

UNDERSTANDEST THOU WHAT THOU READEST? is the King James version of Acts 8:30b.

Acts 8:26–39 tells the story of the conversion of the Ethiopian eunuch. In the middle of that story, the evangelist Philip overhears this man reading from the prophet Isaiah:

> Like a sheep he was led to the slaughter
> and like a lamb before its shearer is silent,
> so he opens not his mouth.
> In his humiliation justice was denied him.
> Who can describe his generation?
> For his life is taken away from the earth. (Acts 8:32, 33, quoting
> Isaiah 53:7, 8)

Philip asked him, "Do you understand what you are reading?" (v. 30), or as the King James Version phrases it, "Understandest thou what thou readest?" The eunuch replied, "How can I, unless someone guides me?"[1]

Like the book of Isaiah, the Song of Solomon (or the Song of Songs, as I will call it throughout this commentary) can be a difficult book to comprehend. The ninth-century Jewish rabbi Saadia likened the Song to "a lock for which the key had been lost."[2] The nineteenth-century German Lutheran

Hebraist Franz Delitzsch wrote, "The *Song* is the most obscure book of the Old Testament. Whatever principle of interpretation one may adopt, there always remains a number of inexplicable passages."[3] More recently, Marvin Pope comments, "[N]o composition of comparable size in world literature has provoked and inspired such a volume and variety of comment and interpretation as the biblical Song of Songs."[4] Daniel Estes adds, "Scholars vary widely on nearly every part of its interpretation. . . . Virtually every verse presents challenges in text, philology, image, grammar or structure."[5]

My favorite example of perspicuity angst comes from Christopher W. Mitchell, who begins his commentary, published in 2003, by reviewing the history of his study of the Song: "My fascination with the Song of Songs began in 1978 . . . when I took a graduate class on its Hebrew text at the University of Wisconsin—Madison. That fascination grew under the tutelage of my doctoral advisor, Professor Michael V. Fox." Mitchell goes on to talk about how he has read commentaries and articles, preached and taught, and since 1992 worked earnestly on his 1,300-page commentary on the Song. He has worked almost thirty years on the Song, but then he writes in his preface about his desire to spend another decade to "delve more deeply into . . . this most difficult book of sacred Scripture."[6]

Scholars who disagree on much of the Song all agree it's a tough text. Thus the need for a guide to uncoil its complexities, solve its riddles, and find that lost key to unlock its door. In this first study I seek to offer some basic directions to help us navigate through the often dark (but so beautiful) waters of Solomon's Song. By means of setting four guideposts in place, I hope to open God's Word, as Philip did, and "beginning with this Scripture," teach you "the good news about Jesus" (Acts 8:35), revealing to you something of the meaning of the "mystery" of marriage (Ephesians 5:32).

Guidepost One: This Is a Song . . .

We start with the first guidepost: *This is a song.*

Our text begins, "The Song . . ." (1:1a). The significance of this simple observation is that it identifies the genre. This is not a letter, gospel, law book, prophecy, or apocalyptic revelation. This is a song. And a song (this is what I've learned after many years of study) is written to be sung. (Aren't you glad I'm your guide?)

Perhaps this Song was originally written to be sung during the seven-day marriage festival.[7] We know that Israelite wedding celebrations lasted this long from Genesis 29:27 and Judges 14:12 and from extra-Biblical Jewish history; and we know from Jeremiah that singing was part of these festivities—"the voice of mirth and the voice of gladness, the voice of the bridegroom and the voice of the bride" (Jeremiah 7:34).[8]

Thus, following the lead of Duane Garrett,[9] I envision the following scenario: Just as there were professional singers and musicians for temple worship (e.g., 2 Chronicles 29:28), so I envision professional singers and musicians poised to sing and play for these week-long weddings. And each day as the bride and groom come out of their chambers, the wine is served, the music begins, and the singers sing. The soprano starts, "Let him kiss me with the kisses of his mouth! For your love is better than wine" (1:2). Then, over the sweet strum of the harp, the tenor softly serenades, "Behold, you are beautiful, my love" (1:15). And throughout the song, as the soprano and tenor call back and forth, from time to time other voices join in—like a chorus in a Greek play or a choir in an oratorio. These voices are comprised of the young maidens, "the daughters of Jerusalem" as our text calls them.

That's what I envision day after day for *seven* days, a *perfect* celebration of the new creation of man and wife as one. Whether or not you envision precisely what I envision matters little. What matters most is that you see the Song as a song, which means music and singing and implies some sort of public celebration.

This also means that this song is not primarily intended to be preached in church or taught in a classroom, but to be sung; and the fact that we don't sing it (or some paraphrase of it) is only to our shame. This is a God-inspired love song! So I suggest we start some new traditions. Let's write songs about the Song. Let's sing those songs at Christian weddings. Let's sing them during the reception. Let's sing them as the couple is whisked away to their honeymoon. Let's follow them to the hotel and serenade them for seven days! This is a song!

Furthermore, when you think *song* you must think *poem* or *lyric poetry*. "This is a song" is the same as saying, "This is a poem set to music." This is obvious everywhere,[10] even in the first verse. Our song begins with a poetic device called consonance: "The Song of Songs, which is Solomon's." Do you hear the repeated *s* sound in the initial consonants: Song . . . Songs . . . Solomon. In Hebrew, a similar *sh* sound is heard: s̲h̲ir has̲h̲irim as̲h̲er lis̲h̲lomoh.[11]

Herein the potential danger lies. We can read and teach the Song, forgetting or neglecting its poetry and quickly run from alliterations to applications. The cry for practical propositions beckons the preacher. It is important that we learn real-life lessons from each poetic pericope. But it is likewise important (nay, necessary) to first understand and feel the power and play of words, what only poetry can do to the human heart and imagination. For there is a difference between saying,

> She walks in beauty, like the night
> Of cloudless climes and starry skies;
> And all that's best of dark and bright
> Meet in her aspect and her eyes.
> Thus mellowed to that tender light
> Which heaven to gaudy day denies.[12]

and saying,

> A woman in a black dress with shiny beads looked pretty when she walked by.

There's a difference between saying,

> Pease porridge hot, pease porridge cold,
> Pease porridge in the pot, nine days old;
> Some like it hot, some like it cold,
> Some like it in the pot, nine days old.

and saying,

> If the pea pudding has been in the pot for nine days, no thanks, I'll pass.[13]

If you turn that simple nursery rhyme into a statement, it loses its punch. Take the poetic structure out—8 syllables, 9 syllables, 8 syllables, 9 syllables—the poetic devices—alliteration (the *p*-words), assonance (the *o*-sound), and the rhyme scheme (hot/pot . . . cold/old)—and you take away the point of the poem: to make you laugh.

The Song of Songs is a song. Thus, as we study each poetic section, I will ask, what is the poetry doing? And together we will try to feel the poetry before we act upon its message.[14] I'll ask you, in a sense (and with your senses), to *smell* the myrrh, frankincense, and aloes, to *touch* the polished ivory, to *taste* the wine and apples, to *hear* the flowing streams, to *see* the gazelles leaping over the mountains . . . yes, to feel the flashes of fire, the very flame of the Lord.

Guidepost Two: . . . a Song about Human Love

That's the first guidepost: this is a song. Here's the second guidepost: this is a song *about human love set in the context of marriage.*

I'll deal with the second part of that sentence first. I've already said that this is a wedding song (also called an epithalamium), but let me now defend that claim. We know it's a wedding song from the cultural context—the sexual revolution of the 1960s hadn't yet reached Jerusalem in 960 B.C. In that place and time, there were only two kinds of love: truly free love between a man and a woman in marriage, and sexual slavery, which is found in adultery and fornication.[15]

So we know this is a wedding song from the cultural context (i.e., in Israel only sex within marriage was celebrated), but also from the language of the Song itself. After the word "wedding" is used in 3:11 (as the wedding day of Solomon is used as a foil), the word "bride" is used of the young woman six times in the next seventeen verses, in chapters 4 and 5. This is the heart of the Song, the section that undoubtedly describes sexual relations.[16] Further support for this marriage-song thesis is found in the language of a permanent pledge, such as "set me as a seal upon your heart" (8:6) or "my beloved is mine, and I am his" (2:16a; cf. 7:5; 8:4).[17]

Thus this is a wedding song that is naturally about what weddings celebrate—*human love*. On the back cover of Tom Gledhill's excellent commentary we read these words:

> At first reading the Song of Songs appears to be an unabashed celebration of the deeply rooted urges of physical attraction, mutual love and sexual consummation between a man and a woman. Tom Gledhill maintains that the Song of Songs is in fact just that—a literary, poetic exploration of human love that strongly affirms loyalty, beauty and sexuality in all their variety.

If you didn't know and weren't influenced by the history of the interpretation of the Song and simply read the Song as is, you would likely surmise—with phrases like "kiss me," "his right hand embraces me," "your two breasts are like two fawns," and so on—that this is *erotic* poetry set within the *ethical* limits of the marriage bed.[18] However, the near consensus of both Jewish and Christian interpretation for at least 1,600 years was that the Song of Songs is not about human love (at all), but divine love. That is, it sings of God's love for Israel and/or Christ's love for the Church or the individual Christian soul.

The reason for this seems to be the presupposition that human sexual love is an inappropriate topic for Scripture. Nicholas of Lyra (1270–1349) could speak of the love between a bride and groom as "proper" but not the proper subject of Scripture and thus not of this Song. Such fleshly love even within marriage has, in his words, "a certain dishonorable and improper quality about it."[19] Similarly, Theodoret of Cyrus (c. 393–c. 457) wrote that those who give the Song a "corporeal [fleshly] interpretation" have committed an "awful blasphemy."[20]

This explains why—from Origen of Alexandria to Charles Spurgeon of London, from the medieval mystics to the American Puritans—Christians allegorized every jot and tittle of the Song, each thigh and breast and kiss and consummation. For example, one commentator said that the phrase "while the king was on his couch" (1:12) referred to "the gestation period of Christ in the womb of Mary," and the "sachet of myrrh that lies between [the bride's] breasts" (1:13) symbolizes "Christ in the soul of the believer, who lies between the great commands to love God and one's neighbor."[21] Those allegories are orthodox (and certainly Christ centered and thus edifying), but they are also exegetically absurd[22] and potentially theologically dangerous.

It is dangerous when Christian commentators, theologians, and pastors think there is a radical dichotomy between the sacred and the secular—praying is sacred; kissing is secular. When we believe that sexuality is the antithesis of spirituality, and that there is a great chasm between *eros* and *agape,*[23] we are in danger of losing not only our witness to the world—"What? Your religion has nothing to say about sex except that it is bad?"[24]—but also vital tenets of the Christian faith—the incarnation (John 1:1, 14), the bodily resurrection (1 Corinthians 6:12–20; 15), and the new heavens and new earth (2 Peter 3:13).

Following Marvin Pope's analogy, I liken the history of interpretation to Hans Christian Andersen's children's tale *The Emperor's New Clothes.*[25] Just as the emperor's ministers and subjects affirmed that he was indeed wearing clothes (when he was not), interpreters kept telling themselves and their readers that the Song is solely about spiritual love (when it's not). But just as a child saw the reality of the situation—the emperor is naked!—so do we see that the characters in the Song are naked. They are naked and unashamed. And today we should share their lack of shame. For the Song is a song that Adam could have sung in the garden when Eve arose miraculously from his side; and it remains a song that we can and should sing in the bedroom, the church, and the marketplace of ideas.

Don't get me wrong here. Its lyrics about tasting and touching are "candid but not crude."[26] They are not prudish, but neither are they immodest. Thus, they are far removed from the sexual anarchy and idiocy of our Top 40 music, as well as the crass love poetry of the ancient Near East. The Song has this beautiful balance: it has adult content, but it is adolescent appropriate. It is not X-rated; it is rated PG—parental (and pastoral) guidance recommended. This Song guides us to see with Scriptural sensibilities that the earth is crammed with Heaven,[27] that the way of a man with a woman is "too wonderful" (Proverbs 30:18, 19), and that marriage is not simply a concession to the necessity of procreation but an affirmation of the beauty, chastity, and sacredness of human love. Amen and amen.

This is a song about human love set in the context of marriage. There you have it. I've pounded that second (sadly necessary) guidepost into place.

Guidepost Three: . . . Found in the Bible

With our second guidepost in place, let me quickly add the third lest we get off course. Just because I think this Song is about human love does not mean I think a-theologically about it, that it has nothing to say about God's love for us or our love for God.

This is not an English poem scribbled on the New York City subway. It is a Hebrew poem, and there is no Hebrew literature of this era that is non-religious. The Song is constructed of imagery that borrows heavily from the rest of the Old Testament. For example, when we read the garden imagery in 4:12—5:1, it's right and natural for us to think of Eden; or when we read about the theme of intoxicating love in 1:2, the command of Proverbs 5:19 to be "intoxicated always in her [a wife's] love" ought to come to mind. This Song of Scripture is saturated with other Scriptural language.

The Song of Songs uses Hebrew words, Hebrew names, Hebrew places, and Hebrew poetic devices *and* has a Hebrew author—"The Song of Songs, which is Solomon's" (1:1). That last word—"Solomon's"—sets this Song within a historical and theological context. So here's the third guidepost: This is a song about human love set in the context of marriage that is *found in the Bible*. What I mean is that the Song of Songs cannot be read properly if it is read outside of its canonical context. We must read its positive marriage imagery in contrast to Israel's unfaithfulness as depicted in the prophets— that while God rejoices over his people as "the bridegroom rejoices over the bride" (Isaiah 62:5), Israel spoils the honeymoon with her spiritual promiscuity and adultery: see the story of Hosea, and read the forthright language of Ezekiel (16:7, 8), Jeremiah (2:2, 19, 20), and Isaiah (54:5–8). And whether we think there are no allusions or a thousand allusions to the Song in the New Testament,[28] we must read it in light of the person and work of Jesus, the very compass of the Christian canon, the one whom John the Baptist calls "the bridegroom" (John 3:29; cf. Matthew 9:14, 15) and Paul our "one husband" (2 Corinthians 11:2), the one whose kingdom and consummation is like a wedding feast (Matthew 22:2; Revelation 19:7).

The Song is a song about human love set in the context of marriage that is *found in the Bible*, and the Bible has as its ultimate reference point Jesus—his birth, life, teachings, miracles, sufferings, death, resurrection, ascension, mediation, and return.

Perhaps an illustration will help you see what I'm saying. If you were to read C. S. Lewis's Chronicles of Narnia, and you didn't know that Lewis was a Christian and used Christian symbolism and parts of the plot of the Bible, then you might never see Aslan, who dies and rises and rules, as a Christ-figure. You might just think he's a lion who talks, a neat character in a nice children's tale. But those who know something about the author and his intentions see more of what he wanted his readers to see—the story beneath the story. You see, the story of Jesus opens our eyes to the subtle details of those Narnian adventures.

Similarly, knowing the story of Jesus opens our eyes to the story of the Song. The love celebrated here has as its source and ultimate illustration Jesus Christ; the loyalty, beauty, and intimacy of human love depicted in this Song point to "that Love that undergirds all of reality and in whose Presence alone all longing can be satisfied."[29]

Therefore, with this third guidepost in place, throughout these studies I will seek, without exaggerating analogies, to be exegetically accurate, thoroughly canonical, and thus "boldly Christological."[30] For I assure you that literary merit and guileless veneration of human sexuality are not the reasons you find love's soft and idyllic voice between Ecclesiastes and Isaiah.

Guidepost Four: . . . Written to Give Us Wisdom

Our fourth and final guidepost is about wisdom. This is a song (guidepost one) about human love (guidepost two) found in the Bible (guidepost three) *written to give us wisdom* (guidepost four).

I say "wisdom" because we can rightly categorize the Song of Songs as Wisdom Literature, thus fitting in with the books of Job, Proverbs, and Ecclesiastes. The most obvious reason I say this is because of 1:1, which reads, "The Song of Songs, which is Solomon's." This is Solomon, the king of Israel, but also the wisest of men, the supreme sage of the Wisdom Literature of the Bible.

In the Christian canon, the order goes Proverbs, Ecclesiastes, and the Song of Songs. Proverbs begins, "The proverbs of Solomon, son of David, king of Israel" (1:1).[31] Ecclesiastes begins, "The words of the Preacher, the son of David, king in Jerusalem" (1:1) = Solomon?[32] Finally, the Song of

Songs starts, "The Song of Songs, which is Solomon's" (1:1). Now, the part translated "which is Solomon's" could indicate:

Dedication: to or for Solomon
Subject matter: about Solomon
Affinity: in the Solomonic literary tradition
Authorship: by Solomon[33]

I take the traditional view,[34] the most natural linguistic view,[35] that Solomon was the author.[36] I take this Song as one of Solomon's 1,005 songs (see 1 Kings 4:32). As the superlative superscription states, the "song of (all) the songs,"[37] it is the very best of all of his prolific songwriting labors.[38]

I also side with the medieval Jewish scholar Rashi that Solomon wrote this Song not in his youth but in his old age[39] and that he did so as an act of contrition. In other words, in view of his idolatrous, polygamous relationships that led his heart away from the Lord (1 Kings 1–11) and away from sexual purity and marital intimacy (it's hard to be truly intimate with 700 wives), he sets himself up as the foil in this Song (as we shall see),[40] and thus he writes this greatest of his songs in a distant "self-deprecating tone"[41] to say to his first readers and to us, "Listen, on this matter of marriage, do as I say, not as I did."[42] Put differently, he says, "Don't emulate my love life. Emulate theirs—this imaginary (or real?) couple. Emulate their simple, monogamous, faithful, passionate love for each other."[43]

That's what I think. But whether you hold this particular view or not,[44] you ought to hold the view that the Song is part of the wisdom corpus,[45] based partly on its association with Solomon, but also on the *wisdom admonition* that functions as a kind of refrain throughout the Song: "I adjure you, O daughters of Jerusalem . . . [do] not stir up or awaken love until it pleases." That refrain is first found in 2:7 and then also in 3:5 and 8:4.

Besides that wisdom admonition, there is another subtle refrain, what I call a *wisdom admission*: "My beloved is mine, and I am his" which is found in various forms in 2:16, 6:3, and 7:10. These two refrains function as a double-sided, serrated key that helps unlock the front door of the Song. They are that important! They are important because they highlight that this is a unified poem, not a collection of random poems pasted together, and because they direct us to the wisdom that Solomon seeks to give to two different groups: the married and the unmarried.

The primary target audience is the unmarried, specifically single young women, "the daughters of Jerusalem." Thrice the refrain begins, "I adjure you, O daughters of Jerusalem."

These "daughters" are the "virgins" mentioned in 1:3 or "the young women" in 2:2.[46] They might be viewed as "bridesmaids,"[47] but they certainly should be understood as young Israelite women (of Jerusalem—Israel's city girls and "local lasses").[48] It addresses women of marriageable age,[49] whose bodies are ripe for sexual love (ages ten to fifteen),[50] who desire marital intimacy but are still unmarried.[51]

These girls are admonished to wait for sexual intimacy. Their bodies are saying "yes." Their instincts for intimacy are saying "yes." Their suitors might even be saying "yes" (or at least "please"). But they are admonished to say "no." The wisdom message to these young women is to wait. Virgins, stay virgins . . . not forever, but for now. Wait for marriage. That's wisdom. That's the simple wisdom offered in this complex book.

Now notice how Solomon artistically does this. The admonition does not come through the voice of a celibate prophet, a learned rabbi, a stern sage, or even a father or mother (as is common in the Wisdom Literature), but through the voice of a newlywed—the bride, a former daughter of Jerusalem herself, one of their peers. This is a book about peer pressure at its Biblical best! Yes, the protagonist in this poem is a young bride.[52] And this newly married woman comes out of her wedding chamber, love scene after love scene (as we shall see), to tell the young ladies, "Wait for this—what I'm enjoying. Wait for this—it's worth it. Cool your passions now, and arouse them later, when it's time." You see, the daughters of Jerusalem who hover around this "poetic drama" (they seem never to leave the scene) are the key to understanding the purpose of this whole wisdom poem.[53]

Let me make this as clear as possible. I'll set this in the context of the Wisdom Literature. The book of Proverbs can be called "a book for boys." The word "son" is used over forty times; the word "daughter" is never used. "My son, stay away from that kind of girl, and don't marry this kind of girl. But marry and save yourself for that girl—Proverbs 31:10–31." That's how the book ends, quite intentionally, for Proverbs is a book for boys. The Song of Songs is a book for girls. And its message to girls is, "patience then passion" or "uncompromised purity now; unquenchable passion then." I'll put it this way: In Proverbs the young lad is told to take a cold shower. In the Song of Songs the young lassie is told to take a cold shower.

However, also in the Song of Songs the married couples (children, close your eyes now)—the newlyweds and not so newlyweds—are told to take a warm shower . . . together. I mean it. God's Word means it. The shower part is optional; the passion part is not. There are two refrains to the Song: one is to the unmarried (young women especially, but also young men); the other is to the married. That second refrain goes like this: "My beloved is mine, and I am his." This addresses mutual compatibility, absolute intimacy—two becoming one.

In an indirect and impressionistic manner, this second wisdom admonition functions as an invitation to intimacy. In Titus 2:3, 4 Paul instructs the older women to "train the young women to love their husbands." Here in the Song, the young woman (the bride) trains the older women to love their husbands. That is, the Song is a like a splash of cold water that some of us old lovers need thrown on our faces. Or, to change metaphors and mix a few from the Song itself, it's like the wind that rekindles a flame that is dying out: "Awake, O north wind . . . come, O south wind! Blow . . ." (4:16)—blow this fizzling spark into an undying flame.

So, the Song asks the Christian couple: How's your love life? Is your wedding bed dead or alive? Is it as cold as a frozen pond in February or as hot as the Florida sand in August? You see, reading, studying, listening to, and feeling the Song of Songs is like attending a wedding and witnessing the ripeness and rightness of young love. This Song is God's provision to sustain loving marriages and renew loveless ones. It is his provision for increased intimacy that reflects the intimacy of Christ's love for the Church, an intimacy that makes the world turn its head to view our marriages and say, "So, that's the gospel. I see it now. Your love—God's love. I get it. What must I do to be made *wise* unto salvation? What must I do to share in that intimacy?"

The Song was written to give us wisdom: to the unmarried, the wisdom to wait; to the married, the wisdom to warm up to each other again . . . and again and again.

My Summary in Sum

We have begun our journey through this difficult book. And as your guide I have put down four guideposts:

1. This is a song
2. About human love
3. Found in the Bible
4. Written to give us wisdom.

Now, I won't ask you yet, "Understandest thou what thou readest?" But I do hope that each step of the way, study after study, your vision of Solomon's Song becomes clearer and clearer.

So, on we journey.

2

Better Than Wine

THE SONG OF SOLOMON 1:2–4

Let him kiss me with the kisses of his mouth!
For your love is better than wine.

1:2

EACH DAY BEFORE SCHOOL, I gather my children for Bible time. I read a short passage from the Bible and then ask them some questions based on it. When I began preparing for this sermon series in the spring of 2010, I read through a number of commentaries. One morning at breakfast Evelyn, my six-year-old at the time, came up to me and asked, "What are you reading?" I said, "A commentary. It's a book that talks about the Bible." Now, in this commentary there was a verse indented from the rest of the text. Evelyn pointed to that verse and said, "Why don't we just read that verse for Bible time?" It was Song 1:4, as translated by Richard S. Hess, the commentator. Here's part of Hess's translation:

> We will indeed rejoice and be happy for you.
> We will indeed recall your *lovemaking* more than wine.[1]

I told Evelyn we would read something else.

Afterward I was just glad she didn't approach me the day before when I was reading Ariel and Chana Bloch's translation of 1:2:

> Kiss me, make me drunk with your kisses![2]

It's hard to explain to my six-year-old daughter how the two things that I will do my best in the next decade to teach her to avoid—kissing boys and comparing such kissing to alcoholic consumption—made it into God's Holy Word, and that they are fitting for *our* Bible time as a church, but not her Bible time as a child.

In this study, as we move from the tame title—"The Song of Songs, which is Solomon's" (1:1)—into the titillating text of 1:2–4, I want you to note that there is "no gradual acclimation" into this Song's theme.[3] The Song does not warm us up to the ideas ahead. Instead it's a baptism by fire. Twentieth-century film director Sam Goldwyn once suggested that "for a successful film you need to start with an earthquake and then work up to the climax!"[4] Well, here's an earthquake of eros.

Let him kiss me with the kisses of his mouth! (1:2a)

That's how it starts! Rupert of Deutz (c. 1075–1129), the medieval Benedictine monk, wrote concerning this verse: "What means this cry, so loud, so startling?"[5] Charles Simeon (1759–1836), the famous vicar of Holy Trinity Church Cambridge, said, "The abruptness with which the poem opens is very remarkable."[6] Indeed it was so very remarkable that first-century Jewish rabbis warned the young men of their congregations not to read the Song until they turned thirty. And Christian preacher Adam Clarke counseled pastors, saying, "I advise all young preachers to avoid preaching on Solomon's Song."[7] This is indeed a delicate and dangerous portion of Scripture. And left to the immature imagination or a godless guide, these inspired words, which were written to make us wise unto salvation—to teach, correct, rebuke, and train us in righteousness (and in *love*!)—could have the opposite effect.

Yes, what a way to start! It's an earthquake of eros. But it's also a "beginning without a beginning," as Bernard of Clairvaux put it.[8] That is, we are introduced to this theme of physical love, but we are not told about the love story. Who is speaking? Who is her man? What is their history? Are they married?

All this is intentional. It's not that their love story is unimportant; rather it's that *the tone* of their love is of primary importance. We will get bits and pieces of their story as the Song unfolds, but here we start with a full-blown flame, a tone that we're to touch. The earth is shaking. The house is on fire. She wants to be kissed—"Let him kiss me" (v. 2)—and she gets more than just his lips: "The king has brought me into his chambers" (v. 4). And then this short opening scene ends with the choir of virgins rising and singing, "We will exult and rejoice . . . in your love," or as Hess puts it, "in your lovemaking." There you have it. Welcome to the Song of Songs. It's the hottest book in the Bible.

What Is the Poetry Doing?

John Milton said that true poetry is "simple, sensuous, and passionate."[9] If so, the Song is certainly true poetry. And this opening poem (1:2–4) is true poetry indeed! In what follows, let me explain this *true* poem and then attempt to *truly* apply it.

The poem begins with a woman's voice. Thus the ESV, like many translations, places "SHE" above vv. 2–4b and then "OTHERS" above v. 4cde. We know it is a woman talking about a man from the gender of the words used—"Let *him* kiss me with . . . *his* mouth." The speaker of verses 2–4b later describes herself with the feminine adjectives in verse 5, confirming that it is a woman talking about her man.

This woman, about whom we will learn more in the next study, is the main speaker throughout this Song—though we never learn quite as much about her as we would like. (There is poetic intention to the vague character descriptions: This woman and man represent every woman and every man who have ever been in love;[10] if you say too much about a character, you limit his or her appeal to a broader audience. This couple appeals to all.) She speaks 53 percent of the time, the man 34 percent, and the others, including the "daughters of Jerusalem," 13 percent of the time.[11] Thus David Hubbard rightly calls her "the star of the Song."[12]

This star begins her first solo with a provocative plea. This ancient woman boldly invites intimacy. She is neither passive nor weak; she is neither silent nor shy. Colorfully and with unbridled expression, she voices her longings and sheer delight in the joyful prospect of the wedding night experience. She wants to be kissed, "and not just a formal peck on the cheek from cold," apathetic lips,[13] but a kiss that is warm and long and loving (and perhaps not limited to her lips!).[14] "Let him kiss me with the kisses of his mouth!" (1:2a).

The sequence of the verb "kiss" with the noun "kisses" provides a nice poetic effect, but the context provides clarity as to what kind of kiss she wants. This is not a kiss of honor for a king ("you may kiss my ring"), or a kiss of peace for a fellow believer (the "greet one another with a holy kiss" of the New Testament), or a kiss of friendship or familial affection ("Oh, Aunt Gertrude, so good to see you"). This is a romantic kiss.[15] This is the climax of the wedding celebration—"You may kiss your bride"—where the first public kiss turns into many private kisses that continue into the bridal chamber and onto the wedding bed and on through the wedding night.

Next, she moves from his lips to his love. She wants to be kissed, not merely because his kissing is so great, but because his love is so great: "For your love [not, your kiss] is better than wine" (1:2b). With this metaphor of wine she stays very tactile. His love is like something you can touch and taste and smell. Wine is something sweet and aromatic, and the overall effect is intoxicating. That's what his love is like.

However, unlike other poetry, she does not employ this metaphor of wine (mentioned seven times in this Song)[16] merely because it connotes intoxication. An Egyptian love song from 1300 B.C. says,

I kiss her,
her lips open,
and I am drunk
without a beer.[17]

More recently, Pablo Neruda wrote,

Drunk as drunk on turpentine
From your open kisses.[18]

Instead of drunkenness, she uses the metaphor of wine to connote pleasure. In the Bible, wine often symbolizes pleasure or the greatest earthly delights, as in Psalm 104:15 where wine is said to "gladden the heart of man," or Judges 9:13, where "wine," we learn, "cheers God and men."[19] Jesus first manifested his glory by turning water to wine at a wedding (John 2:1–11); and he showed humanity the joy that he alone can bring to earth, a joy we celebrate in the Lord's Supper, our "love feast" of bread and wine (cf. 1 Corinthians 11:17–34), and a joy we will celebrate eternally at the Messianic banquet, where the finest wine will never run out.

In verse 3 she continues her praise by moving from a physical description to a nonphysical one, as she did in verse 2, from the way he smells ("your anointing oils are fragrant") to his character ("your name is oil poured out; therefore virgins love you"). Sexual attraction, as perfume companies well know, comes as often through our noses as through our eyes. Her lover would have worn perfumes to mask his natural body odor. So the oils of the perfume and the oils of his body likely produced a scent that was uniquely his, a scent that now represents his very person.

When my wife is gone and I'm sleeping alone, I have on occasion rolled over onto her pillow and given it a whiff because her pillow has her smell, which I like. Sometimes in secret, as I'm picking out clothes to wear for

Sunday morning, I lift one of her dresses to my nose and take it all in. That's my Emily. I love *her* smell.

Now, let's move past my strange smelling obsessions, as this young woman does her lover's smell. Beyond this physical, sensuous attraction, she is likewise attracted by the fragrance of her lover's *name*. In the Bible, one's name represents one's character (e.g., 1 Samuel 25:25; Ruth 4:14). We are baptized in the name of the Father, Son, and Spirit (Matthew 28:19), and there is no other name than Jesus under Heaven given among men by which we must be saved (see Acts 4:11, 12). What she is saying here is that his name—his fine reputation and noble character—is irresistibly attractive to her.

So the physical fragrance of his perfume and the metaphorical fragrance of his character overwhelm her. Thus she continues her plea:

Draw me after you; let us run.
The king has brought me into his chambers. (1:4)

Her refrain throughout this Song is to wait for love. Three times she addresses her virgin bridesmaids, "[Do] not stir up or awaken love until it pleases" (2:7; 3:5; 8:4). But she has waited all her life for this moment—for her wedding day; thus, she is now justifiably impatient. Now is the time for her to arouse and awaken love.

However, note that as much as she has been aggressive—"kiss me . . . draw me"—she hasn't reversed traditional gender roles. She asks the man to come and kiss her and whisk her away.[20] There is actually a beautiful give and take. She is not like the leading ladies in today's movies. She doesn't pull his tie and kiss him deeply. No, she pulls his tie and says, "Kiss me deeply." Then she waits willingly for him to come and carry her into his chambers, the bridal chambers, his bedroom (1 King 1:15; cf. Judges 15:1; Joel 2:16). Yes, it's like the old picture of the groom lifting his bride over the threshold into their new house, kicking the door closed with his foot.

As we move to the final lines of this opening poem, I want you to notice some of the subtle poetic details. For example, see how she shifts from addressing her lover in the third person to addressing him in the second—"him" has turned into "you." This occurs in the middle of verse 2 and remains until verse 4a. This slight grammatical alteration, a common device found in Hebrew poetry,[21] is used to enhance the intimacy of the scene, an intimacy that grows with each verse.

She begins, "Let him kiss me." That sounds far off, as if she is calling out from her balcony. Then she says "your"—"your love . . . your anointing oils

. . . your name." He is close enough to hear her. But then . . . then he's there! *You* "draw me after you." *You* take me away. Has he climbed up to her? Who knows? Who cares? She doesn't. *You* are here!

So we move from "him" to "your," then to "you." Finally, we move from third person (him) to second person (you) to first person plural: "Let us run." The two have become one. And then grammatically (isn't grammar fun?), verse 4 creates some distance by switching back to third person— "the king." This final switch, however, I suggest is the most intimate verse yet. I say that because of what she says: "The king has brought me into his chambers." She calls her lover a "king." She will describe him as a shepherd in 1:7. He could be a king and a shepherd literally, like King David. But it is more likely that he is a shepherd literally and a "king" metaphorically.[22] "He is her *king*,"[23] her "triumphant king."[24] In other words, she reaches for an image to adorn his honor, worth, and greatness in her eyes. King? Yes that will do.

In the Orthodox Church today, the bride and groom are called "king" and "queen" for their wedding day. I remember attending a wedding of a child-hood friend, and the Orthodox priest placed a crown upon the groom's head, and then all the men surrounded him and congratulated him as king. King for a day! It's a wonderful, Bible-based tradition.

To her, he is a king. And to her their first night together is majestic. It has a royal righteousness about it. She is not whisked away by some joker at a singles bar to some cheap motel or the backseat of an old Buick. Rather, she is taken captive by the king and brought into his private chambers.[25] There the lights dim, the dark curtains close, the scene ends, and the kissing with the kisses of the mouth begins. It is the ideal wedding night.

The only thing left is for the choir to sing. And that they do. Announcing their approval, boasting of their blessing, the voices of the virgins fills the air: "We will exult and rejoice in you" (v. 4c). Yes, your man is right for you. Yes, your time for pleasure is now. Yes, your love, in your own words, dear bride, is better than wine.

What Are We to Do?

So that's what the poetry is doing. I hope you understand it and *feel* it. I hope you get close enough to feel the flame. Now we turn from the question, what is the poetry doing? to the question, what are we to do? In other words, how do we apply this ancient Hebrew poem to our contemporary American lives? Below are four applications.

Desire Is Not Demonic

The first application is this: *desire is not demonic*. Or if you'd like: *Eros is not evil*. Pick whichever alliteration you like better. That is, this desire for sexual intimacy expressed here so obviously is not only natural but can be (should be) naturally good.

When God created the world he said, "It is good . . . good . . . good . . . good . . . good . . . good" (Genesis 1:4, 10, 12, 18, 21, 25). And when he created the pinnacle of his creation—human beings made of flesh and bones and with desires for intimacy—he said, "It is very good" (Genesis 1:31). Although we are now fallen creatures and cover our bodies in shame (as we should), and our natural desires can so easily be distorted and debased (contrast 1 Corinthians 7:9 with 7:37), there is still something very good about this natural desire for intimacy.

However, we must be careful. Our desires are dangerous. Ask Tiger Woods. Ask Bill Clinton. Ask Jim Bakker, Jimmy Swaggart, and Ted Haggard. This is why we are warned throughout Scripture that we must battle against immorality and that giving in to sexual desires outside of the covenant of marriage is evil, what Paul calls "the works of the flesh [the sinful nature]" (Galatians 5:19), such as fornication (sex before marriage), adultery (sex with someone other than your spouse), and homosexuality (sex with a person of the same gender as you). Eros alone is not evil, but eros outside of God's ethics is. Thus, Christians are repeatedly told in the New Testament to "put to death . . . whatever is earthly in you: sexual immorality, impurity, passion [i.e., lust], evil desire"; and we are told to do so because of God's judgment: "On account of these the wrath of God is coming" (Colossians 3:5, 6; cf. Hebrews 12:16). It is natural to desire, but don't let the natural neutralize the ethical. We are to glorify God with our bodies (1 Corinthians 6:20), and glorifying God means playing by his rules.

The Bible doesn't deny strong sexual desires before marriage and in marriage. It acknowledges them, warns of their potential danger, but also rejoices in their right expression. And that's what we have here. In this passage, intimacy within marriage is received with thanksgiving, as all of God's created gifts should be (see 1 Timothy 4:4). Here right love is rightly exalted. Here desire and the fulfillment of that desire are celebrated.

So, desire is dangerous but not demonic.

Let me add one disclaimer to this first point of application. Desire is natural, and the consummation of that desire in marriage is good, but it is not necessary. People have died falling from ladders. People have died by being stung by a swarm of killer bees. People have died for lack of food and water. But no one has died for lack of sex.

I'm not denying that we are sexual beings, but I am denying the myth that to be truly human is to be sexually active. While it's true that the human race would go the way of the woolly mammoth or the stilt-legged llama without sex, you individually would not. This is an important point. It's important because the most fulfilled human being ever—our Lord Jesus Christ—lived without it. And so did John the Baptist and many of Jesus' followers who came after him. Jesus was and is a virgin. That's an important reality to remind ourselves of today and every day.

Thus when considering eschatological realities—the kingdom of God being at hand and soon to come in full glory (1 Corinthians 7:29–31)—Paul writes that it is "even better" if one remains unmarried (v. 38). He says earlier that "it is better to marry than to burn with passion" (v. 9), but it is "even better" to be so gospel centered that sex is not only unnecessary but also undesirable when compared to one's devotion to the Lord.

For all of us the lesson is this: putting Christ and his kingdom first means putting sex second or third or fiftieth; and for those gifted with singleness, putting God's kingdom first means sex never. Jesus is celibate. And Jesus celebrates the celibate, those who have, in his words, "made themselves eunuchs for the sake of the kingdom of heaven" (Matthew 19:12). He celebrates celibacy. And so should we.[26]

Character and Chemistry Both Matter in the Matters of Love

The second application is that *character and chemistry both matter in the matters of love.* In our text we see two reasons why she loves him. The first reason is his character. She esteems his name. He is a king to her. She respects him, and so do her friends. His good reputation has spread like perfume. Both verses 3 and 4 say that the virgins "love" him. In other words, they highly approve. They aren't saying to themselves, "What does she see in him?" No, they see the same character traits she sees.

The second reason she loves him is their chemistry. He loves her (v. 2), and she likes that he loves her. This is the first time this persistent theme in the Song is made. Throughout the Song, their touches and talks (and teases!) are filled with chemistry.

Both character and chemistry matter in the matters of love. Know that. Apply that. To marry someone who lacks character—"but she's so stunningly beautiful," or "he's so filthy rich"—is just stupid. Don't be stupid. Young ladies, you are to look for a man who *now* emulates the characteristics of the godly husband in Scripture: a man who is "understanding" (1 Peter 3:7), "not . . . harsh" (Colossians 3:19), sacrificially loving like Christ (Ephesians 5:25, 28), and able to lead and nourish you in your faith (Ephesians 5:23, 26–29).[27] Young men, you are to look for a woman who *now* emulates the characteristics of the godly wife: a woman who has a submissive spirit (Colossians 3:18; Ephesians 5:22, 24; 1 Peter 3:1, 6), is pure in conduct (1 Peter 3:2), and values the internal "beauty of a gentle and quiet spirit" more than external beauty (1 Peter 3:3, 4).

So, character counts, but so also does chemistry. When looking for the right person to marry we should ask: "Is his/her character commendable?" But we should also ask, "How do I feel about him/her?" When William Smith, a pastor in Alabama, interviews couples wishing to marry, before he addresses their readiness to sustain a lifelong commitment, he first asks, "Do you love each other with Song of Solomon love?"[28] That is, are there "hot emotions, physical desire and rich romance" in your relationship?[29] That's what the Bible is asking here in an indirect way. You see, Jane Austen wasn't the first to bring to the world's attention that one shouldn't marry for convenience, economic security, or social advancement. The Bible teaches that same truth here, and even as early as Genesis it depicts a love-struck Jacob who will work fourteen years for beautiful-eyed Rachel. The Bible is not against chemistry, as we call it: two people marry because they romantically love each other. Although it might be true that covenant loyalty and godly character are listed above chemistry, chemistry is listed nevertheless. It's listed, in my reading of the broad Scriptural witness of what it means to love another person, a close third. So don't dismiss it in the matters of love.

That First Flame Need Not Fizzle

The third application is that that first flame of desire (which is depicted colorfully here) need not (ought not!) die out after the honeymoon. Put more succinctly: *that first flame need not fizzle.*

Often when I meet one-on-one with the men of my church—"Mondays with a Man," is what I call it—I will ask the married men, "Do you love your wife?" I have yet to have a man fold his arms and say, "No." Thus far everyone has said, "Yes." And that "yes" is simply the "yes" of commitment. Yes, I love her enough not to divorce her and to stay faithful to her. Now, the man can mean more than that, but he certainly (and thankfully so) at least means that. He loves her. Love equals commitment.

But then sometimes I will follow up with a second question: "Do you like her?" Those who have a healthy and enjoyable marriage will often laugh and say, "Of course. Yes, I like my wife very much." But those who are struggling in their marriage—whether they have been struggling for a long or short time, over a major or minor issue—won't laugh. Instead they'll open up. They'll share—"Recently things haven't been that great"—and on they go.

I have yet to add a third question (one I think is based on this text): "Do you *desire* your wife?" The American Puritan poet Edward Taylor described his desire for his wife as "a golden ball of pure fire."[30] (Oh, so puritanical!) Husband, does your love for your wife burn like a golden ball of pure fire? That's my new question.

Do you desire your spouse? If so, thank God for that gift. If not, I'll give you three steps to renew your marital intimacy. The first step is to *pray*. Ask God, who is in the business of changing hard hearts, to soften yours and your spouse's.

I came across a wonderful poem by Steve Scafidi called "Prayer for a Marriage," in which the poet talks about him and his wife kissing on their wedding day, and he prays that the desire they shared then will not fade—"from the wild first surprising [kisses] to the lower dizzy ten thousand infinitely slower ones." He ends, "and I hope while we stand there in the kitchen [later in life] making tea and kissing, the whistle of the teapot wakes the neighbors."[31] Pray for your marriage. Pray for desire. Pray for prolonged kissing in the kitchen.

My second step is to *remember*. Remember what fueled that first flame.

The other night when my wife and I were lying in bed, I reached over and placed Emily's hand in mine. I then shared with her how the first time I reached over and grabbed her hand (when we were dating) was the most wonderful physical sensation I have ever experienced. Honestly. And she said, "I know what you mean." She then added, "You're crushing my hand." And I was, I was holding it so tightly.

That short recollection (and the laugh about me crushing her hand) brought us closer together. We desired each other more. After that, to continue the playful mood, I asked her, "So, am I the best kisser you've ever known?" (She has never kissed anyone but me—that's why I asked.) She responded, "You are the best kisser I've known . . . and the worst." (Another good laugh . . . for her, and maybe for you.)

Step one—pray (ask for God's help); step two—remember (recall old times; ask your spouse today why he/she first loved you); and step three—*understand* (grasp that desire follows love). That's what is in our text. She wants to be kissed (she desires him) because/"for" (v. 2b) he loves her. Start loving each other.

Men, especially, take the lead and start loving your wife. I tell Emily that when I desire her physically, "It's my way of saying, 'I love you.'" She will then say to me, "Hmm, no, when you discipline the kids, wash the dishes, or pick up after yourself—when you sacrifice for me—then I know you love me . . . and then I desire you." Men require twenty-four seconds of foreplay, women twenty-four hours. But how healthy! If we men never had to learn to love, we would never be desirable to our wives.

In his book *Sex, Romance, and the Glory of God*, C. J. Mahaney gives a memorable word to men on this point. He writes, "Before you touch her body, touch her heart and mind."[32] Isn't that great? (The wives reading this are nodding.) Before you touch her body, touch her heart and mind. Husbands, do you ever study your wife the way you did when you were trying to win her? Do you know what pleases her, excites her, honors her, encourages her, refreshes her, and helps her?[33] Do you spend any time during the week thinking about what she might like—a weekly date (that you plan), a daily phone call, a spontaneous love letter, a gift of clothing, jewelry, a book, a vacation, or two hours free from the kids?[34]

Pray (step one), remember (step two), and understand (step three)—these three steps will keep that first flame aflame.

Desiring Christ

Our final application is an application to all Christians, and it has to do with our desire for Christ: Just as your desire for intimacy with your spouse is a reliable indicator of your marital health, so too your desire for intimacy with Christ is a reliable indicator of your spiritual health.

Here I'm not making a connection with Christ by means of allegory— that when the bride sings of kissing, it is the Church singing of its spiritual union with the King of kings or whatever. I'm merely making a thematic connection, which is done throughout Scripture when the topic of marriage is addressed. In Ephesians 5, for example, when Paul is talking about husbands and wives, he naturally moves from that theme to the theme of the relationship of Christ and the Church (v. 32). And he doesn't even explain the shift. He just shifts, assuming his readers are saturated enough with the Bible to grasp the shift. The same happens in Hebrews 1:8, 9, where the author quotes Psalm 45:6, 7—a wedding poem—drawing reference to Jesus as the divine representation of the Davidic king. So, within the canon of Scripture, one should not think of marriage without thinking of Christ, and this is because marriage was always intended to point to him.

Our desire for Christ is a good indication of the health of our relationship. We are saved by faith alone in Christ alone. But genuine faith has its effects on our affections. Those who are in Christ, not always (all the time) but often (most of the time), desire him. It's our overall disposition. I'll put it this way, the way Jesus puts it: there is a greater love for Christ than anyone or anything else (see Matthew 10:37; 1 Corinthians 16:22). So, if you can pant as Paul does in Philippians 1:23 as he speaks of his "desire . . . to depart and be with Christ," or as Bernard of Clairvaux phrased it, "Jesus, the very thought of thee with sweetness fills the breast; but sweeter far thy face to see, and in thy presence rest," then thank God. Thank God for those God-given affections. That's what we all want and need. But if you are struggling to desire the divine Bridegroom, then I offer some free marital counseling: the same three steps in reverse order.

Step one: *Understand.* Understand that desire follows love. Here, of course, the roles are reversed. As his bride we lose our desire for Christ, but not because he's a bad husband. There is no greater love than to lay down your life for a friend, and Jesus has laid down his life for friends and enemies alike. The bride is to blame here. We are to blame.

The barrier to intimacy with Christ is sin. Jesus said, "If you love me, you will keep my commandments" (John 14:15). Since we sin and don't obey his commandments perfectly, this is evidence that we don't love and desire him the way we should. If a husband comes to me and says, "My wife and I are having difficulties lately; oh, by the way, I'm having an affair." What! I will counsel him, "Stop the affair!" Yes, Christians, stop having affairs with the world. You don't desire Christ because you're not living for Christ. You're cheating on him spiritually. You're denying him as Lord. Each time you indulge in this or that sinful activity, you are saying, "I do not love Christ. I do not desire intimacy."

Step two: *Remember.* This is what we do when we partake of the Lord's Supper. We remember what Jesus has done for us. It is important to remember both the benefits of Christ's death and how God has worked in the past so we can love, trust, and desire him in the present. Psalm 73 is a wonderful example of this. In that Psalm, the psalmist is at first envious of the arrogant. Why do the bad guys get off scot-free? And why do they prosper? But then he remembers God's justice in the past, which leads him to trust God in the present for future vindication. Once he grasps this, he ends by saying,

> Whom have I in heaven but you?
>   And there is nothing on earth that I desire besides you.
> My flesh and my heart may fail,
>   but God is the strength of my heart and my portion forever.
>   (Psalm 73:25, 26)

If you want to desire Christ more, remember his person and his works.

Step three: *Pray.* Fittingly, John Piper begins his book *When I Don't Desire God* with these words: "I hope you will not be offended if I open this book by praying for you. There is a reason. When all is said and done, only God can create joy in God." [35] Yes, only God can create desire for God. So, if you have lost your first love (see Revelation 2:4), pray for it. Pray 1 Peter 1:8, that "though you have not seen him, you [would] love him." Or pray Psalm 51:12: "Restore to me the joy of your salvation." Or pray one of the great hymns of the faith, such as Augustus Toplady's "Compared with Christ, in All Besides":

> The sense of thy expiring love
> Into my soul convey;
> Thyself bestow, for thee alone,
> My all in all, I pray. [36]

> My eyes are dry
> My faith is old
> My heart is hard
> My prayers are cold
> And I know how I ought to be
> Alive to you and dead to me

> But what can be done
> For an old heart like mine
> Soften it up
> With oil and wine

> The oil is you
> Your spirit of love
> Please wash me anew
> With the wine of your blood

Or pray the words of that old Keith Green chorus, lyrics linguistically and thematically fitting to end on:

> My eyes are dry
> My faith is old
> My heart is hard
> My prayers are cold
> And I know how I ought to be
> Alive to You and dead to me.

> But what can be done
> For an old heart like mine
> Soften it up
> With *oil and wine*
> The oil is You, Your Spirit of love
> Please wash me anew
> With the wine of Your Blood. [37]

3

The Metaphors and Metamorphosis of Loving Words

THE SONG OF SOLOMON 1:5—2:7

I am a rose of Sharon, a lily of the valleys.
As a lily among brambles, so is my
love among the young women.

2:1, 2

YOU'RE SOMETHING SPECIAL.

"You won't amount to anything."

"You are so beautiful."

"You make me sick."

Words have power, and we all know it. Words can build up or break down. Words can heal or hurt. Words can cure or kill.

I remember in seventh grade hanging out with a group of close friends. One of the girls, Cara, had an extremely bad complexion. Yet she was well-loved for her attractive personality. She was kind, generous, and warmhearted. I was always glad to be in her presence. Well, as this group was hanging out and chitchatting, I mentioned something nice about Cara to one of the other boys. And he said, loudly enough for everyone to hear, "You mean Pizza-face over there?" Silence. Everyone stared at Cara. And you could see her start to shrivel up on the inside. It was awful. She would have preferred a stick to the stomach or a stone to the head than to have those five cruel words crammed through her ears and down into her heart.

The Bible has much to say about words. Giving perhaps the strongest statement on the topic, our Lord Jesus declared, "I tell you, on the day of judgment people will give account for every careless word they speak, for by your words you will be justified, and by your words you will be condemned" (Matthew 12:36, 37).

The power of words is also a prevalent theme in the Wisdom Literature of the Bible. Job cries out to his friends, "How long will you torment me and break me in pieces with words?" (Job 19:2). In Ecclesiastes, "the Preacher [who] sought to find words of delight" (12:10) wrote these delightful words: "The words of the wise heard in quiet are better than the shouting of a ruler among fools" (9:17). Proverbs says, "The words of the reckless pierce like swords, but the tongue of the wise brings healing" (12:18, NIV), and "Death and life are in the power of the tongue" (Proverbs 18:21a).

Here in the Song of Songs (which I take as part of the wisdom corpus) we have more wisdom on words. But here it is not an admonishment or axiom but rather an image. So often poetry paints a picture, and 1:5—2:7 paints a picture of the transformative power of kind, romantic, sweet, affirming words—what I've entitled *The Metaphors and Metamorphosis of Loving Words*.

Her Perception of Herself

Our text begins with the woman's words of self-perception:

> I am very dark, but lovely,
>   O daughters of Jerusalem,
> like the tents of Kedar,
>   like the curtains of Solomon.
> Do not gaze at me [or look down upon me],[1] because I am dark,
>   because the sun has looked upon me.
> My mother's sons were angry with me;
>   they made me keeper of the vineyards,
>   but my own vineyard I have not kept! (1:5, 6)

Later she adds this about herself:

> I am a rose of Sharon,
> a lily of the valleys. (2:1)

Note a few things about these verses of self-perception. First, these are overall negative reviews: the first of her body (1:5, 6), the second of her being (2:1).

In 1:5, 6 she describes her body as unattractive in at least two ways. First, she is too tan. She is "very dark" (v. 5). She is very dark because that *angry* "sun has looked upon" her (v. 6) and because her *angry* half-brothers (her "mother's sons") made her work outside.

This is a Cinderella story with minor character alterations. There is the beautiful young girl forced to labor in the vineyard, work that according to Isaiah 5:2 entailed digging ditches, clearing stones, planting vines, building a watchtower, hewing out a wine vat, picking grapes, and sometimes driving away thieves and wild animals, such as foxes (Song 2:15) and boars (Psalm 80:13, 14). We don't know why the brothers were angry. Was she being lazy around the house? Was she "too pretty" to get her hands dirty? Whatever the reason, their insensitivity was unjustified. Whatever the circumstances, brothers should protect their sisters. In 8:8, 9, we learn that they did protect her virginity; but here they did not protect her attractiveness. And in her mind this lack of protection—protection from the sun especially—has permanently tainted her skin.

She is an Israelite.[2] She is not the daughter of Pharaoh, as some have thought.[3] She is not African. So she is not saying, "Black is beautiful," or "I'm black; therefore I'm not beautiful." There is nothing racial here. Rather she is saying, "My already dark Mediterranean skin is 'very dark.' It's too dark—as dark as those tanned Bedouin hides ('the tents of Kedar')."

Now, why is too dark too bad?

Every culture has its reasons for what is considered beautiful. For many Americans today the beautiful woman is lean, muscular, and tan, which is far removed from the European Renaissance, for example, when beautiful women were always painted pale and plump. Well, pale and plump is what the woman in our text would have been quite content with. And that is because slender and dark meant low social status.[4] Darker skin meant working class, while lighter skin meant upper class. When compared to the posh ladies of Solomon's court, Pharaoh's harem, or even the ladies in waiting—those daughters of Jerusalem—her skin is too dark.[5]

Furthermore, her problem is not just her outdoor job in the vineyard, but that her body—what she calls her "vineyard"—is "not kept."

> [T]hey made me keeper of the vineyards,
> but my own vineyard I have not kept! (1:6b)

What she is saying here is that she does not have the time to "attend to her own attractiveness."[6] Unlike Queen Esther, she hasn't been getting her twelve-month beauty treatments—her skin softened with oil of myrrh for six months, and then spices and ointments for another six months (Esther 2:12). She has a working-class complexion, *and* her hair is undone, *and* her attire is unattractive. She has been on her feet all day pruning vines or picking grapes, shooing away sneaky foxes. And when she gets off her shift, she calls it a day. No time for a manicure and pedicure, and certainly no time to powder her sunburnt cheeks.

That's what she thinks of her body. Here's what she thinks of *her being*. When she looks at the ladies around her, she compares herself to "a rose of Sharon, [that is] a lily of the valleys." Now, that sounds nice. She at least thinks she's a flower, not a weed. And she does call herself "lovely" in 1:5. She's a natural beauty, and she knows that. (In 1:5 she compares herself, in her darkness, to Solomon's dark but finely crafted curtains.[7]) She doesn't have the negative self-image that is all too common today. Rather, she has a realistic self-assessment. She's not emotionally oversensitive; she's emotionally sensible. She's lovely, and she's like a lily.[8]

But this analogy with the flowers is not an overly positive one. She basically says, "There's nothing special about me. I'm like a common countryside wildflower. I'm not like an orchid that has been planted, trimmed, and watered. I'm pretty . . . *pretty* common."

His Perception of Her

That's what she says of herself (overall not a high assessment). But what does her beloved say about her and to her? Here is where the metaphors of love metamorphose her very body and being. Watch as she is transformed by the power of loving words. Three times he calls her "beautiful" (1:8, 15a, 15b), and to her common flower metaphor he says,

> As a lily among brambles,
>   so is my love among the young women. (2:2)

In other words, "A lily? Okay, you're a lily. We'll stay with that analogy. Lilies are lovely. Common lilies are uncommonly beautiful flowers. Lilies are carved into the pillars of Solomon's temple,[9] and not even king Solomon 'in all his glory was arrayed like [a lily]' (Matthew 6:28, 29), as a wise man would one day say. And you, my lily, are like a lily *among thorns*. Line up all the ladies, and let me look. Yes, to me they look as briars and brambles compared to you. You are the best looking. You are the only one worth looking at."[10] That's what he says to her here (cf. 5:9, 6:1).

And can't you just see her opening up like a flower to the warm rays of his affection and the gentle rain of his words? Can't you see desire being aroused and awakened in her?

So, he calls her a lily among brambles. That's a compliment. He also calls her . . . a horse (another compliment?):

I compare you, my love,
to a mare among Pharaoh's chariots. (1:9)

Here we might be tempted to say to the poet, "Okay, pal, why not stay with the flower metaphors, like 'My Luve's like a red, red rose' (Robert Burns). Or change the metaphor to something like the weather: 'Shall I compare thee to a summer's day? Thou art more lovely and more temperate' (Shakespeare). But stay away from the animal analogies." That would be our advice. But here the man calls his love a mare *intentionally*. Why? Well, despite what we may think about the mare metaphor, note that both he and she think it's a compliment. It might be that he is intentionally contrasting conventional images of beauty (as, for example, in Shakespeare's Sonnet 130), and she gets this. She thinks it is kind of cutting-edge cool. But more likely it is an image that makes sense to both of them. Note it is not her value, strength, vibrancy, or animal magnetism (sex appeal) but rather her beauty that is compared to this animal's beauty.

Let me start there, with *her beauty*. While men today don't say of a beautiful woman, "Oh, she trots like a Clydesdale," or "Her disheveled hair flows like the mane of a Kiger Mustang," nevertheless, the concept of a beautiful horse is not unfamiliar to us. Think of the classic book *Black Beauty*. Or think of the movie *The Black Stallion* as the boy watches this untamed creature run along the shore in the moonlight. That horse is beautiful. Similarly, this young woman is a black beauty. She is dark, and she has this unkempt quality about her, like a wild horse with long, healthy, glossy black hair.

And now she is *his*!

And his love has captured, tamed, and beautified her. She has been removed from the vineyard, and now in 1:10, 11 she somehow (this is poetic license) stands before her king as a stunning queen. He says, "[Wow!] Your cheeks are lovely with ornaments, your neck with strings of jewels." Her bridesmaids add, "We will make for you ornaments of gold, studded with silver" (v. 11).[11]

The focus here is on her natural beauty, now enhanced externally by beautiful jewelry.[12] In fact, the mare metaphor is largely about the jewelry she now wears. As Duane Garrett observes, "[T]he only actual visual similarity" between the bride and the horse is that they both are "adorned in splendid ornamentation."[13]

> I compare you, my love,
>   to a mare among Pharaoh's chariots.
> [That is] Your cheeks are lovely with ornaments,
>   your neck with strings of jewels. (1:9, 10)

We know from ancient Egyptian art that the mares for Pharaoh's royal chariot wore elaborate headdresses lined with jewelry.[14] This bride is adorned in a similar way, likely in her wedding gown. (Israelite women wouldn't wear elaborate jewelry unless it was their wedding day.[15]) So, with silver and gold adorning her hand, head, ears, cheeks, and neck, and (if you'll allow me some license for visual effect) her body clothed in our traditional white wedding dress, the white accenting this dark beauty, she stands before her jaw-dropped husband.

So he gives her three compliments. First (in my ordering), she is a lily among thorns. Second, she is a black beauty, a magnificent mare. And third, she has those eyes.

> Behold, you are beautiful, my love;
>   behold, you are beautiful;
>   your eyes are doves. (1:15)

It is not uncommon in love poems and love songs to talk about a woman's eyes, from D. L. Lawrence's "Green"[16] to Van Morrison's "Brown Eyed Girl." That's because most eyes are beautiful, so they work well for that reason, but also because they well represent the whole person.[17] The eyes are the window of the soul. Or as Jesus put it, "The eye is the lamp of the body" (Matthew 6:22).

Now, the poet compares her eyes to "doves." It is possible that this expression describes *disposition*, "that the girl's eyes are somewhat timid, they glance and flutter and dart around, like a pair of shy doves,"[18] or *color*, that "iridescent quality, a scintillating pearly-grey, speckled with flecks of brighter colors as in Swinburne's *Felise*: Those eyes the greenest of things blue, the bluest of things grey,"[19] or *shape*—oval or almond shaped eyes, like those you would find on an Egyptian tomb-painting or statue, like the contours of the bird's body when it's "stretched down to pick up scraps from the ground."[20] However, I think the "eyes are doves" analogy symbolizes intimacy and innocence.

I say *intimacy* because in order to describe someone's eyes you have to be close enough to see them. The picture here is face-to-face, eye-to-eye intimacy. And I say *innocence* not only because Jesus uses that analogy—"be wise as serpents and innocent as doves" (Matthew 10:16), but also because of what this man doesn't say and what this woman does say.

Here he doesn't speak about her other body parts. Later he will talk of her most private parts—we'll learn about her navel, thighs, breasts, and so on. But here he only describes (a) her overall beauty, (b) her external beauty (the part about the jewelry), and (c) her eyes. That's fairly innocent.

He speaks innocently because she is innocent. In 1:7, where she is searching for him during his midday siesta, she doesn't want to run out into the countryside even in broad daylight (this is not a midnight liaison!) to find him because she doesn't want to be viewed "like one who veils herself beside the flocks of your companions." In other words, she doesn't want to be thought of as a harlot, for a veiled woman was often a prostitute (e.g., Genesis 38:14, 19). Even though she expresses urgency about being with him—"Tell me, you whom my soul loves" (1:7a); "I am sick with love" (2:5b)—she won't throw caution to the wind. She won't go into the men's locker room to retrieve him. Think of it that way. She drinks her "wine" responsibly.[21] Think of it that way. To her, love never justifies reckless behavior. There is not even a hint of impropriety—"nothing sleazy or shady . . . nothing seedy or sordid."[22]

What she does in 1:7 she says in 2:7. This poem ends with her exhortation to innocence. She tells the daughters of Jerusalem to stay innocent (sexually inexperienced) until their wedding night. I'll further explain and apply that verse in the next study.

So, to summarize this final compliment, when he says "your eyes are doves," he is certainly commending her beauty but also, as argued above, her overall character, especially her innocence. That is what is so attractive to him. "Behold, you are beautiful, my love; behold, you are beautiful"—your body and your whole self.

Application to Husbands

All that to say: Husbands, compliment your wives.

Husbands, you should compliment your wife's beauty. It's nice to compliment her cooking, intelligence, or work ethic. But from time to time she wouldn't mind being called "beautiful."

I know a Christian businessman who shared with a group of men at a men's retreat what he does in order to resist lusting after an attractive woman. He said he simply finds something unattractive about her and focuses on that.

One could run into complications, however, with this line of protection. For example, imagine being on an airplane sitting next to an attractive woman, and as you begin your ritual (but righteous) gazing, she turns to you and says, "May I ask what you are doing?" and you admit, "Oh, sorry, I'm just looking for imperfections. This should only take a few seconds."

While I doubt the wisdom of my friend's practice, I think the reverse of it is quite wise when it comes to my wife. That is, I should regularly ask myself, "What do I find beautiful about her?" I would imagine that when you were dating, as you watched the way she walked, dressed, laughed, or flipped back her hair, you could regularly sing, "Every little thing she does is magic."[23] Then it was easy to compliment her because your love was fresh and exciting. But you can make it fresh and exciting again if you would stop moping around the house singing, "You've lost that loving feeling." You've lost that loving feeling because you've stopped looking.

The first time you saw a rainbow it was awe inspiring. You could look at it all day. But now do you stop to take a glance? "Oh, it's just a rainbow." Yeah, it's just a rainbow, but it's hasn't changed its awe-inspiring attributes. You've changed. Familiarity has bred contempt, or at least complacency. You've neglected such beauty. Some men "would rather die than praise their wives."[24] But it is their own funeral, the deadly chill of their once warm marriage bed. Flattery will get you nowhere, but honest praise will always get you somewhere, and sometimes it will get you into "the banqueting house" of love (2:4), literally "the house of wine,"[25] where there is (rumor has it) intoxicating kisses of the mouth (1:2).[26]

That is my counsel to the husbands. Here is my word to the wives.

Application to Wives

Throughout this poem there is give and take between the man and the woman. He compliments her. She compliments him. And through *her compliments* she gives *him* that same sense of acceptance and assurance that he needs. Just look at what she says about her "beloved."[27] Like the previous poem (1:2–4), she calls him a "king" (1:4, 12). This title and the mention of Solomon in 1:5 has led many to conclude that the king of verse 12 is Solomon. I have argued already (see Chapter 1 of this book) and will argue later (see Chapter 10) that is not the case. Solomon is the author but not the beloved. Her man is a shepherd (1:7), whom she repeatedly views as a king when it comes to the lovemaking scenes. She compliments him as a king and also as "a sachet of myrrh" (1:13), "a cluster of henna blossoms" (1:14), and "an apple tree" (2:3)—teeming with life,[28] things my wife is always saying about me.

Moreover, she compliments him by taking his compliments and firing them back at him, which is actually something my wife often does to me (truly). He says to her, "You are beautiful" (1:8, 15a, 15b), and she says to him, "You are beautiful" (1:16). She also echoes his adoration in 2:3. After he says, "As a lily among brambles, so is my love among the young women" (2:2), she says, "As an apple tree among the trees of the forest, so is my beloved among the young men." (A man would rather be called a fruit tree than a pretty flower, and she knows that and adjusts her metaphor accordingly.)

In 2:3–6 she is likely describing foreplay or sex. But again notice the modesty,[29] and notice that she doesn't focus on the physical as much as she does the emotional. "His left hand is under my head, and his right hand embraces me!" is an erotic picture. The exclamation point in the ESV is appropriate. But her focus is on joy and protection. She is in this safe place with the man she trusts with her body (the body that she wasn't too thrilled with a minute ago). They are in this wooden cottage (literally? metaphorically? who knows?) made of strong cedar (1 Kings 4:33; cf. Ezekiel 31:3, 6) and shady evergreens.[30] They are lying together on a couch (note that it is not *his* couch but *"our* couch," 1:16), the lush and luxuriant royal bed used for feasting.[31] And like Eve under "the tree of life" (Genesis 2:9), she sits "in his shadow" (Song 2:3b). What a picture of protection and provision, of security and shade (unlike her harsh brothers who provided no shade from the sun, this gentle man provides all she needs)![32] His "banner over [her is] love" (2:4). And there she eats from the fruit of the tree (2:3b), apples and raisins that are sweet to her taste, fruit that was part of the garden of Eden in all its pre-fall glory,[33] fruit that sustains and strengthens her, fruit that overcomes the love-sickness she had in 1:5–7. It is all very innocent. It is all very good. There is no snake slithering in the background, taunting them, "Hath God said?" God has said, "Take and eat," and they have taken and *are* eating.

Application to All

So mutual admiration in marriage is important. Husbands and wives are to *complement* one another by *complimenting* one another. And as it should be in the church, so it should be in marriage: we are to speak the truth in love (Ephesians 4:15; cf. v. 25). We are not to let any unwholesome talk come out of our mouths, but only what is helpful for building each other up (v. 29). We are to get rid of all bitterness, rage, anger, brawling, and slander (v. 31). We are to be kind and tenderhearted to one another, forgiving one another, just as God in Christ forgave us (v. 32).

As you think about your marriage or any relationship you are in, perhaps you are wondering why you should speak the way I'm teaching you to speak. Or perhaps your question is not why, but *how* you can speak in that way. The answer to both those questions is the gospel: God in Christ forgave us.

One of the things I did to prepare for the sermon series that became this book was to read through the New Testament twice with one question in mind: What further light does the revelation of Jesus Christ shed on the Song of Songs? I have discovered many interesting and potential connections. But the one connection relating to the theme we are studying now is the connection between their love and God's love.

Now that connection may not blow you over. "Wow, Pastor, you made a connection between the theme of love in a love song and God's love. Revolutionary! Genius!" No, it's not the connection that is so startling, it's the reality: God is love, and God in Christ has loved us![34]

This I Know

I know my Bible well enough to know that in the Old Testament God selected Israel from all the nations and set his love upon her without any natural beauty in her whatsoever (see Deuteronomy 7:6–8). She was very dark, *and* she was very *unlovely*. There was no pale, plumb righteousness about her that made her more appealing to God or made her stand out like a lily among thorns.

And I know what goes on in Israel's long history, that even in all her spiritual "blackness"—not a mere external suntan of sin, but an external and internal apostasy—God loved and re-extended his loving mercy. I know, for example, how the book of Hosea ends, which is about their apostasy and is illustrated through real-life adultery. That book ends like this:

> I will heal their apostasy;
> I will love them freely. . . .
> [Israel] shall blossom like the lily . . .
> take root like the trees of Lebanon . . .
> his beauty shall be like the olive,
> and his fragrance like Lebanon.
> They shall return and dwell beneath my shadow . . .
> they shall blossom like the vine;
> their fame shall be like the wine of Lebanon. . . .
> It is I who answer and look after you.
> I am like an evergreen cypress;
> from me comes your fruit. (Hosea 14:4–8; cf. 2:16–20)

I know these things about God's love for his people under the old covenant. And I know of his love for his people under the new covenant. I know that just as God set his love on Israel, so in Christ he has set his love on the Church.

Matthew Henry wrote, "True believers are *black* in themselves, *but comely* in Christ."[35] Gregory of Nyssa said, "When [the Lord] takes some black soul to himself, he makes it beautiful by communion with himself."[36] Along the same lines, Samuel J. Stone wrote in his great hymn of the faith:

> The Church's one foundation
> Is Jesus Christ her Lord,
> She is His new creation
> By water and the Word.
> From heaven He came and sought her
> To be His holy bride;
> With His own blood He bought her
> And for her life He died.[37]

I know that.

And I know those verses in the New Testament that speak of this love. Romans 5:8 says, "God shows his love for us in that while we were still sinners, Christ died for us." Romans 8:35–39 asks and then answers, "Who shall separate us from the love of Christ? . . . [No one; nothing shall] separate us from the love of God in Christ Jesus our Lord." Similarly, 1 John 3:1 explains, "See what great love the Father has lavished on us, that we should be called children of God!" (NIV).

I know all that. But what I often don't know, or dwell on as much, I should say, is God's personal love *for me*. I don't mean anything narcissistic by this. What I mean is what Paul wrote in Galatians 2:20b, "I live by faith in the Son of God, who *loved me* and gave himself *for me*." What I mean is what Charles Wesley wrote:

> And can it be that *I* should gain
> An interest in the Savior's blood?
> Died He *for me*, who caused His pain—
> *For me*, who Him to death pursued?
> Amazing love! How can it be,
> That Thou, my God, shouldst die *for me*?[38]

What I mean is that *bowels-of-affection yearning* that Christ has for his people (see the Greek text of Philippians 1:8), the kind of personal affection he had for his disciple John, "whom Jesus loved" (John 13:23), the kind of affection he had for Mary, Martha, and Lazarus—"Now Jesus loved Martha and her sister and Lazarus" (John 11:5). He loved them personally, so much so that when he came to Lazarus' tomb he was so "deeply moved" (v. 38) that "Jesus wept" (v. 35). Tears fell down before Lazarus rose up.

That's what I mean.

Do *you* know what I mean?

Have you stopped lately to dwell on the love of God in Christ *for you*? Yes, as Samuel Crossman put it, "Love to the loveless shown, that they might lovely be." Such love changes sinners into saints, enemies into friends, a harlot into a bride. This is love that makes your soul soar and your voice sing, "O who am I, that for my sake my Lord should take frail flesh and die?"[39] Who am I, O Sovereign Lord (2 Samuel 7:18)? I am unworthy (Genesis 32:10). Why am I so favored (Luke 1:43)? Why me, Lord? Why set your love on me?[40]

Every morning I get up at 5:30. I walk downstairs and pull two books off the shelf (one being the Bible). I start the coffee. As the coffee is brewing, I take out my homemade daily prayer sheet that helps me know what to say to God, and the first prayer I offer every morning is this: "Lord, open my heart to rejoice in you, and fill me with a spirit of gratitude." I pray for gratitude for grace, gratitude for the gospel, gratitude for the love of God in Jesus Christ for me . . . that love that changed and continues to change me, that love that changes everything, even this old, very dark tongue, to sing God's praises and to lovingly affirm those around me—to love God and love neighbor as I already love myself.

Why should we and how can we show love with loving words? The answer is the gospel: God in Christ forgave us.

4

The Voices of Spring

THE SONG OF SOLOMON 2:8–17

*My beloved speaks and says to me: "Arise, my love,
my beautiful one, and come away, for behold, the
winter is past; the rain is over and gone. The flowers appear on the earth, the time of singing has come,
and the voice of the turtledove is heard in our land."*

2:10–12

MY WIFE AND I HAD AN INTERESTING COURTSHIP. Right after I finished grad school, we went on five dates. Emily then went on a summer college trip to the Holy Land, where despite our five fine dates and a dozen or so overseas "love" letters, she fell for another guy. Yes, she returned to tell me, "I will never be interested in you." Those were her exact words.

Well, time passed . . . slowly . . . but it passed. A year or so after that unholy land incident, we both decided separately to be part of our church's first church plant in Chicago. During that time, I roomed with her brother (bonus), and the pastors paired Emily and me as small group coleaders (double bonus). It was there and then that the walls of hostility were broken down. Put differently, she finally gave in after months of persistent pursuit. "Yes, I will be your girlfriend" is what she wrote in a letter she placed in front of my apartment door.

After dating for a while—one week!—I gained the courage to tell her just how I felt about her. Cupid had struck me through the heart. The setting was perfect. We were sitting at a campfire at a retreat center. We were alone. The evening was cool, the fire was warm, and I was warm on the inside, though cool on the outside. As I remember it, I wrapped a blanket around her shivering body and said with deepest sincerity, "Emily, I love you." All was well in the world. That is, all was well until she replied, "That's nice." The rain began to pour, then sleet, then snow. The moon crashed to earth. And I pulled the arrow out of my heart. Stupid Cupid!

That was the fall of 1998.

But then came the spring, the time when, as Tennyson put it, "a young man's fancy lightly turns to thoughts of love."[1] The trees were green again, the flowers were all abloom, and the birds returned to chant and coo. The time was at hand. I was ready to propose.

The only problem was I got the flu the day the proposal was to transpire. Her brother was supposed to walk her (just by chance) into this ornate old chapel near the University of Chicago, and there I would be at the piano, in my three-piece suit, singing a song I wrote on the Song of Songs (no less!) upon her entrance. But alas, my death was near. I had a high fever and was in bed all day. But when Emily, the sympathetic soul that she is, came to visit, I changed my mind and the plan. I kindly asked her to go the store to buy me some fruit for my ailments. In retrospect, she said I barked out orders like I always do when I'm sick. Whatever the case may be, off she went, dutifully and dourly.

Meanwhile, Plan B took effect. I got out of my pajamas, put on my three-piece suit, pasted the poems I'd written to her on the wall (including my song on the Song), and poised my unshaven, sick-faced self for proposal. Needless to say, she was surprised when she returned. But this time she was also receptive. I genuflected before her, told her I loved her, and asked her to marry me. She said yes, and she also said (finally!), "I love you too." I kissed her on the check and went back to bed.

How very romantic.

The text before us (if we can turn to that at last) is a text about timing—"Arise, my love, my beautiful one, and come away, for behold, the winter is past; the rain is over and gone. The flowers appear on the earth, *the time* of singing has come" (2:10–12a). The time of singing, as Jeremiah would put it, by the bride and bridegroom (Jeremiah 33:11). With this text, we look at this theme of time—the timing of intimacy within marriage and before marriage. And as we look at 2:8–17, I will exhort you to *trust God's timing for intimacy within marriage*, and then as we reflect on 2:7 I will exhort you to *trust God's timing for intimacy before marriage*.

Trust God's Timing for Intimacy within Marriage

Evangelical scholars do not debate whether the sexual intimacy described in the Song of Songs takes place within or outside of marriage. They all agree that a book in the Bible would only affirm such relations taking place within marriage.[2] But evangelical scholars do debate at what point the first erotic encounter takes place within the Song.

The majority opinion is that 4:1—5:1 describes the first encounter. It's a poem about the wedding night. Thus, 2:8–17 is about the proposal, 3:1–5 the prewedding jitters, and 3:6–11 the wedding ceremony. Others think the Song starts in the bedroom with a love scene, and from there on it is one earthquake of eros after another. In plainer language, the whole Song is set in the context of marriage. I stand in this camp.

That is, I believe almost every section has imagery of sexual intimacy, including the first two: *Poem One* (1:2–4), which ends with the "king" having "brought" (which is a key word for intimacy throughout the Song, cf. 2:4; 3:4) her into his chambers for deep kissing, and *Poem Two* (1:5—2:7), which ends with the "king" again having "brought" her into the banqueting house (2:4), where they lay on "our couch" in "our house" (1:16, 17) and where they engage in intimate touching—"his left hand is under [her] head, and his right hand embraces [her]" (2:6). Both of these scenes connote lovemaking through eating and/or drinking metaphors.

Having stated that the Song describes sex within marriage, let us now turn to the Song itself and see *why* we should view the text this way. This poem (2:8–17) is filled with the *language* and *actions* of marital intimacy. The language is most obvious. In verse 15 he speaks of "our vineyards." Whether he is speaking literally (they together own some land) or metaphorically (their bodies are their vineyards), either way they possess these vineyards together. Then look at what they call each other—"my beloved" (vv. 8, 9, 10, 16, and 17) and "my love" (vv. 10, 13), and then, "My beloved is mine, and I am his" (v. 16a). That's language of mutual possession. That's Bible talk for "leave and cleave [ESV, hold fast] . . . [and] become one flesh" (Genesis 2:24; cf. Hosea 3:3; 1 Corinthians 7:3, 4).[3] That's covenant formula language—"I will be their God, and they will be my people" (Jeremiah 7:23; 11:4; cf. 1 Peter 2:9, 10).[4] That's the material of marriage vows—"Do you take this man to be *your* husband? And do you take this woman to be *your* wife?"

Let's move from this language of mutual possession to his invitation. He repeats it twice for poetic effect, not because she is hard of hearing, although she may be playing hard to get. He says, "Arise, my love, my beautiful one, and come away" (vv. 10, 13b). Here he is inviting her to sexual intimacy. I say that with confidence because the next time we hear that language, "Come with me . . . come with me" is in 4:8, a text in which every scholar agrees he is inviting her to bed.

Next let's look at some of the animal imagery and activity. If we have learned one thing about this couple thus far, it is that they really like calling each other names. Nice names. Animal names. Here he compares her to a dove—"*my* dove" who is hiding in "the clefts of the rock, in the crannies of the cliff" (v. 14a). Why is she acting inaccessible to him? Is she just naturally shy? Has she had a rough go of it in their first few encounters? Why the need for his tender words of wooing? We don't know. But woo he must, and woo he does. "Let me see your lovely face and hear your sweet voice" (see v. 14). "Come, fly away with me, my dove, my love" is the sense of it.

So, she's a dove, but what is he? Is he a roaring lion, a wild boar, an untamed tiger? No, he's not a powerful, dangerous animal but rather a gazelle—a swift, handsome, cautious, curious, strong but not violent, easily excitable, and sexually eager animal, especially in the spring.[5]

> Behold, he comes,
> leaping over the mountains,
>   bounding over the hills.
> My beloved is like a gazelle
>   or a young stag.
> Behold, there he stands
>   behind our wall,
> gazing through the windows,
>   looking through the lattice. (vv. 8b, 9)

He's not a Peeping Tom. Rather, he's a Curious George or an eager beaver or . . . a yearning young stag. "Please let me in!" he pleads.

Now, notice in verses 16, 17 that his wooing has worked. This dove has stopped playing hide-and-seek and has come out to play more adult games. This poem ends with these words of intimacy:

> My beloved is mine, and I am his;
>   he grazes among the lilies.
> Until the day breathes
>   and the shadows flee,
> turn, my beloved, be like a gazelle
>   or a young stag on cleft mountains.

What's going on here? This final verse (v. 17), along with the first verses

(vv. 8, 9) share some of the *same* words, notably "gazelle/young stag" and "mountains" (thus, this section is undoubtedly a poetic unit).[6] But notice also what's *different*. There is what I'll call a "climatic inclusio." In verse 17 she invites him to act like an animal, in a good way: "My beloved, *be* like a gazelle or a young stag on cleft mountains."[7] Be like a gazelle!? How so? He is to graze and climb. In verse 9 he is *gazing*, and in verse 16 he is *grazing*. In verse 8 he is leaping *over* mountains, but in verse 17 he is invited to "be" *on* the mountains. He went from over to on, from gazing to grazing (looking to touching). What the "lilies" and "mountains" symbolize, I will leave to your sanctified imagination, or until we get to 4:6 and 7:8 where it is clear what the mountains symbolize. Has he climbed her breasts (cf. 4:6; 7:8)[8] and deflowered her vagina (see 6:2, 3 especially) or her lips (5:13)?[9] Perhaps he has.

One final intimate action that adds to my argument that our text takes place within marriage is this bit about the foxes. Oh, the foxes, what shall we do with the foxes? This verse has plagued commentators, and it has plagued me as well.[10] So I'm slipping in these sneaky foxes here, hoping that I'm putting them in the right place, but if I haven't, at least I'll be done with them in less than a minute.

The final word (and I think the ESV has it right—i.e., he is the speaker) of his invitation to intimacy is, "Catch the foxes for us, the little foxes that spoil the vineyards, for our vineyards are in blossom" (v. 15). Here is what I think is going on here. We know from 1:6 that her job before marriage was attending her family's vineyards; and we know from Scripture that part of that job entailed keeping foxes out when the grapes were ripe. So he seems to be speaking to her metaphorically here: "Get rid of anything that spoils our *feasting on fruit* together." In other words, "Whatever inhibitions you might have toward lovemaking, put them aside, and let's eat. 'Our vineyards'—your body and mine—'are in blossom.' It is the right time and the right season for love. And so, before these foxes come in and take away what we have together, let's 'refresh' each other with fresh fruit (2:5). Let's eat our 'choicest fruits' (4:16). Yes, let's 'eat . . . drink, and be drunk with love!'" (5:1).[11]

You see, if you focus on the foxes to the exclusion of the fruit (what the foxes want or will ruin),[12] you miss the facts. But if you focus on the fruit—"our vineyards are in blossom"—the symbolism makes sense. For throughout the Song eating fruit always equals intimacy. Below are the three most obvious examples:

And his fruit was sweet to my taste. (2:3d)

I say I will climb the palm tree
    and lay hold of its fruit.
Oh may your breasts be like clusters of the vine,
    and the scent of your breath like apples,
and your mouth like the best wine.
It goes down smoothly for my beloved,
    gliding over lips and teeth.
I am my beloved's,
    and his desire is for me.
Come, my beloved,
    let us go out into the fields
    and lodge in the villages;
let us go out early to the vineyards
    and see whether the vines have budded,
whether the grape blossoms have opened
    and the pomegranates are in bloom.
There I will give you my love.
The mandrakes give forth fragrance,
    and beside our doors are all choice fruits,
new as well as old,
    which I have laid up for you, O my beloved. (7:8–13)

I would give you spiced wine to drink,
    the juice of my pomegranate.
His left hand is under my head,
    and his right hand embraces me! (8:2c, 3)

So here is my summary of their language and actions of intimacy in this poem (2:8–17):

1. He approaches her with great interest for intimacy (vv. 8, 9).
2. He invites her to intimacy—"Come away with me" (vv. 10–15); that is, let's
    eat before the fruit is spoiled and the time has passed.
3. She accepts: "Yes, take me away!" (vv. 16, 17).

Until the day breathes
    and the shadows flee [all night long?],
turn [toward me], my beloved, be like a gazelle
    or a young stag on cleft mountains. (v. 17; cf. 8:12–14)

Obviously there is nothing prudish here. You might be prudish, but the Song is not. The Bible is not. God's Word is fully aware of desire, seduction, rape, polygamy, homosexuality, adultery, and sex after age ninety. And that's just Genesis. So if you are shocked by what I'm saying (what this poem is saying), you shouldn't be. Let your sensibilities be shaped by Scriptural sensibilities. This poem is an invitation to sexual intimacy within marriage.

Back to the Practical Point

Having done a lot of work with the poetry, let me get back to the original point of application: *Trust God's timing for intimacy within marriage.*

In many ways the point of this poem echoes Ecclesiastes 3:5, which is part of that great text on time: "For everything there is a season, and a time for every matter under heaven" (3:1). Ecclesiastes 3:5 reads, "[There is] a time to cast away stones, and a time to gather stones together; *a time to embrace*, and a time to refrain from embracing.*" The point of our poem is that there is a time for embracing, so embrace! Married couples, God "has made everything beautiful in its time" (Ecclesiastes 3:11), including the timing for intimacy within marriage. So when the time is right (and take time to make the time right), embrace. Yes, embrace to the glory of God!

Under this first point, let's talk briefly about the second part of that Ecclesiastes verse: there is "a time to refrain from embracing." That is, I want to be clear as I'm teaching through the Song of Songs that a passionate love life, a warm marriage bed, is good, but it's not all there is to having a healthy marriage. I'll put it this way: there are more important things than sexual intimacy within marriage.[13]

There are some obvious examples, like a man who is fighting in a war, who is overseas on mission for months at a time, who willingly sacrifices (if he is a godly man) his personal pleasures with his wife (and she sacrifices too!) for the good of our nation. That is a noble thing, as noble as Uriah, who when David brought him back from battle wouldn't sleep in the same house with Bathsheba during a time of war (2 Samuel 11:9–11). Another example is that of a wife whose husband is dying, whether it is of old age or prematurely of some disease or accident, a wife who day after day, perhaps month after month, stays by his side, nursing him, loving him, holding his hand through the valley of the shadow of death. That is intimacy within marriage, which is at a much higher level than sexual intimacy.

So there is "a time to embrace, and a time to refrain from embracing." We might refrain for the good of a nation, for the care of a dying spouse, or for many other valid reasons. Another valid reason to refrain is for the sake of the gospel—whether it is frontline missions or bedtime prayer. This is what Paul teaches in 1 Corinthians 7. On one hand, he exhorts singles to remain single as he is, "to secure . . . undivided devotion to the Lord" (v. 35). On the other hand, he exhorts husbands and wives to "not deprive one another, except perhaps by agreement for a limited time, that you may devote yourselves to prayer" (v. 5). In other words, fast from sex for the sake of prayer. From time to time, when your bodies are saying, "Let's eat," one or both of you should say, "Let's pray." Let's pray because the undivided devotion to the Lord and seeking first the kingdom of God and his righteousness takes precedence over all. It takes precedence over our marriage. It takes precedence over our marriage bed. There are more important things than sexual intimacy in marriage. There is a time to embrace and a time to refrain from embracing.

Trust God's Timing for Intimacy before Marriage

Timing. That's what this text is about. Having talked about trusting God's timing for intimacy within marriage, we now turn to trusting God's timing for intimacy *before marriage*. Look at 2:7. This is the first of three times in the Song that the bride gives her wise admonition, "I adjure you, O daughters of Jerusalem, by the gazelles or the does of the field, that you not stir up or awaken love until it pleases."

Notice a few facts. First, notice that she is addressing the "daughters of Jerusalem," who are the target audience of the Song. These are young, single Israelite teenagers, ripe and ready for love. Second, notice that her counsel is to keep in check sexual arousal and activity "until they can be fulfilled with the right person and at the right time," and "the right person for sexual intimacy is one's spouse, and the right time is after the commitment of marriage."[14] Third, notice that she is very serious about her warning to wait: "I *adjure* you."

She adjures or puts them under oath "by the gazelles or the does of the field."[15] What does she mean by this animal adjuration? Those animals—gazelles and does—are now familiar to us. In fact, they are the feminine counterpart to what she calls her beloved in verses 9 and 17. He is a male gazelle or young stag. Here in 2:7 we have the female gazelle and the female young deer, a doe. What we are perhaps not familiar with are some subtle nuances of the language used. The Hebrew word for "gazelles" (s^eba'ot) sounds like the word for "hosts" or "armies," which is part of a common name for God in the Old Testament: "Lord of hosts." Furthermore, some scholars argue that the Hebrew phrase "does of the field" (*'ay^{e}lot hassadeh*) has a similar sound as "El-Shaddai," the ancient patriarchal name for God.[16] The language here is no slip of the tongue. These allusions are meant to heighten the seriousness and strength of her admonition.[17] So, think of it this way: she puts them under oath: "Do you pledge purity, complete purity, *so help you God*?"

With all that said, let me put 2:7 in the context of what we considered in the previous study. There we looked at 1:5—2:7. That poem starts in the pasture and (with great poetic license) ends in a palace of some kind, whether it is indoor or outdoor, literal or metaphorical. In 1:5–11 she seeks and finds her lover. Then (let me put it this way) the director says, "Cut." The actors change their postures and perhaps their costumes, and then comes act 3, scene 2, take 1. *And . . . action!* It's the bedroom scene, a scene filled with verbal foreplay. It starts in 1:12 and ends in 2:6 with "his right hand embraces me!" *And cut.* The scene ends—well, almost ends. The bride peeks her head out of the bedroom window, and before she closes the shade she says, "You girls wait—patience now, passion later (2:7). Promise? Do you pledge purity, complete purity, so help you God?"

"We promise."

So that's 2:7. Trust God's timing before marriage—wait for your spouse and your wedding day. Wait.

Why Wait?

But why wait? Why on earth would anyone wait, especially today? This is A.D. 2010, not 1010 B.C. We have the pill, condoms, and as a last resort, abortion tablets (for the day after) and clinics (for the months after). Why wait? The answer, implied throughout, is to wait because it's worth waiting for. It's the motive of delayed gratification.

Other portions of Scripture would answer the "why wait" question with the reply that you wait because there are serious consequences if you don't.

There are *social* consequences. Imagine a society where everyone was just picking partners (whomever, whenever) the way they pick cell phone accessories at the shopping mall. Imagine the social chaos and economic disaster of unwanted pregnancies, single mothering, the spread of sexually transmitted diseases, the revenge of angry husbands or boyfriends. Well, we don't have to imagine, do we?

The Bible speaks of social consequences. But the Bible also speaks of *spiritual* consequences—a seared conscience (what Paul talks about in Romans 1:18–32) and the coming judgment of God (what Paul talks about in 1 Corinthians 6:9, 10 and Galatians 5:19–21).

Thus, other parts of the Bible answer the "why wait" question by speaking of the serious social and spiritual consequences to sexual activity outside the marriage covenant. But here in the Song of Songs we find a different answer. Here it's not negative but positive reinforcement. You wait because there are serious blessings. It's worth the wait. It's the motive of delayed gratification—opening your Christmas presents on Christmas morning, not on Thanksgiving eve.

Let me ask you, Christian: do you believe in delayed gratification? Let me be more specific: do you hold out in faith for the promises of God? Do you wait for the bridegroom like those five wise virgins, lamps burning, ready to meet him and then enter the marriage feast (Matthew 25:1–12)? Do you join in Paul's elation for the future, longing for that "crown of righteousness" that is laid up for you, "which the Lord . . . will award" to you on the day of judgment (2 Timothy 4:8)? Can you say with the apostle, in his radical heavenly-mindedness, "For to me to live is Christ, and to die is gain" (Philippians 1:21)? Death is gain because only Heaven offers full comfort, satisfaction, salvation, sonship, and inheritance.

Christian, do you believe in delayed gratification? You see, whether it comes to something as grand as our salvation or to something as good as our sexual activity or inactivity, delayed gratification is as foundational to a Christian ethic as love of neighbor.

So, in a world that says, "Change *now*" and "a half-a-million-dollar mortgage on a $30,000-a-year paycheck *now*," and "sexual freedom *now*—with whomever, whenever, however," more than ever we need to say, "No. Not *now* but *then*." Delayed gratification! That principle would save our economy, renew marriages, eventually (if practiced by all) abolish AIDS, wipe out unwanted pregnancies, and socially revolutionize our country and the world. Do I exaggerate? I don't know. Let's give God's wisdom a whirl.

Trust in God's Forgiveness through Christ

We are to *trust God's timing for intimacy within marriage*, and we are to *trust God's timing before marriage*. We are to wait. Why? Because it's worth it. But what if we haven't waited?

Thankfully, the Bible has one more grand point: *trust God's forgiveness through Christ*.[18] Or if we want to keep with the time theme: trust that in the fullness of time God sent forth his Son to redeem us from "the elementary principles of the world" (see Galatians 4:3, 4), such as that popular principle, "If it feels good, do it."

Listen, I'm not ignorant of the world we live in. Temptations toward sexual immorality hang over us like a thick, dark blanket. The light of purity is obscured by things as obvious as click-of-the-button pornography or the less obvious mockery of virginity in the movies. Sure, we don't have temple prostitution or the easy acceptability of concubines to deal with, but we have enough troubles for the day. In our society sex is off the rails, and some of us are riding that train.

I'm not ignorant of the world we live in, and God is not ignorant either. God knows that human beings are sinful. God knows that human beings are sexually sinful. But God has not left us to ourselves. He has sent his Son to heal the sick, free the slaves, and forgive the debtor.

On one occasion Jesus was invited to dinner at Simon the Pharisee's house. Luke tells us in his Gospel what happened:

> [Jesus] went into the Pharisee's house and reclined at table. And behold, *a woman of the city*, who was a sinner [likely a prostitute], when she learned that he was reclining at table in the Pharisee's house, brought an alabaster flask of ointment, and standing behind him at his feet, weeping, she began to wet his feet with her tears and wiped them with the hair of her head and kissed his feet and anointed them with the ointment. Now when the Pharisee who had invited him saw this, he said to himself, "If this man were a prophet, he would have known who and *what sort of woman* this is who is touching him, for she is a sinner." And Jesus answering said to him, "Simon, I have something to say to you." And he answered, "Say it, Teacher." "A certain moneylender had two debtors. One owed five hundred denarii [$10,500], and the other fifty [$1,050]. When they could not pay, he cancelled the debt of both. Now which of them will love him more?" Simon answered, "The one, I suppose, for whom he cancelled the larger debt." And he said to him, "You have judged rightly." Then turning toward the woman he said to Simon, "Do you see this woman? I entered your house; you gave me no water for my feet [the traditional sign of hospitality], but she has wet my feet with her tears and wiped them with her hair. You gave me no kiss [the traditional greeting], but from the time I came in she has not ceased to kiss my feet. You did not anoint my head with oil [another traditional custom], but she has anointed my feet with ointment. Therefore I tell you, her sins, which are *many*, are forgiven— for she loved much. But he who is forgiven little, loves little." And he said to her, "Your sins are forgiven. . . . Your faith has saved you; go in peace." (Luke 7:36–48, 50)

Perhaps you are asking, "But what if I haven't been sexually pure? What if I haven't waited for marriage? What if I'm *that sort* of a woman or man?" The answer is that God offers forgiveness for sins through Jesus Christ; trust in that forgiveness. Jesus came for sinners. Jesus lived with sinners. Jesus dined with sinners. Jesus died for sinners. Jesus rose for sinners. And Jesus stands now ready to accept all sinners who repent and trust in him. Jesus did not come for the righteous but for sinners . . . like you and me. So come to him.

I did twenty years ago. I came to Christ as a sexual sinner.

I grew up in a very devout Roman Catholic home where virginity was prized and where I was taught to wait for marriage, not because "it's worth it" but because "it's right, and you do what is right." But I knew that "love" is what justified sex. If you were emotionally mature enough, if you had a consenting partner—someone who had deep feelings for you and for whom you had deep feelings—then what happens happens. Well, "what happens happens" happened to me. I fell in love, and in my mind this feeling justified anything and everything.

Such love also, sometimes even when you are very careful, produces children. And that's what happened to me as well. At age eighteen my girlfriend was pregnant, and at age nineteen I was the father of a baby boy. And when my boy's mother moved on from me—our "true love forever" didn't last forever, not even twenty months—God's saving grace moved me toward Christ. "Jesus, forgive me," I prayed one night. "And clean me up on the inside, for I'm full of lust and pride." And you know what? He forgave me and cleaned me up.

I share that because I want you to know that when I say "trust in God's forgiveness through Christ," I mean it because I've experienced it. I used to be that, and now I'm this. I've been washed, sanctified, and justified in the name of the Lord Jesus Christ and by the Spirit of our God (see 1 Corinthians 6:11).

I share that so you might come to the living waters of Jesus Christ, waters that cleanse our sins and quench our thirst (see John 4:14). I share that so you might come to your Creator (Christ), the One who holds all things together (Colossians 1:17), who created the world, renews creation each spring, will bring about the new creation—the new heavens and earth, and who even now creates new creations by saving sinners who grow into Jesus, the firstborn of all creation, and who are now as fragrant as flowers, as sweet as pomegranates, as melodious as the tunes of turtledoves.

I share that so you might hear the voice of the Bridegroom (John 3:29; cf. John 10:3, 4, 14, 27), who says, "Your sins are forgiven" (Luke 7:48) . . . "Neither do I condemn you" (John 8:11) . . . "Go in peace" (Luke 7:50)—and so that the joy of forgiveness might be yours.

I share this so you might know the love that surpasses all understanding, the love of Christ, the King who will come in power to judge when the fig tree ripens (see Mark 13:28), but who has already come in love (as a shepherd who laid down his life for his sheep) to offer forgiveness to all who claim in faith, "My beloved is mine, and I am his."

5

Greater Than Solomon

THE SONG OF SOLOMON 3:1–11

Go out, O daughters of Zion,
and look upon King Solomon,
with the crown with which his mother crowned him
on the day of his wedding,
on the day of the gladness of his heart.

3:11

IN HER PLAYFUL, SATIRICAL POEM "The Betrothal," Edna St. Vincent Millay writes:

> Oh, bring me gifts or beg me gifts,
> And wed me if you will.
> I'd make a man a good wife,
> Sensible and still.[1]

Neither Sensible nor Still

At the beginning of our text (3:1–4), the woman of the Song is neither sensible nor still. She is not *still*, but rather out of bed seeking "him whom [her] soul loves." She is not *sensible*, but rather out at night searching for him in the dangerous city streets and squares. She is neither sensible nor still, and yet she makes a man a good wife.

I say that because of the "story" that unfolds. Beginning in verse 1, "On my bed by night," she says, ". . . I sought him, but found him not." Here she is either dreaming or lying awake daydreaming about her husband's return

65

(i.e., seeking him in her thoughts). I favor the second scenario. I do so because there is a similar scene in 5:2ff., where she says, "I slept, but my heart was awake," and when her husband knocks on the front door, she is reluctant to open the door for him. Perhaps her attitude there is, "Hey, I'm tired. What are you doing coming home this late? I waited up as long as I could. I'm not getting out of bed. You can sleep on the front porch. You were supposed to be home at 10. It's now midnight!" Her attitude will change in that poem. She will let him in (in more ways than one, see 6:2, 3). In chapter 5 she is cold at first. But here in 3:1 she is in bed but not asleep. In fact, she is so awake that she gets right out of bed (contra 5:3) and goes on a search and rescue mission, or as I call it, "a sought and brought mission." Note the repeated words "sought" ("seek") and "found" as well as the important word "brought."

On my bed by night
I *sought* him whom my soul loves;
    I *sought* him, but *found* him not.[2]
I will rise now and go about the city,
    in the streets and in the squares;
I will *seek* him whom my soul loves.[3]
    I *sought* him, but *found* him not.
The watchmen *found* me
    as they went about in the city.
"Have you seen him whom my soul loves?"
Scarcely had I passed them
    when I *found* him whom my soul loves.
I held him, and would not let him go
    until I had *brought* him into my mother's house,
    and into the chamber of her who conceived me. (3:1–4)

Watchmen were patrolling the city streets and squares because such places were not always safe at night—think of the incident in Sodom in Genesis 19:1–11 or the Levite's concubine in Judges 19:15–30. But she's not afraid. She is on a mission, "drawn by the power of love,"[4] willing to risk life and limb.

I will talk more about the "mother's house" soon,[5] but now I will simply state what she is saying in verses 1–4. As she moves from the private space of her bed to the public spaces of the city and then back *with him* to the private place of their home and chamber (the latter has, as Daniel Estes puts it, "undeniable sexual overtones"[6]), here she is saying, "I brought him home, to the place of security;[7] and I brought him to bed, to the place of the intimacies of lovemaking."[8]

To say "lovemaking" is appropriate for two reasons. First, we have the placement of the refrain in verse 5: "I adjure you, O daughters of Jerusalem, by the gazelles or the does of the field, that you not stir up or awaken love until it pleases." The refrain comes always in the context of heightened sexual attitudes or actions.[9] Think back to 2:7 (the first time the refrain appears) or ahead to 8:4 (the last time). Right before those two occurrences we have the phrase "his right hand embraces me," which at the very least means that he is touching her body somewhere. (It is very intimate.)

The second reason that 3:4 likely refers to lovemaking is due to the word "brought." The two other times we have seen that word, it referred to such intimacy both times. In 1:4 she has been "brought" into his chambers for those deep kisses she wanted in verse 2. Then in 2:4 she has been "brought" into the banqueting house, right after she says, "His fruit was sweet to my taste," and before she says, "His banner over me was love." So it is my contention that in 1:4, 2:4, and 3:4 the word "brought" refers to being brought to bed. This also fits the pattern we have seen thus far, with each poem ending with sexual intimacy.

In summary, here is 3:1–5 as I see it, with (if you'll allow me) some contemporary embellishment just for fun:

> She's in bed. She can't sleep. She can't sleep because her husband is not home yet. So she gets out of bed. She searches the city for him. She finally finds him. She hugs him, perhaps kisses him, and then she tightly holds his hand and leads him home. She has been waiting for him and for intimacy. They walk through the front door. It's the house she grew up in, her mother's house that is now somehow theirs.[10] He wants to unpack and watch the late show. But she won't let go of his hand. "Come, hither, husband," she beckons and flutters her long eyelashes. He complies happily. They walk into the bedroom, her parents' old bedroom, yes, the "chamber" in which she was conceived years ago, which she sees as a beautiful thing, a continuation of a family romance and potentially the family tree. She had been tossing and turning, but the bed is still ready for love. She has planned it all. The tea light candles are still burning, now burning very low. Subtle sprays of her Chanel No. 5 perfume the air. And Andrea Bocelli's *Romanza* is playing in the background. She says, "Let the intimacy begin . . . oh, for me, dear daughters of Jerusalem, not yet for you."

An Aggressive Wife Is Not an Unorthodox One

Let me stop here, catch our breath again, and give an application. Here it is. Are you ready for it? You might not be. Application number one: *An aggressive wife is not an unorthodox one.*

I realize that this is poetic fiction and not a historical narrative, and certainly not a theological treatise. Thus there is a higher risk of proposing applications without textual warrant. There is no explicit command here: "Wife, be like this wife." However, the Scriptures often express imperatives in ways other than propositional statements. In Proverbs 31:10–31, although the writer gives no explicit command to wives, he is nevertheless instructing wives, "Be like her." As we read the stories of Sarah or Hannah or Esther or Ruth, it is right and natural to say, "Be like her." Yes, Ruth, who went out at night to the threshing floor to meet her man. She sought Boaz, found him, married him, and then was brought home to bed. "So Boaz took Ruth, and she became his wife. And he went in to her" (Ruth 4:13), and that's where Obed came from. Obed was the father of Jesse, the father of David (Ruth 4:17, 22), the father of (guess who?) Solomon.

To be clear, I'm not nullifying Paul's teaching about gender roles within marriage—that the man is lovingly to lead and the wife respectfully to submit. What I am saying, however, is that the desirous attitude and aggressive actions of the wife in this Song are Scriptural. When she says, "Let him kiss me with the kisses of his mouth" (1:2) to start the Song, when she says, "Be like a gazelle" and climb these "mountains" in 2:17, and here when she gets out of bed to bring him to bed, our application is not, "Men, as the leader of the home, you must always make the first move."

Here we have a picture of pursuit—*her* pursuit of *him*. She is not fanning herself in the drawing room, covering her eyes, dressed in her vice-proof Victorian gown. She is no stiff thorn, and neither is she a passive wallflower. She is eager and aggressive. After she has abandoned comfort and even safety, she courageously ventures out to grab him,[11] risking her life for the reward of love.

I am not suggesting *Sex in the City* femininity—impulse immorality. What a disaster that is for everyone involved! Nor am I suggesting the more sanctified but still deadly philosophy (or should I say theology?) of *Eat Love Pray* femininity. One movie reviewer described this book turned film as "a contemporary *Pilgrim's Progress*, in which a scattered, baffled modern woman finds happiness by figuring out what God desires from her, and acting accordingly." According to the main character, "God dwells with me, *as* me." And what does this "God" want? God wants just what a "willful, capricious, self-indulgent Western woman with too much time and money on her hands [wants]": to divorce her husband for selfish reasons, "shack up with a handsome young man then dump him, travel the world," there to "get religion"—that is, to learn how to meditate and how to "forgive herself," and oh . . . and then to "fall in love with a new guy."[12] When I say an aggressive wife is not an unorthodox one, I don't (God forbid!) mean that. Rather, I mean that it is not unorthodox, unethical, or inappropriate for a married woman from time to time to move "from a passive desire to a focused determination to bring her [husband] to bed."[13]

Two Poems, One Point

In verses 1–5 we have the ideas of *sought, found, brought,* and *wait.* And then, starting in verse 6, we have the arrival of King Solomon.

> What is that coming up from the wilderness
>   like columns of smoke,
> perfumed with myrrh and frankincense,
>   with all the fragrant powders of a merchant?
> Behold, it is the litter of Solomon!
> Around it are sixty mighty men,
>   some of the mighty men of Israel,
> all of them wearing swords
>   and expert in war,
> each with his sword at his thigh,
>   against terror by night.
> King Solomon made himself a carriage
>   from the wood of Lebanon.
> He made its posts of silver,
>   its back of gold, its seat of purple;
> its interior was inlaid with love
>   by the daughters of Jerusalem.
> Go out, O daughters of Zion,
>   and look upon King Solomon,
> with the crown with which his mother crowned him
>   on the day of his wedding,
>   on the day of the gladness of his heart. (vv. 6–11)

What's going on here? What is obvious is that Solomon is coming to town—"Behold, it is the litter of Solomon!" (v. 7); "Go out . . . and look upon King Solomon" (v. 11).[14] What is also obvious is that his coming is a big deal. There are sixty elite solders (nearly twice as many as King David had, see 2 Samuel 23:13–39)—armed and able to protect even at night, marching beside this carriage or palanquin.[15] And this carriage smells good (it's perfumed with expensive imported goods from places like India and Arabia) and looks good. It has a beautifully designed exterior and luxuriously inlaid interior, made of rare and costly cloths, metals, and lumber, made of the same materials as the royal palace and the tabernacle (Exodus 35) and temple (1 Kings 5, 6).[16] The Rolls-Royce Limited meets the ark of the covenant! It's a spectacular (almost theophanic) sight!

With the smoke and the smells and the soldiers, and the king lounging in the litter with his crown, likely "a crown of fine gold" (Psalm 21:3; cf. Zechariah 6:11),[17] this whole scene is the picture of importance and opulence. You can almost hear the triumphant tune of "Crown Him with Many Crowns." This is the Davidic king in all his glory (cf. Psalm 45).

Connecting the Two

But what does that have to do with verses 1–5 ? What's the connection between these two sections?

I have found some similarities and contrasts that connect the two. Both poems end with similar characters. There are two mothers: the wife's mother is introduced in verse 4, and then Solomon's mother is mentioned in verse 11. Twice the "daughters of Jerusalem" are addressed: once in verse 5 and again in verse 11, where they are called "daughters of Zion," which is just a poetic variant.[18] Here "Zion" stands for "Jerusalem,"[19] for Zion, as Keel notes, "was the most distinguished part of ancient Jerusalem, the site of the royal fortress (2 Sam. 5:7) and the temple mount (Isa. 29:8)."[20] Those two similarities show there is likely some connection between verses 1–5 and verses 6–11. It's the poet's way of saying, "Read these two poems together."

There are also contrasts. In verse 5 the daughters are told to wait for their wedding; in verse 11 we learn of Solomon's wedding and the "gladness of his heart" associated with it (no more waiting). There is also the contrast between the unprotected woman and the overly protected king. She is vulnerable, walking alone through the city streets at night, while Solomon is protected, traveling in broad daylight in an ornate and bulletproof tank, lifted up above the action, with sixty armed Green Berets by his side. Furthermore, the opulence attached to Solomon and his marriage is contrasted with the simple, unadorned love between the woman and "him whom my soul loves."

In other words, Solomon is used here as a foil, "someone or something that serves as a contrast to another."[21] If this is not obvious here, it will be obvious when we get to 8:11–14, where she contrasts Solomon who has these vineyards (which may be an allusion to all his women, his illicit harem, or simply a description of his incredible wealth[22]) with her vineyard: "You, O Solomon, may have the thousand" (8:12b), but "my vineyard, my very own, is before me" (v. 12a). Then, in verse 14, she calls on her husband (who is not Solomon), "Make haste, my beloved, and be like a gazelle or a young stag on the mountains of spices." Therefore I agree with Tremper Longman when he writes, "The Song is not about Solomon as such."[23] I also agree with Duane Garrett who argues that in chapter 3 Solomon "is not a character in a story but serves as a symbol."[24] Indeed, the pageantry of Solomon's postwedding procession (vv. 6–11) and his love life in general[25] are used as an ironic contrast to the unspectacular, single-minded, committed love of this couple in verses 1–4 and throughout the Song. She is saying, "Ladies, think of Solomon's coming to town with all its grandeur and gladness. Well, my love and my man are greater than Solomon in all his glory."

Thus, these two poems, with their similarities and contrasts, are poetically paired to make this point: This wife's seeking, finding, and bringing her husband back to bed was not in vain because her beloved—who is greater than Solomon, the beloved of the LORD (2 Samuel 12:24, 25)—is worth the risk.

Wise unto Salvation through Faith in Christ

The second application is: The Song of Songs (even this text!) can make you wise unto salvation through faith in Jesus Christ.

There is a long history of Christians making a connection between the heart of our text (3:1–4) and John 20, the tomb scene where Mary Magdalene encountered the resurrected Jesus. Hippolytus (Bishop of Rome from 222–235), was the first to point out the possible parallels between the Song and this Gospel scene, arguing that our text is a prophecy.[26]

I too see the similarities: (a) Mary, who loves Jesus and whom Jesus loves (as a disciple), came to the tomb "while it was still dark." (b) She has come to Jesus' tomb because she is seeking to find him (Jesus says to her, "Whom are you seeking?" [John 20:15]). And then, (c) once she has found him and recognizes him, she clings to him.

Those are similarities (fair enough), and they are interesting and perhaps intentional. But such similarities are not enough to convince me that the first part of Song of Songs 3 is a prophecy. I say that because even some of the most striking similarities are different. For example, Jesus and Mary are not married. Jesus also tells Mary to let him go: "Do not cling to me, for I have not yet ascended to the Father" (John 20:17a). The talk and tenor of "don't touch me now" is very different from our text.

Now, I admire the effort to make connections to Christ. I'm trying to do it every time I preach on the Old Testament. I do so because all Scripture points to Christ in the sense that he is the climax of redemptive history to which every Old Testament pericope either leans toward or reflects upon. But in general, with the Song, we are to make connections to Christ not by means of typology (e.g., King Solomon = King Jesus) or mere linguistic similarities (e.g., the word "seek" is found there and also here). Rather, we are to make the connections thematically.

Here's how it works: Each week I turn on my *Internal Scripture Scanner* (play along with me) and I say, "Okay, what do we have? We have this 'seek, find, and brought home' theme in verses 1–5 mixed with this 'greater than Solomon' theme in verses 6–11. Now, where in the New Testament do some or all of these themes come together?" So I put in all the data, shake it around, and out pops Luke 19:1–10, the story of Zacchaeus, the tax collector, that sinner who got saved. What came to mind was this: Zacchaeus sought Jesus (v. 3), found Jesus (v. 4), and brought Jesus home (vv. 5, 6; cf. vv. 8, 9). Well, there you have it—our Christological connection. And for extra theological interest and value I can add verses 9, 10:

> And Jesus said to him, "Today salvation has come to this house, since he also is a son of Abraham. For the Son of Man came to seek and to save the lost." (cf. Ezekiel 34:16)

But wait. Zacchaeus sought and found Jesus. That's the story. True, he did. But Jesus sought and found Zacchaeus—that's the bigger story.[27] Jesus came out of his safe home to seek after sinners like Zacchaeus, people who are lost in the city streets and squares, and to bring them home to the security and intimacy of his love.

Now that will preach! It will preach because it's true. It's the gospel! It's the good news that we believe. It's the life-changing power that we have experienced. So is Luke 19:1–10 the perfect connection to Christ? Well, maybe.

How about something simpler? How about this: Isn't the Bible amazing? It has a whole book—the Song of Songs—that is "primarily an unabashed celebration of the pleasure of physical intimacy."[28] And what if God designed this short song as an entry place to his long love story?[29] What if part of the intention of this wisdom book is to make the world wise unto salvation by getting the attention of people who wouldn't normally be interested in religious themes—the building of temples, the sacrifice of animals, the teaching of ethics? What if this book is designed in part to open the door to outsiders, to those who would never come to church, lift a Bible, or listen to a sermon?

Think with me for a moment. Imagine a woman coming to church for the first time in ten years. She hears the sermon that became this book chapter. When she returns home after the service, her husband is reclining on the couch, watching the football game. It's a commercial, so he generously mutes the television and asks, "So how was it?"

"Fine," she says.

"Well, what did the pastor talk about?"

"Oh," she says, "he talked about how wives should be more aggressive in bed."

"What!" He turns off the TV.

"Yeah, he said something about how wives should be more aggressive in bed. It's in the Bible, I guess. Some book called the Song of Songs."

"Really?"

"Yeah, really."

He looks down, rubs his chin, and murmurs, "So, what time is the service next week?"

According to Paul, the whole Old Testament was written to make us wise unto salvation through faith in Christ (2 Timothy 3:15). I believe that the Wisdom Literature especially was written partly to draw outsiders inside. Think of the book of Job with its question, "Do bad things happen to good people?" and Ecclesiastes with its question, "What is the meaning of life?" Those are still Top Ten questions.[30]

What if the Song of Songs was written not only as a celebration of pure passion but also as an antidote to immoral intimacies? And what if that antidote was used by God to open eyes (even your eyes) to the "Beloved"—God's beloved Son, Jesus—who is greater than Solomon?

Greater than Solomon in his wisdom.

Greater than Solomon in his purity of heart.

Greater than Solomon in his obedience.

Greater than Solomon in his sacrificial seeking of sinners.

Greater than Solomon in his glory—Christ's heavenly glory, as he now sits enthroned as King of kings and Lord of lords, the one who will come in glory to judge the living and the dead.

What if?

A Detective Finds God

This week I was listening to a sermon by Sinclair Ferguson. In it he shared a story from the life of David Suchet, the famous British actor, best known for his portrayal of Agatha Christie's quirky Belgian detective, Hercule Poirot, on London Weekly Television's series *Poirot*.

One night Suchet was in a Manhattan hotel room when for the first time in his life he had the overwhelming desire to read the Bible. He knew the Gideons leave Bibles in every hotel room, so he searched the room, but he couldn't find one. Determined he went out and searched the city streets and squares looking for an open bookstore. He finally found one, bought a Bible, brought it to his room, and opened it randomly to Romans 8:

For I am sure that neither death nor life, nor angels nor rulers, nor things present nor things to come, nor powers, nor height nor depth, nor anything else in all creation, will be able to separate us from the love of God in Christ Jesus our Lord. (vv. 38, 39)

Upon reading this he was converted. God's Word worked on his heart miraculously, the same way it worked on Augustine centuries before with the same epistle and nearly the same text,[31] and the same way it has worked on many of us. God's Word was opened, and your heart was opened to Christ.

My prayer is that God would use the Song of Songs, even what we studied here, to make you wise unto salvation, to make you aggressively seek and find the Savior who came to seek and find you.

6

A Love Feast in the Beautiful Garden

THE SONG OF SOLOMON 4:1—5:1

I came to my garden, my sister, my bride,
I gathered my myrrh with my spice,
I ate my honeycomb with my honey,
I drank my wine with my milk.
Eat, friends, drink,
and be drunk with love!

5:1

BEFORE HE CONVERTED TO CHRISTIANITY, the famous British journalist Malcolm Muggeridge wrote to his father about an eye-opening incident that happened while he was living in India. Each night, as the sun was setting, he would go down to the river to take a swim. One night at the river he saw a woman in the distance.

> She came to the river and took off her clothes and stood naked, her brown body just caught by the sun. I suddenly went mad. There came to me that dryness in the back of my throat; that feeling . . . of wild unreasonableness which is called passion. I darted with all the force of swimming I had to where she was, and then nearly fainted, for she was old and hideous and her feet were deformed and turned inwards and her skin was wrinkled and, worst of all, she was a leper . . . [u]ntil you have seen one you do not know the worst that human ugliness can be. This creature grinned at me, showing a toothless mask, and the next thing I knew was that I was swimming along in my old

way in the middle of the stream—yet trembling. . . . It was the kind of lesson
I needed. When I think of lust now I think of this lecherous woman.[1]

Years later, after Muggeridge became a Christian, he wrote these memorable words: "[N]o desert is so dreary, monotonous and boring as evil," and
"Nothing is so beautiful, nothing so continually fresh and surprising, so full
of sweet and perpetual ecstasy as good."[2]

As we turn to the most erotic text in the Song, I want us to see that there
is nothing so beautiful, continually fresh, and surprising, so full of sweet and
perpetual ecstasy as love and lovemaking under the rules of our loving Maker.
And I want us to see this in the light of the leprous nature of lust, the way the
world so often thinks about sex today.

In the last study I spoke of the Song as an antidote. Its innocent eros is an
antidote to guilty and godless pleasures. Take a steady dose of this Song—ten
weeks straight—and you'll start to see straight and live straight. You will walk
straight on the straight and narrow way, the only way that leads to life, joy,
fulfillment, and eternal salvation.

Unlike the previous studies, let's jump right to the applications, what I
call my *three antidote applications*. Like the method of the master-teacher,
Jesus—"You have heard it said, but I say to you . . ."—I want to contrast what
you have heard (what *the world* says about sexual intimacy) with what God
says to you (what *the Word* says about the same subject).

Antidote Application One: Beauty

Antidote application number one is: The world says, "Show all; tell all." But
the Word says "Show him; tell her."

We live in a show-all-tell-all world. That is, fully nude and lewd images
are everywhere. When I was a boy, pornography was first gaining ground. But
it was underground. In my case someone's father had to order a magazine,
get it in the mail, and then some sneaky schoolmate had to steal it for a day
and secretly show a page or two at the playground. Then it all went back
underground.

But today if a boy were to type the word "girl" into an Internet image
search, even on the safest of search engines with the "safe search" feature on,
I doubt the results would be so safe. It's everywhere. Showing-all-to-everyone
is everywhere. There is no shame and no sacredness attached to nudity. And
this lack of shame and holiness is seen in something as obvious as pornography
but also as subtle as a midriff, where a junior high girl shows her navel, what
the Song will see (as we shall see in two chapters) as something highly erotic.

We live not only in a show-all world but also a tell-all world. I don't have a TV. I never go to news networks on the Web. I barely look at blogs. I don't buy or read the newspapers. I am the least informed human being on the planet. And yet somehow I know that there are shows like *Desperate Housewives* and *The Real Housewives of New Jersey*, which feature married women openly sharing about their love lives and gossiping about their friends' lovers. Furthermore, I know the lurid details of the adulteries of politicians and princes, sports stars and rock stars. It's all in here (my brain) because it's all out there. Ladies and gentlemen, boys and girls, we live in Tabloid Town, where real news is not news, and where the idiocies and idiosyncrasies of everyone-who's-anyone is everywhere. The world says, "Show all and tell all." The fig leaf has fallen, and no one gasps anymore.

So, what's the antidote to that? The antidote is Song of Songs 4:1–7, where the Word says in essence, "Show him and tell her." Show your husband your body; and tell her, husband, how beautiful she is.

We know from the refrain throughout the Song (2:7; 3:5; 8:4) and the woman's firm admission at the end of the Song (8:10) that she has kept her virginity until marriage. She has saved herself for him. But now she stands before him with very little on. She has a veil (4:1b, 3b), a necklace (v. 9), and her long dark hair (v. 1c), only enough to make her more enticing (she has learned the secret of Victoria's Secret). As a "symbolic demonstration of perfect honesty, perfect trust, perfect giving and commitment,"[3] she stands before him unclothed and unashamed (cf. Genesis 2:25).

And he has seen nothing like it. "Behold [or "Wow," we might translate it[4]], "you are beautiful, my love, behold [let me say it again], you are beautiful!" That's how he begins (4:1a). He ends similarly: "You are altogether beautiful, my love; there is no flaw in you" (4:7).

No flaw? Really? Is she a perfect ten? She certainly didn't think so. Remember what she said about herself in 1:5 and 2:1? She is not blind to her imperfections. But he is. It's blind love at its best. The blemish here and the bulge there he notices not. Instead, to him her eyes, hair, teeth, lips, cheeks, neck, and breasts—those *seven* (!) body parts (she's perfect)—represent her complete beauty. She's "altogether beautiful." She's his realized eschatology!

In Middle Eastern wedding ceremonies this "inventory of another's body" is called a *wasf*[5] and in Renaissance love poetry an *emblematic blazon*. This is the first of four such affectionate inventories, one in which the woman praises the man (5:10–16) and three in which the man praises the woman (4:1–5; 6:4–7; 7:1–5). In these three, the man moves, in all but one (7:1–5), downward. Here in chapter 4 it is from head to breasts.

To him, her *eyes* are pure and luminous. Her *hair* is awe inspiring;[6] it's thick, silken black, and flowing, "a dark waterfall of waves."[7] Her *teeth* are glistening white; they're even, straight, complete, and matching (a rarity in those days before the advent of orthodontics and cosmetic dentistry). Her *lips* are red and "as shapely as a perfectly tied bow."[8] Her *cheeks* are rouged, full of color and health. Her *neck*, which is layered with jeweled necklaces, is long, strong, thin, dignified, and elegant.[9] And her *breasts* are tender, young (recently matured), symmetrical, round, sprightly, and playful.[10]

He will soon get to "her garden" in verse 12, but here in verse 5 he stops at her breasts. No shame in that. This is his wife. He stops to stare and sing. He sings of enjoying this sweet "mountain" and that scented "hill" all night long:[11]

Until the day breathes
    and the shadows flee,
I will go away to the mountain of myrrh
    and the hill of frankincense. (v. 6)

To him, there are "[t]wo hundred [years] to adore each breast."[12] To him, from head to heart to heel, she is altogether beautiful.

She is altogether beautiful if you don't press the metaphors too literally.[13] Do that and she might (and does) sound and look "bizarre, comic, even grotesque."[14] Her hair is like . . . goats!

The key to understanding these metaphors is to understand the language as sensory and emotive. We are not so much to see what he sees but to feel what he feels. We are to smell, taste, and touch. He wants us to take in "his joy, awe, and delight."[15] For to him, her body, made in the image of God and for his completion as a man, is "the most awesome thing in creation."[16] It is good, good, good, good, good, good . . . very good! It's the pinnacle of perfection. It is the best of God's creation (a flock of goats leaping or halves of a pomegranate) combined with the best of what man has done with God's creation (a scarlet thread or the tower of David). She's "altogether beautiful."

God's "Blind" Love

I don't know about you, but when I think about this man's love (which as much as his eyes are open to her, we might rightly label "blind" love), I think about God's "blind" love for us in Christ. It's called the doctrine of forensic justification. Not a beautiful name, but it is a beautiful reality: You and I are made beautiful through Christ's bloody atoning death.

Oddly enough, one of the places this doctrine is illustrated is in Ephesians 5:25–30, which speaks of the mystery of marriage between Christ and the Church and how through Christ's sacrificial love he will present the Church to himself "holy and without blemish." Yes, Christian, in him you and I are "altogether beautiful."

Antidote Application Two: Unity

Antidote application number two is this: The world says, "Sex means nothing." But the Word says, "Sex means unity." Put differently, sexual intimacy means spiritual union.

My church sponsored a teaching series on the local college campus called *Christian Sex.* The second speaker in the series, Dr. Stanton Jones, gave a talk entitled "King of the Bed: Should Faith Meddle with Our Sexuality?" He began by sharing common challenges to the Christian view of sex, the first being evolutionary materialism. This idea advocates that material reality is all there is, and thus life is just a blind, ruthless struggle to propagate our genes. It's all biology, baby. (Not the most romantic view.) Now, if you combine that view with the sex and contraception revolutions, you arrive at "sex means nothing" or "sex means whatever you want it to mean." It is merely a natural and necessary biological act and thus ethically neutral. Sadly, this has become our culture's predominant perspective.

As Jones was debunking this philosophy, he shared that anthropologists have studied sex in a variety of cultures around the world and have noted how rare this evolutionary materialism view is. To most of the world, even today, sex means something. That is why sex is surrounded with ceremonies and regulations and also why there are taboos and punishments associated with living outside the norms. "For your own good and the good of the society, you can't just do whatever you want with that biological body of yours"—that's the shared sentiment.

To those who haven't been caught up in our "highly scientific" but wholly unnatural view of sex, sex means something. And what the secular anthropologists today have discovered is what our sacred book has taught for thousands of years: sex means unity—deep, physical, personal, emotional, and spiritual union.

In Genesis, after woman was formed out of man (Genesis 2:21, 22), and as the first husband and wife stood naked before each other (v. 25), Adam sang of Eve, "This at last is bone of my bones and flesh of my flesh" (v. 23a). Then the author of Genesis adds his commentary: "Therefore a man shall leave his father and his mother and hold fast to his wife, and they shall become one flesh" (v. 24). "One flesh"! In Matthew 19:6, after Jesus quoted that Genesis text in his argument against easy divorce, he added his simple summary, "So they are no longer two but one flesh," and then he added his theocentric application, "What therefore God has joined together, let not man separate."

The world says, "Sex means nothing." But the Word (the Word of God incarnate no less) says, "Sex means unity," an inexplicable, God-ordained unity—"my beloved is mine, and I am his."

Now, this theology—sex means unity—is what we find expressed poetically in 4:8—5:1, the second half of our text. The scene is simple, and the outline obvious:

> 4:1–7 "How beautiful you are!" He compliments her beauty.
> 4:8, 9 "Come away!" He invites her to intimacy.
> 4:10–15 "How beautiful is your love!" He compliments her lovemaking ability.
> 4:16 "Come in." She invites him into her (cf. Genesis 16:2).
> 5:1 He goes in. He complies, and everyone praises this act of love. Their private matter gets public praise.

Everyone (and we are to join in) "celebrates the beauty and goodness of sexual love."[17] You see, in the Song of Songs sex is at the center. I mean that literally. It's at the exact center of this Song. As Tom Gledhill points out, there are "111 lines from 1:2 to 4:15 and 111 lines from 5:2 to 8:14."[18] So 4:16—5:1 is "the centre of gravity,"[19] "the heart of the Song . . . the central pivot around which the rest of the Song revolves,"[20] "the centerpiece and crescendo."[21]

It's about sex!

But what is sex about?

It's about unity!

Do you know what the most repeated word in this section is? Many words are repeated here—Lebanon, spices, garden, bride. The most repeated word, however, is "my" (twenty times), 5:1 having the highest concentration in all the Old Testament (nine times!).[22] In Hebrew "my" is not a word by itself; it is a suffix (a first-person possessive suffix). It attaches itself to the word it's modifying, which I think is a fitting visual. "My" doesn't stand alone. Look at 5:1: "I came to *my* garden, *my* sister, *my* bride, I gathered *my* myrrh with *my* spice, I ate *my* honeycomb with *my* honey, I drank *my* wine with *my* milk." That verse (the virtuously veiled sex verse)[23] contains all the key concepts. He came into his wife—who is his bride, his sister (a word of deep family union and intimacy),[24] and his garden (a place of pleasure,[25] perhaps paradise regained)[26]—and has enjoyed it. And now her body is not only his wonderland, but it's the promised land (see Exodus 3:8).[27] "I ate . . . my honey, I drank . . . my milk." She's a land flowing with milk and honey. Yes, he could just eat her up (cf. Proverbs 30:20); and he does eat her up and drink her in.

So the world says, "Sex means nothing. It's recreational. It's like sipping a caramel frappuccino, eating a hamburger, or going to the bathroom. It's no different than any other biological function." But the Word says, "Sex means unity." It's an inexplicable act of mutual passion, possession, and submission: I give my total self to you, and you give your total self to me. You eat me up and drink me in, and I eat you up and drink you in. You become a part of me, and I become a part of you.[28]

"Awake, O north wind, and come, O south wind![29] Blow upon *my* garden," she says in 4:16a.[30] And then notice the change in verse 16b: "Let my beloved come [in]to *his* garden." Here she is not merely "a garden" (4:12, 15), but now through lovemaking she is "his garden." In 4:16 *she says* of her most private part, it's "my garden" (4:16), and in 5:1 *he says* of this usually inaccessible (it's "locked" and "sealed," 4:12) and watery (it's "a spring," "a fountain," and "a well of living [and "flowing"] water," 4:12, 15) place, it's "my garden" too. She has fully and unreservedly given herself to him. She has come down from the mountain peaks of Lebanon and the dangers of lions and leopards (4:8), into his safe arms—his left arm is behind her head, and his right arm now embraces her.

This is pure consummation—the "undefiled" (Hebrews 13:4) and yet aflame marriage bed. This is God's antidote for immorality! Drink it in. Eat it up.

Antidote Application Three: Worship

The third and final antidote application is this: The world says, "Sex is a god." But the Word says, "Sex is not a god, but rather a blessing from and a bridge to God."

I find it highly ironic that in a world that thinks "it's all biological"—that sex doesn't matter—it sure seems to matter to so many people. Sex is an idol and perhaps the most prevalent one today. It has its own houses of worship (strip clubs, brothels, bookstores, etc.) and its own priests and priestesses (porn stars, suggestive pop singers, lingerie models, etc.) and billions of worldwide parishioners who pay money and give homage. And that's just the start. There are billions more—sadly, some professing Christians included—who bow the knee. I have yet to hear a congregant say that Islam or Judaism or Hinduism or atheism has compelled him to do something, but how often I have heard, "Love made me do it."

"Love? Do you mean carnal desires? Do you mean seemingly uncontrollable sexual urges?"

"No, it was for 'love' that I left my wife and kids."

Love? Is such "love" sacred? A god?

You see, there is a world of difference between "God is love" and "love is god." When people depend on the feeling of love and the act of sex to be the answers to life's troubles and the sources of life's meaning, something good turns wicked. C. S. Lewis said it this way: "Love, having become a god, becomes a demon."[31] In his book *The Four Loves*, Lewis explains:

> Years ago when I wrote about medieval love-poetry and described its strange, half make-believe, "religion of love," I was blind enough to treat this as an almost purely literary phenomenon. I know better now. Eros by his nature invites it. Of all loves he [Eros] is, at his height, most god-like; therefore most prone to demand our worship. Of himself he always tends to turn "being in love" into a sort of religion.
>
> Theologians have often feared, in this love, a danger of idolatry. I think they meant by this that the lovers might idolize one another. That does not seem to me to be the real danger; certainly not in marriage. The deliciously plain prose and businesslike intimacy of married life render it absurd. So does the Affection in which Eros is almost invariably clothed. Even in courtship I question whether anyone who had felt the thirst for the Uncreated, or even dreamed of feeling it, ever supposed that the Beloved could satisfy it. As a fellow-pilgrim pierced with the very same desire, that is, as a Friend, the Beloved may be gloriously and helpfully relevant; but as an object for it—well (I would not be rude), ridiculous. The real danger seems to me not that the lovers will idolize each other but that they will idolize Eros himself.[32]

Sex is an idol. But we'll have none of that. To this idol, Christianity comes with its hammer. "Hear, O Israel: The LORD our God, the LORD is one. You shall *love* the LORD your God with all your heart and with all your soul and with all your might" (Deuteronomy 6:4, 5; cf. Matthew 22:37; Mark 12:30; Luke 10:27). That's the greatest commandment. God first! Jesus restates that command in this way *regarding himself*: "Whoever loves father or mother . . . son or daughter [and I'll add here 'husband or wife' or even 'sex between husband and wife' or 'between any two people'] more than me is not worthy of me" (Matthew 10:37; cf. 1 Corinthians 16:22). You can't have sex first and Jesus second.

Christianity seeks to destroy in our hearts the idea of sex as a god and erects in its place the understanding that sex is a blessing from and a bridge to God.

It should be obvious from a passage like this that sex is a *blessing from God*. Some scholars even argue that the final voice in 5:1—the "Eat, friends, drink, and be drunk with love!"—is God's voice of approval.[33] I don't know if I agree with that view, but I like the point it makes. It's the point I'm making. Not only is everything under the gaze of God, but God enjoys our enjoyment of sex. He loves our lovemaking. He takes pleasure in those bodies he has carefully designed for pleasure having pleasure.[34] He's our "cheering section,"[35] if it can be phrased that boldly, affirming what is happening here in the marriage bed as wholesome and proper, and thus glorifying to him.[36]

Sex is a blessing from God. But sex is more than that. It is also a *bridge to God*. What I mean is that even the highest pleasures and sweetest intimacies are designed to leave us wanting something more. Sex creates a hunger for something infinitely more beautiful, pleasurable, and satisfying: God! Dan Allender and Tremper Longman write:

> God gave us sex to arouse and satisfy a hunger for intimacy. Sexuality arouses a desire for union. Sexual consummation satisfies the desire, but it also mysteriously creates a hunger for more—not only for more sex, but also for a taste of ultimate union, the final reconciliation with God.[37]

According to Scripture, sexual intimacy is for unity, comfort, offspring, help against sexual temptation, and pleasure. But it's also designed to point us to God, the Lord of love, in whom all longings are ultimately satisfied.

This is taught in the Song through all the garden imagery.[38] To the groom, his bride is like the garden of Eden *and* the temple, which was decorated like Eden.[39] To them, lovemaking is the closest thing to the promised land. In other words, their love is like being in the presence of God. That is what Eden, the promised land, and the temple all have in common. He mixes all these metaphors to say that sex is a signpost that points to *God's intimate presence* with his people.

Throughout the Old Testament there is an ongoing theme not of Eden restored but of "Eden fulfilled and transcended."[40] The prophets speak of this salvation that is to come in garden/temple terminology (e.g., Isaiah 58:11; cf. Jeremiah 31:12). In the person of Jesus the very presence of God comes to us in bodily form, with eyes, hair, teeth, mouth, etc. And those who come into his presence now by faith are promised final salvation that is portrayed in the New Testament as a wedding feast with lots of food and drink (see Matthew 8:11; Revelation 19:7, 9; 21:6) in the city of God (which is like a garden, with its river and trees and fruits). In that place at that time those in Christ "will see his face" (Revelation 22:4a). This will be the ultimate ecstatic encounter with God!

Augustine had a term for this reality. He called it *totus Christus* ("the whole Christ"), that is, "Christ together with his church, who together will enjoy God in the consummation."[41] This consummation will make sexual consummation seem insignificant, even silly, like two teenagers throwing matches into a roaring bonfire.

The incomplete satisfaction sex gives is intentional.[42] Sex is not god. Rather it is a blessing from and a bridge to God. What C. S. Lewis said of the beauty found in books, music, or memories, I say of sex: it is "only the scent of a flower we have not found, the echo of a tune which we have not heard, news from a country we have not visited."[43] This explains Jesus' teaching that there is no marriage in Heaven (see Matthew 22:30), which I think implies that there is no sex in Heaven. Why? Because it's not needed. Why? Because it's not even desired! To *know* God is to need nothing.

Thus the Song of Songs is God's antidote for sexual immorality and idolatry. It teaches us to appreciate the beauty of the human body, it teaches us that sexual intimacy means unity, and it teaches us that sex is a blessing from and a bridge to God. Yes, it teaches us that "nothing is so beautiful . . . so continually fresh and surprising . . . so full of sweet and perpetual ecstasy"[44] as God, our ultimate good.

7

A Reprieve and Return to Eden

THE SONG OF SOLOMON 5:2—6:3

My beloved has gone down to his garden
to the beds of spices,
to graze in the gardens
and to gather lilies.
I am my beloved's and my beloved is mine;
he grazes among the lilies.

6:2, 3

IS IT LAWFUL TO DIVORCE one's wife for any cause?" That was one of the questions with which the Pharisees tested Jesus. After Jesus answered their question, Matthew 19:10 records the disciples' reaction to Jesus' no-easy-divorce policy: "If such is the case of a man with his wife, it is better not to marry."

I love that. I don't love their reaction (it's sinful), but I love their realism (it's not so saintly). "You mean, Jesus, I'm stuck with this woman because God has 'joined us together' and now we are somehow 'one flesh' and that mystical union trumps whatever transgressions I can trump up against her, legitimate reasons in my mind for divorce—like her overbearing mother, her overdrawing the bank account, or her overtoasting the toast? If such is the case . . . it is better not to marry."

Why do I start this way? Well, thus far in the Song of Songs we have had far more idealism then realism. For six studies we have walked into the bedroom of this committed couple and witnessed their pillow talk, beautiful bodies, tender touches, and passionate lovemaking. We have seen their Edenic love. But now in 5:2ff. we walk east of Eden. We take a brief reprieve from relational paradise. Momentarily we leave the "uninterrupted revelries" of idealism (1:2—5:1) and step into the inevitable "realisms of married life."[1] We step out into the night and hear the crunch of thorns and thistles beneath our feet, the slithering of the snake, and even "the brooding presence of death" in the distance (8:6).[2] We witness more than the expected harshness of half-brothers (1:6) and peskiness of "little foxes" (2:15). Now we see a husband's sweet-talking insensitivity (5:2), a wife's sleepy selfishness (5:3), the violent brutality of men (5:7), and perhaps the subtle disdain of women (5:9). Yes, it is midnight outside the garden of God.

Yet soon the sun shall rise, the morning dawn, and love arouse itself again. "I am my beloved's and my beloved is mine; he grazes among the lilies" (6:3). That's how our poem ends, with emotional and physical intimacy. But it begins like this:

> I slept, but my heart was awake.
> A sound! My beloved is knocking.
> "Open to me, my sister, my love,
>   my dove, my perfect one,
> for my head is wet with dew,
>   my locks with the drops of the night."
> I had put off my garment;
>   how could I put it on?
> I had bathed my feet;
>   how could I soil them? (5:2, 3)

Poetry: What Is the Poetry Doing?

Here is the start of the story. I say "story" not because this is a historical narrative featuring real people and real events. It's poetic fiction, "the poetic creation of the author of the Song, put on the lips of the girl."[3] It's like reading Dante's *Divine Comedy* or Chaucer's *Canterbury Tales*. You are not to ask, did that really happen? Did Virgil really say that? Did the Wife of Bath really do that? No. Think poetry. Poetic license and literary embellishment are permitted. They are permitted to create a mood and make a point. The mood here is tense, and the point (to borrow from Shakespeare) is that "the course of true love never did run smooth."[4] The point is that they're having a spousal spat. All is not Edenic.

And so we enter this "story"—life after the honeymoon in a fallen world.

She says, "I slept, but my heart was awake." She's asleep. But she awakes because she hears the *tap, tap, tap* of her coming-home-too-late lover. She has locked the door. Is it a literal door or *her* "private" door? Scholars disagree. A door and a hand going through the small opening in the door, and then the arousal that follows is an easy target for double entendres.[5] "My beloved put his hand to the latch, and my heart was thrilled ['I trembled to the core of my being'[6]] within me" (5:4).

Modest man that I am, I will take a *moderate* position. I think the situation is something between the literal and metaphorical. They had scheduled a time for intimacy. She washed her body, slipped on her negligee, and then waited for him to get home. She waited for hours. Finally she gave up. She blew out the candles, sealed the bottle of myrrh, locked the door, took off her negligee, and went to sleep. Meanwhile, he doesn't know the plans have changed. Sure, he's a few hours late, and he's tired too, but he is more than ready for their rendezvous. He gets home. He puts his hand on the doorknob. It's locked. Hmm, what shall he do? Ah, he'll just sweet-talk her into submission. That will work (it has always worked thus far). "Open to me, my sister, my love, my dove, my perfect one. It's almost morning. I've been out all night. There's dew on my hair; my locks of love that you love, my love, are getting cold. Come on, my little honeypot, my sweetie pie, my buttercup, just open up and let me lie with you as planned."

In a half-asleep daze she hears all this mumbling mush through the keyhole. And she yells, "What?[7] It's late. It's too late. Why didn't you call?"

"Call?" he says. "Because phones haven't been invented yet! That's why I didn't call."

"I don't care if they haven't been invented. You should have called!"

"What!"

"I'm not getting up to let you in. Sleep outside for all I care. You're not coming into this warm bed . . . or body."

She has played her cards—and pretty well, she thinks.

Now, whatever he does in verse 4 to awaken her to love, it works. She gives in. She'll now gladly let him come in. She quickly opens the bottle of myrrh and pours this expensive oil on her body.[8] She then slowly and proudly trots to the door ("his dreams shall come true," she thinks to herself). But then we read of her nightmare. She has overplayed her hand.[9] Her teasing revenge has backfired.[10]

> I arose to open to my beloved,
>   and my hands dripped with myrrh,

my fingers with liquid myrrh,
    on the handles of the bolt.
I opened to my beloved,
    but my beloved had turned and gone.
My soul failed me when he spoke. (vv. 5, 6a–b)

Now what? Her newfound passion turns to panic. She must do something. She'll just get out of bed, find him, and bring him back. She has done this before (3:1–4). It is certain to work again. Ah, but this time . . .

I sought him, but found him not;
    I called him, but he gave no answer.
The watchmen found me
    as they went about in the city;
they beat me, they bruised me,
    they took away my veil,
    those watchmen of the walls. (vv. 6c, 7)

This whole scene is awful. Her husband, who thus far has been her protector, leaves her unprotected. I don't think she was literally beaten and perhaps raped by the watchmen.[11] But that's how she feels. She feels defenseless and defeated.[12]

Suddenly, while she is still in this nightmarish world, the daughters of Jerusalem appear (where did they come from?). Maybe this is a dream, as many suggest. The illogical character and scene shifts remind me of my own dreams. One minute I'm getting called out by my college basketball coach for not hustling for a loose ball, and the next minute Emily and I are at a grocery store, and she's squeezing a head of lettuce, I'm picking up a bag of potatoes and biting into it, and then she turns and asks me, "Did you remember to turn off the moon?" Basketball? Potatoes? Moon? Bizarre!

I don't know what transpired between verses 7 and 8, but, behold, there's the virgin chorus. She sings, "I adjure you, O daughters of Jerusalem, if you find my beloved, that you tell him I am sick with love." Then they sing,

What is your beloved more than another beloved,
    O most beautiful among women?
What is your beloved more than another beloved,
    that you thus adjure us? (v. 9)

Their question might have a sarcastic, disdainful tone to it: "O wonder-woman, what's so special about your super-man?" Thus this poor bride gets a one-two punch. First, in verse 7 she receives injustice from *the men* of justice who are supposed to protect the unprotected, and then in verse 9 she receives ridicule from *the women* of the wedding, her bridesmaids who are supposed to extol their love. Perhaps this is the case. Or the young women serve merely as perfectly placed poetic devices that get us to where the poet wants to get us—namely, this poem within the poem about the bridegroom's body.

Below you will see that verses 8–16 comprise a poem within the poem. We know it's a separate poem because of its chiastic nature. A chiasm is a common literary device in Hebrew poetry that uses parallel concepts or words to make a point. The center of the poem (vv. 11b–15a) describes the man's body parts—hair, eyes, cheeks, lips, and so on. That description is surrounded by the same or similar words or ideas that parallel each other. Othmar Keel divides it as thus:

a   v. 8b   O daughters of Jerusalem . . . tell him . . .
b   v. 9ac   What is your beloved more than . . .
c   v. 10b   distinguished among . . .
d   v. 11a   His head is the finest gold
d'   v. 15b   [his feet are] gold
c'   v. 15d   choice as . . .
b'   v. 16c   This is my beloved
a'   v. 16d   O daughters of Jerusalem.[13]

Note that "gold" is at the center. His head and feet are golden. That's her way of saying, "From top to bottom he is magnificent, pure, costly, divine—like gold. He is superior to all others."[14] That's the point of the poem. Thus, to answer the question of verse 9, she replies that her guy—this god-like statue, her larger-than-life lover—is worth going after and risking her life to seek, find, and bring back to bed.[15]

In our previous study we saw that the *wasf* was the man's description of the woman's body. Here it is the woman's description of the man's body. (Other than the symbolic bodily descriptions of Jesus in Revelation [1:12ff.; 2:18b; 19:11–16], this is the only inventory of a man's features in the Bible,[16] and one of the few extant in the ancient world.) The man focused on the woman head to breasts. Here the woman gives a full-body scan. While she admires his body in general ("His body is polished ivory" and his complexion is "radiant and ruddy") and takes note of his strong arms ("rods of gold") and legs ("alabaster columns"), her focus is on his face—his distinguished, elevated-above-the-crowd head, his wavy, black hair, his moist, sparkling, lively eyes,[17] his sweet-smelling cheeks and lips (perhaps his beard),[18] and his sweeter-tasting mouth.

Her description of him is slightly more modest than his description of her. She is interested in personality, we might say, what's above the shoulders rather than below. Oh, she thinks he's more masculine than Michelangelo's *David*, but it's not his biceps that she misses most. Rather, it's his companionship or friendship—"This is my friend" (v. 16). That's mostly why she needs him to return.

So, that's 5:2–16. She falls asleep. He comes home late. She doesn't let him in. He takes off. She takes off after him. She runs into the watchmen and then the women. The watchmen are violent, the women are curious. They ask their question, and she gives her response. "What's he like?" "Well, let me tell you: Think cedars of Lebanon. He's tall, strong, and handsome. And he's mine—my lover, my friend. There's your answer. Any more questions, ladies?"

"Oh, yes," they say, "Just one: where is he? 'Where has your beloved gone, O most beautiful among women? Where has your beloved turned, that we may seek him with you?'" (6:1).

Answer: Why look! Surprise. Surprise. He's right here.

> My beloved has gone down to his garden
>   to the beds of spices,
> to graze in the gardens
>   and to gather lilies.
> I am my beloved's and my beloved is mine;
>   he grazes among the lilies. (6:2, 3)

What's going on here? Has she found him? Has he found her? Did they ever leave each other's presence? Was this all a bad dream? We don't know, and it doesn't matter, for the poetic point is clear. The chasm of separateness has been filled emotionally and *physically*. We don't hear the "I'm sorry, please forgive me" . . . "No, I'm sorry, please forgive me," and we don't see the hug of absolution. We only hear the results of reconciliation—the start of his passionate kisses and the renewal of their vows.

He has returned to "his garden," which we learned in the last study is her private part,[19] or more broadly her body or even her whole being.[20] And there, in this garden, he gathers the lilies and grazes among them. This is a reference to kissing (see 5:13—"his lips are [like] lilies") or to sexual intimacy (cf. 2:16) or both.[21] "I am my beloved's . . . [and] my beloved has gone down to his garden."[22]

Propositions: What Should the Poetry Do to Us?

In summary, this is a reprieve (5:2—6:1) and a return to Eden (see especially 6:2, 3). The cherubim have put down that flaming sword and let the man and his wife back into the garden of God. That's what the poetry is doing. But what should this poetry do to us? What lessons are we to draw from this text?

Get Real

The first lesson is: *Get real.* That is, all of us need a realistic view of marriage. East of Eden, where we all live now, the "realistic rhythm of married life is that of frustration and delight,"[23] but marriage allows us to work through difficulties in order to become more Christlike.

One morning in adult Sunday school at my church, the teacher ended the class with this question: "Do you think we have a realistic or idealistic view of our pastors?" Emily was the first to reply. She yelled out, "Realistic!" Everyone laughed as my halo slowly dissolved. Now, by God's grace I am qualified to be an elder, but it's also true that I am a sinner, and no one knows that better than that sinner wife of mine. She is married to "a difficult man."[24] Or is it the other way around? I forget. Oh, I suppose we are both difficult at times, and thus we have had our difficulties.

On a recent pastors' retreat, we had a wonderful conversation with our associate pastor Andrew Fulton and his wife Rachel. They asked if we had any conflicts in our marriage. It was a humorous moment for Emily and me. We immediately looked at each other and laughed. We laughed because our honest answer is that I've been happily married for twelve years but she for only five. I'll explain.

When I took my first job as an associate pastor, it was an extremely difficult time for Emily. She was a new mom and pregnant (again!), we moved into a new house, and my junior-high-aged son moved in with us. I was oblivious to her stresses. When she most needed a husband and father—a pastor at home—I was counseling church members and shepherding the church's children. I was preaching the Word of God to the household of faith!

One particular weekend I was scheduled to preach, so I needed some time on Saturday night to gather my final thoughts and go through my sermon. The kids were crazy. My wife was crazy. And I was crazier than all those crazy-heads. Once the children were subdued by sleep, Emily gave me a lecture on how much she needed my help. She broke down and cried. I got angry and lectured her on how stressed I was with work and how much I needed her support. She didn't understand. I didn't understand. I walked out of the bedroom, grabbing a pillow, a blanket, and my sermon manuscript. I walked into my office, opened the closet door, closed it, locked it, *and slept in it!* True story. A picture of hypocrisy? Perhaps. A snapshot of marriage outside Eden? Certainly.

Brothers and sisters, get real. Get realistic about two sinners saying "I do" in an undone world. Unmet expectations are our unexpected undoing. I thought he'd be this; I thought she'd be that. I thought we'd "live happily and effortlessly ever after."[25] The idol of the perfect marriage is as dangerous as the idol of eros. Love and marriage make wonderful bedfellows but terrible gods.

Sex is not god. Marriage is not god. God is God. And marriage is part of his plan. It is part of his plan to sanctify you. It's designed to do so. This is what is so beautiful about the covenant of marriage.

Will you take this man . . . ?

I will.

Will you take this woman . . . ?

I will.

Yes, I will love you when you come home too late, when you are cruel with your tongue, when you lock yourself in the closet. I will love you for richer or for poorer, in sickness and in health . . . till death do us part. That's marriage. That's the liberation of exclusive love![26]

Difficulties will stretch but not sever the covenant bond. They will stretch it, and if you allow them—through grace and forgiveness—strengthen it. Get real. Marriage is for your sanctification.

Deny Self

The second lesson is just as terse and just as difficult to get into our heads and put into practice: *deny self*. Put positively and practically, selfless submission overcomes obstacles to intimacy.

For whatever reasons, we all tend to focus on the external rather than the internal. That is, couples might argue about money, sex, or the in-laws (all externals). But I have found that the root problem in marital conflict and the greatest obstacle to intimacy is selfishness.

Isn't that what we see in our text? They are both selfish. He is selfish because he has come home too late, and even if they planned something upon his return, he should have been more considerate. Instead of treading on holy ground, asking to enter the garden temple with respect and reverence, he thinks he's at the Burger King drive-thru window: he wants it his way right away. He's inconsiderate. He's demanding. He's foolish.[27] He's selfish.

But she's selfish too. She is unhesitant in her unwillingness to let him in because it's inconvenient. She's too tired, and thus erotically unenthusiastic. Verse 3 is dominated by that egocentric "I": "I had put off my garment . . . I had bathed my feet." Not now, honey. Your way? No way!

He's selfish. She's selfish. But then what happens in verse 4 and following?[28] He takes some initiative, and she responds. We don't know if any change has happened in his heart (we can assume something did), but we do know something has happened in hers. She is the focus here, as she is throughout the Song.[29] We are all to learn from watching her.

And what do we see her do? Here she stops thinking about self (v. 3) and starts thinking about him (every verse in 5:4—6:3 except verse 7 is about her "beloved"). In verses 5, 6 that egotistic "I" turns into an altruistic "I"—"I arose . . . I opened . . . I sought him . . . I called him." She is now aroused, and her "single-hearted desire" is to "find her lover" to cure this lovesickness.[30] But look at what she does. She does the least convenient thing imaginable—she gets out of bed in the middle of the night and searches the city streets. How highly inconvenient. How highly dangerous! She risks her reputation.[31] She risks her life for him. And even after the guards beat her (5:7), she gets up and goes. Why? Because now *she* is not her focus. *He* is her focus. So much so that in verses 10–16 she will sing a song about how special he is! From there, once she has found him, she will sing again, "I am my beloved's and my beloved is mine" (6:3).

That closing verse especially shows this shift. In 2:16 she said nearly the same thing: "My beloved is mine, and I am his." Conversely, here in 6:3 she states that she belongs to her beloved first ("I am my beloved's"), and then that he belongs to her second ("and my beloved is mine").[32] Perhaps this is not significant, but perhaps there is a shift from selfishness to selflessness. Either way, 5:3 and 6:3 are worlds apart, and the chasm of their separation has been bridged by selflessness—"I am not my own; I am my beloved's."

Three Selfless Steps

I'll get even more practical with this poem at this point. I have talked about getting real and denying self. Under the heading "denying self," I'll add three selfless steps toward intimacy: open eyes, open mouth, and open door.

First, you should have *open eyes*. By this I mean that you should see your spouse the way you first saw him or her, looking again with loving eyes that overlook a multitude of sins. Not the eyes of ingratitude or indifference, but the eyes you had on your favorite date, your wedding day, or the moment of the proposal.

Recently I was walking down the street, and I saw a man come out of a jewelry store. He was smiling. A woman was sitting on a bench, and she was smiling too. As I got closer he knelt down, said something, and placed a diamond ring on her finger. I saw all this as I walked by. But they never looked at me. They didn't even notice I was there. They were in their own world. When I was a few paces beyond them, I turned around and saw him take her face in his hands and kiss her. It was deep and passionate, too deep and passionate for a public sidewalk. But it made me smile because this man and woman were so in love with each other. They had loving eyes *only* for each other.

Daniel Estes writes:

> In marriage, it is easy to lose sight of how special one's spouse is. The inexorable duties of life can dilute the delight of intimacy, so that what used to provoke excitement now evokes only a yawn. Indifference is a lethal blow to intimacy, because it communicates that the relationship is not as valued as it should be.[33]

Don't lose sight of how special your spouse is. Open your eyes to your beloved. What do you admire about him or her? What is outstanding? What are you grateful to God for—the way she looks, the way he talks, the way she cares for you, the way he sacrifices for you, his or her friendship? And do you ever go overboard with your mutual admiration—"I admire my husband's 'solid, immovable, firm and steadfast' character, his Lebanon-like imposing permanence."[34] Or "I admire my wife's flawless beauty—I'm talking rounded thighs like jewels, the work of a master hand" (see 7:1b). You get the idea.

Second, you should have an *open mouth*. Did you notice in this text (in fact in every text thus far) how this couple speaks to each other? Words matter in the matters of love. They are constantly complimenting and affirming each other. They are always using terms of endearment—"my dove, my perfect one, my beloved, my friend." In fact, they often borrow from each other's language. Their normal pattern of speech is "honest, considerate, constructive and tender."[35]

Do you ever open your mouth? If so, what do you say? Anything nice? Do you ever sound like they sound? I hope so. Do you have pet names for each other—honey, sugar, sweetie, babe, gorgeous, love, bride, or Bob Dylan's term "covenant woman"? Is she your "Covenant woman/Got a contract with the Lord"? And is he your covenant man? I hope so.

Third, you should have an *open door*. As a pastor, I hesitate sharing anything personal on this final point. But in the end I decided that if I could share about the closet, I could share about the door. Emily and I have an "open door policy." This policy is not based on the text of our study, though it could be. It's based on 1 Corinthians 7:1–5, where Paul writes:

> Now concerning the matters about which you wrote: "It is good for a man not to have sexual relations with a woman." But because of the temptation to sexual immorality, each man should have his own wife and each woman her own husband. The husband should give to his wife her conjugal rights, and likewise the wife to her husband. For the wife does not have authority over her own body, but the husband does. Likewise the husband does not have authority over his own body, but the wife does. Do not deprive one another, except perhaps by agreement for a limited time, that you may devote yourselves to prayer; but then come together again, so that Satan may not tempt you because of your lack of self-control.

Paul gives this as "a concession, not a command" (v. 6). He wishes the Corinthians' sex-crazed culture didn't have such an effect on the church. But he's realistic, and so he concedes to what Emily and I call an "open door policy." My beloved is mine, and I am hers. We are one flesh. Therefore anytime I need or want to be intimate with my wife and she doesn't want to be intimate with me (or vice versa [this has yet to happen]), she says, "Open door. If you want to, you can." And sometimes I say, "Yes, I want to." Other times I say, "Okay, I'll wait." That may sound, especially to newlyweds, negative and dutiful. But it's not; "it's positive and dutiful."[36] It is positive and *selfless*. In this case my wife is saying, "My husband's needs and desires become mine." It's a selfless attitude.

So, open eyes, open mouth, and open door—those are the three selfless steps I commend to you.

The Benefits of Self-Denial

As you reflect upon these two lessons—get real and deny self—perhaps you are thinking, "Okay, I get the *get real* part, but remind me again why I should ever *deny self*—that's a very counterintuitive claim." There are at least two reasons: (1) it will help your marriage—it's heavenly living with a selfless person, but it's hellish living with a selfish one; and (2) you're a Christian, and thus your marriage mirrors the gospel, *and* at the heart of the gospel is self-denial!

Below I've provided the logo for Desiring God Ministries, which is composed of four arrows pointing inward that form a cross:

⊞ desiringGod

That's the perfect picture of this text. Anyway you turn it, it points us to the cross, to Jesus who is "altogether lovely" (Song 5:16, KJV)—lovely in his person, glory, majesty, resurrection, ascension, grace, power, wisdom, pardon, *and in his selfless incarnation and death.*[37] Jesus is the epitome of self-denial. He did nothing from rivalry or conceit, but in humility he counted others better than himself, so much so, that

> though he was in the form of God, [he] did not count equality with God a thing to be grasped, but emptied himself, by taking the form of a servant, being born in the likeness of men. And being found in human form, he humbled himself by becoming obedient to the point of death, even death on a cross. (Philippians 2:6–8)

A cross! Is your marriage characterized by self-sacrifice? Does it look "like a crucifixion"?[38] Well, in some ways, it should. Your marriage should look like a crucifixion, where selfless love and selfless submission collide (see Ephesians 5:21–33), where both husband and wife can say, "God has given me a lover who preaches to me every day the gospel,[39] a spouse who sings to me the story of our salvation—of God having reconciled selfish sinners through his selfless Son."

Deny self because it will help your marriage (and any relationship you are in) and because it mirrors the glorious gospel of Jesus Christ,[40] a gospel that the world so desperately needs to *see.*

8

How Beautiful!

THE SONG OF SOLOMON 6:4—8:4

You are beautiful as Tirzah, my love,
lovely as Jerusalem,
awesome as an army with banners.

6:4

IN MY OFFICE I HAVE A WHOLE WALL of Bible commentaries. On that wall are works by two older commentators whom I especially trust and often reach for when I prepare to preach: John Calvin and Matthew Henry. Astonishingly Calvin commented in detail on most books of the Bible. I have twenty-two volumes on one shelf. But he did not (perhaps wisely) touch the Song of Songs.[1] I wish he had. Matthew Henry wrote a six-volume commentary titled *Exposition of the Old and New Testaments*, which covers every verse in the Bible, including the Song of Songs.[2] Concerning Henry's commentary, Charles Spurgeon said, "Every minister ought to read [it] entirely and carefully through once at least."[3]

I too commend Matthew Henry's old commentary to you . . . with one reservation. I do not commend his view of the Song of Songs. In his introduction to it he wrote, "When we apply ourselves to the study of this book we must not only, with Moses and Joshua, *put off our shoe from off our foot* [we are on holy ground, but we must also] . . . forget that we have bodies."[4] Forget that we have bodies!?

My master's thesis was on the history of interpretation of the Song of Songs. In my studies I learned there were over one hundred Latin commentaries written on the Song from the second through the sixteenth centuries.[5]

Compare that number to six commentaries on Galatians, nine on Romans, thirteen on Mark, and sixteen on John![6] This trend continued even during and after the Protestant Reformation. For example, from 1515–1550 (the heart of the Reformation), ten commentaries were written on John, six on Romans, and yet twenty-seven (!) on the Song.[7] In the 1640s, during the Westminster Assembly, the Westminster divines noted some 500 commentaries available on the Song (yes, the Puritans and their progeny loved this love song as well).[8] More remarkable than those statistics is that all these commentaries agreed with Matthew Henry's remark, either implicitly or explicitly.[9] Thus, in light of the history of interpretation, his remark is not remarkable. Allowing for a few voices crying in the wilderness, pre-twentieth-century Christian exegetes agreed that we must "forget that we have bodies" when we read this book!

But how? How are we to forget that we have bodies when we read 6:4—8:4?

And why? Why are we to forget that we have bodies when we read, "Your *neck* is like an ivory tower"? Why are we to forget that we have bodies when we read four large poetic sections *on the human body*, two of which are in our text (6:4–10 and 7:1–9a)?

Why interpret the Song only spiritually and never literally, such as Matthew Henry does with 7:8, where he views the bride's "breasts" as the Church's "pious affections towards [Christ]"?[10] The reason is the influence of Neo-Platonic dualism. The spirit of Plato (or at least Greek thought) hovered over the Church[11] and still hovers there today, just a little higher than it used to. The body is "the tomb of the soul," as Orpheus taught,[12] or it is "Brother Ass," as St. Francis famously phrased it, this useful but infuriating beast.[13] It's a necessary evil. In many instances, we'd be better off without it, they thought.

One of the earliest commentators and certainly the most influential on the Song was Origen of Alexandria. He wrote, "I advise everyone who is not yet rid of the vexations of the flesh and blood and has not ceased to fell the passions of this bodily nature, to refrain from reading the book and the things that will be said about it."[14] I'll paraphrase: "Anyone who is human should not read this book." Okay, that's an exaggeration. He says, "Anyone who is still struggling with natural bodily passions should not read this book." Is there a difference? Not really.

Now don't get me wrong. I love church history and have studied it most of my Christian life. So by starting this study this way, please understand that I am neither a chronological ignoramus nor a chronological snob. I just think that for too long too many Christians held an un-Biblical view of the body and bodily pleasures within marriage. So much so that Bertrand Russell's infamous critique of Christianity's attitude toward sex—that it is "morbid and unnatural"[15]—while overstated and partly ill informed, is not completely unwarranted.

Did you know that on the table (for discussion and vote) at the Council of Nicea (A.D. 325) was the proposal that all clergy give up not only relations with their wives but also living with their wives?[16] The proposal did not pass, but sadly the perspective did. By that time celibacy had become the supreme symbol of piety, and sexual pleasure (even within marriage!) was frowned upon and seen as inherently sinful.[17] Later Augustine's perspective, which has been prevalent since he advocated it, was that sex was only to be engaged in for the begetting of children.[18] Procreation was positive, but the passion and pleasure of procreation was not.

"When we apply ourselves to the study of this book we must . . . forget that we have bodies."

Really? Says who? Certainly not the Bible! When we open the Bible we don't find a separation of body from soul, matter from spirit, or godly purity from physical passion. There is no devaluing of the human body.[19] Think of the incarnation![20] Think of the bodily resurrection! There is no belittling of sensual delights. Think of Jesus celebrating a wedding by providing his miraculous vintage wine. There is no dichotomy between spirituality and sexuality,[21] between loving God with heart and soul and loving one's wife or husband with heart and flesh—with eyes and hands and mouth and . . . well, you know what.[22]

That is what the Song of Songs brings to the table. And thank God! Thank God that the answer to the question, "What do you think of the human body?" is "It is good." And thank God the answer to the question, "What do you make of physical pleasure within marriage?" is no different. Both *bodily beauty* and *pure passion* are very good. Thus saith the Lord.

Bodily Beauty

Bodily beauty and *pure passion* are the two themes in this study because they are the two clear themes in our text.

We begin with bodily beauty. My core idea for that theme is this: all of creation, especially the beauty of the human body, points to the beauty of the Lord, our Creator. So by saying "bodily beauty" I ultimately have God in mind. I want to arouse your affections toward him by looking at her, the beautiful bride of Solomon's Song.

The Bible is a very balanced book. It warns about the demise and danger of beauty. The demise: "Beauty is vain" (Proverbs 31:30). The danger: "Do not desire [the adulterous woman's] *beauty* in your heart, and do not let her capture you with her eyelashes" (Proverbs 6:25).[23] However, the Bible also notes (and likely values) beauty, especially feminine beauty.[24] Abraham's wife Sarah was "a woman *beautiful* in appearance" (Genesis 12:11); she was "*very beautiful*" (Genesis 12:14). Isaac's wife Rebekah was also "*very beautiful*" (Genesis 24:16, NIV). Other women in the Bible who were called "beautiful" include Rachel (Genesis 29:17), Abigail (1 Samuel 25:3), Tamar (2 Samuel 13:1), Esther (Esther 1:11; 2:7), and the daughters of Job (Job 42:15).[25]

So, Biblically speaking, beauty is like a cut rose. It's worth beholding even though you know it is withering away. It's worth beholding even though its thorns can prick. It's worth beholding because the flower's beauty in that moment points to the beauty, not of Mother Nature, but of Father God.

As Bible-believing Christians we must not lose an aesthetic element to our faith. The Bible is neither hostile to nor dismissive of beauty. It recognizes and extols it, and nowhere more than in the Song of Songs, where "beauty is everywhere," as Leland Ryken notes, "—in the exalted poetry, in the pictures of nature, [and even] in the attractiveness the lovers find in each [other's bodies]."[26] Bodily beauty.

Finally we come to our text.

The word "beautiful" is an important word in the Song. It occurs sixteen times in the book,[27] four of which are here in our text (6:4, 10; 7:1, 6). All four occur in these *wasfs*, the descriptions the man gives of his bride. The opening words of both *wasfs* say it all—"You are beautiful" (6:4), and "How beautiful" (7:1). And what is so beautiful? Her eyes, hair, teeth, cheeks, feet, thighs, navel, belly, and breasts. Those are all body parts, right? Yes! Her body is beautiful.

With such a large section in front of us, I'm not going to unpack each image (especially those we have already seen). Instead I will make three summarizing observations of these two bodily descriptions in 6:4–10 and 7:1–9a.

One: He gives a full-body view.

Although he does not cover every imaginable body part—there is no meditation on the left earlobe—he does cover feet to face, with an emphasis on her facial features. This is likely because the face is a person's most distinctive feature and physically represents one's personality.[28]

Note that in the second *wasf* (7:1–9a) he gives the most intimate inventory thus far. He focuses on her face, but he features what is between the face and feet. He especially features (again, cf. 4:5) her breasts, twice speaking of them. He also includes, for the first time, her thighs, navel, and belly. Those are body parts that only a husband *would* see in an ancient Near Eastern culture and that only a husband *should* see in our culture, and certainly in the Church. So it is a comprehensive and intimate description.

Two: The imagery he uses here is sensory and symbolic. We have already learned this lesson about Hebrew poetry. In fact, we have learned it with some of the same metaphors. Song 6:5b–7 repeats 4:1b, 2, 3b nearly verbatim. So her nose is not literally as big as "a tower of Lebanon" (7:4) but is like this tower symbolically. To an Israelite, this tower was "a symbol of excellence, a recognized standard of value."[29] It is like a sports announcer saying of a basketball player, "He's money!" That is, when he shoots the ball you can count on its going in the basket. He's not literally made of money.

I'll give three more examples, and you can do the rest yourself. When he says, "Your rounded thighs are like jewels, the work of a master hand" (7:1b), he is simply saying that her thighs are beautifully and perfectly shaped. When he says, "Your belly is a heap of wheat, encircled with lilies" (7:2b), he envisions her slim or svelte waist. Can you picture wheat gathered and tied together tightly and the curvature that creates? She has an hourglass figure, and this describes the bottom half of that hourglass.

Finally, when he says, "Your head crowns you like Carmel" (7:5), he means that her head is like Mount Carmel. This mountain range sits above the plains and juts out into the Mediterranean Sea, making it "strikingly beautiful,"[30] and this striking beauty is noted several times in the Old Testament (e.g., Amos 1:2; 9:3). Here the poet uses it as just the right image for her majestic beauty and grace, which to him distinguishes her above all others.[31]

With that image explained, the third observation follows.

Three: When you put all the images together, the point of the whole picture is that his bride is unique and awesome. Her uniqueness is highlighted in 6:8, 9:

> There are sixty queens and eighty concubines,
>   and virgins without number.
> My dove, my perfect one, is *the only one,*
>   the *only one* of her mother,
>   pure to her who bore her.
> The young women saw her and called her blessed;
>   the queens and concubines also, and they praised her.

They all see what he sees: this "Shulammite" (6:13)[32] outshines them all in bodily beauty. Every lady agrees with the man's assessment: "In mine eye she is the sweetest lady that ever I looked on."[33]

She is *unique;* and she is *awesome.*

> But, soft! what light through yonder window breaks?
> It is the east, and Juliet is the sun.[34]

His bride is as awesome as the sun and as beautiful as the moon, the two great heavenly lights. She is out of this world! And she is as awe-inspiring as the grandest cities—Tirzah and Jerusalem (cf. Psalm 48:1, 2; 50:2; Lamentations 2:15).[35] She is *terrific* in both senses of the word: she looks great, and she has this terror to her, like an army in battle formation—"an army with banners" (that's his inclusio in the first *wasf*; see 6:4, 10). He gets nervous in her presence. He can't look her in the eyes for long—her eyes "overwhelm" him (6:5). Her head and hair are so royal, majestic, and powerful that he is entrapped, "held captive in the tresses" (7:5)—her long, flowing, purplish-black hair.

Bodily Beauty—a Theological Theme?

In these two *wasfs*, the groom uses sensory and symbolic imagery to give a comprehensive and intimate description, a full-body view, which describes his bride as unique and awesome. That's my summary of these two sections on bodily beauty. But let's not stop with that. Let's think theologically about this theme. What is the purpose of bodily beauty or any beauty we might witness in creation? Giovanni Leone got the idea right but overstated it when he said, "The strongest evidence to prove that God exists is a beautiful woman."[36] More broadly and Biblically I would say it this way: all creation, especially the beauty of the human body, points to the beauty of the Lord, our Creator.

How can I say that? I can say that because Paul said it. In Romans 1:18–25 he taught that when people look at creation they are to look up in gratitude to God and acknowledge him as the Creator.

> What can be known about God is plain. . . . For [God's] invisible attributes, namely, his eternal power and divine nature, have been clearly perceived, ever since the creation of the world. (vv. 19, 20)

It follows that when we look upon the beauty of the human body we should look beyond the *image of God* to *God*.

According to Genesis, humans are the pinnacle of divine creation, because only humans (soul and *body*) are the image of God, something of God's divine glory and beauty.[37] That fact is emphasized (with the world's biggest exclamation point!) in that the second person of the Trinity didn't become a stone, a plant, or a donkey. He didn't become a penguin or a petunia.

He didn't become wind or water. He didn't become the North Star or a black hole. He became a man. And ironically, the most amazing part of the incarnation was that the Lord would die, that he who "had no form or majesty that we should look at him, and no beauty that we should desire him" (Isaiah 53:2) was so "beautiful and glorious" (Isaiah 4:2) upon that tree. Yes, "behold the king in his beauty" (Isaiah 33:17)! "How great is . . . his beauty!" (Zechariah 9:17), a marred beauty that has made many marred sinners beautiful through faith in him (cf. Isaiah 60:9). Richard Hess writes:

> [A] proper recovery [of an aesthetic theology] lies in an appreciation of the incarnation and the ultimate exhibition of Christ on the cross—at once a terrible and horrifying spectacle and yet also the sacrifice of love that transcends all other forms as the most beautiful and desirable subject the world has ever known.[38]

Amen to that!

Pure Passion

We have examined and applied the first theme, *bodily beauty*. The human body can be quite beautiful. We should all acknowledge that, and if married we should appreciate and enjoy that. Yet the beauty of the Lord is better than the beauty of the body.[39] Now we move onto the second theme, *pure passion*.

I say "passion" because that is the theme covered in the remainder of our text—sexual passion. We find some of this in the HE sections. (In the ESV, HE is above the sections where the man speaks, and SHE above where the woman speaks.) Most of the HE sections cover this theme of bodily beauty. He says, "Your body is beautiful." But notice that in 7:6 he moves from seeing to touching (and smelling and tasting!): "How beautiful and pleasant you are, O loved one, with all your delights!" He says not simply, "How beautiful is your body," but "How beautiful are your delights," that is, what her body does to him. He's talking about lovemaking.[40] And if you think I'm wrong, just keep reading. Read about his rugged desire and determination to enjoy such high delights:

> Your stature is like a palm tree,
>   and your breasts are like its clusters.
> I say I will climb the palm tree
>   and lay hold of its fruit.
> Oh may your breasts be like clusters of the vine,
>   and the scent of your breath like apples,
> and your mouth like the best wine. (vv. 7–9a)[41]

Now that's passion. Anytime a man talks about mounting a tree and eating its fruit, I say he is talking about passion.[42]

I need not go further to prove the point. But I will. Interestingly, the SHE sections are dominated by this theme of passion as well. Look first at 6:11, 12:

> I went down to the nut orchard
>   to look at the blossoms of the valley,
> to see whether the vines had budded,
>   whether the pomegranates were in bloom.
> Before I was aware, my desire set me
>   among the chariots of my kinsman, a prince.

What is she saying here? You know it's a tough nut to crack (pun intended) when commentators who are unanimous on nearly nothing in the Song are unanimous that verse 12 is "the most difficult in the Song and one of the most difficult in the Old Testament to make sense of."[43] And you know it is difficult when one of the most prominent Wisdom Literature scholars, Roland Murphy, says it "has resisted all attempts at translation."[44]

However, enough of the pieces of this many-piece puzzle can fit together to form some picture. With verse 12, for example, it's not difficult to see that she (again!) desires her man and that this "desire" is what moves her toward her prince. And if you place that piece next to verse 11, here's what comes in view: she goes down to this orchard to see if the fruit is ripe. (Mandrakes or "love-apples" were an aphrodisiac, while pomegranates, with their many seeds, were seen as a symbol of fertility.) There she is investigating whether the time is ripe to arouse and awaken desire. The answer to that inquiry is hinted at in 6:12 and answered clearly in 7:9b—8:4. There the answer is twofold. Is it the right time to arouse and awaken passion? Yes, it is for us (7:9b—8:3), but not yet for you, O daughters of Jerusalem (8:4). One translation renders 8:4 this way:

> Daughters of Jerusalem, swear to me
>   that you will never awaken love
> until it is ripe.[45]

With 8:4 we move from "this is just a text about passion" to "oh no, this is a text about *pure* passion."

The first subpoint is this: *Pure passion is patient.* The implication of 8:4 (and 2:7 and 3:5) is that pure passion waits for the proper time and the proper person. The proper time is marriage, and the proper person is one's spouse, one man and one woman lawfully wed.[46]

God-given boundaries are for our good and the good of society. One of those boundaries is marriage. Passion must wait for the proper time and the proper person. But my second subpoint is that within those boundaries *pure passion can be pleasurable.* It's okay to *enjoy* lawful carnal knowledge. That's what 7:9b—8:3 teaches.

By 7:9a he has worked his way up to her mouth, and there he sings that her kisses are "like the best wine." (Wine again represents the world's greatest pleasure.) Then in 7:9b it's as if she interrupts him. She opens her mouth and says, "You've taken the words right out of my mouth." Yes, my beloved, that wine you speak of "goes down smoothly . . . gliding over lips and teeth." In other words, his kisses "flow from his lips to mine" (MESSAGE). This is pleasurable passion—bodies created by God to experience intense physical sensations.

Next, look at 7:10, where she speaks about their mutual solidarity ("I am my beloved's") and his passion for her ("and his desire is for me"). In 6:12 she spoke of her desire, and here (although it's a different Hebrew word[47]) she speaks of his.

The word used for "desire" here is interesting. It is only used three times in the Old Testament, the first time most famously. In Genesis 3:16, after God curses the woman with "pain in childbearing," he says to her, "Your *desire* shall be contrary to your husband, [but guess what?] but he shall rule over you." The sadly ironic picture is this: she will have this "unhealthy, clinging, and controlling" desire for her husband, and yet her husband will rule over her as a cold, oppressive ruler,[48] *and* as the one who will bring her (of all things!) children (who will hurt her coming out). But here in the Song, where Edenic love is on display, it is like the curse has been lifted.[49] Here we find marital love set within a garden of delights—there are fields and vineyards and trees and fruit.

As throughout the Song, the language here is erotic, but tasteful and reserved. The couple wants to be passionate with each other outside and inside—in the "fields" and "vineyards" (7:11, 12) as well as in her mother's house (8:2). But note that the couple does not lose themselves in themselves.[50] Rather, they see themselves within God's creation and within the restraints of society. In 7:11–13 she says:

Come, my beloved,
 let us go out into the fields
 and lodge in the villages;
let us go out early to the vineyards
 and see whether the vines have budded,

whether the grape blossoms have opened
and the pomegranates are in bloom.
There I will give you my love.
The mandrakes give forth fragrance,
and beside our doors are all choice fruits,
new as well as old,
which I have laid up for you,[51] O my beloved.

In 7:8, 9a he invited her to intimacy, and here she invites him. She wants to be intimate with the right person (her beloved) at the right time (early in the morning) and in the right place (the secluded private fields).[52]

Then in 8:1–3 she wants what has been *private* and *outside* (in 7:11–13) to be *public* and move *inside* (and based on v. 3 it seems as though it does).

Oh that you were like a brother to me
who nursed at my mother's breasts!
If I found you outside, I would kiss you,
and none would despise me.
I would lead you and bring you
into the house of my mother—
she who used to teach me.
I would give you spiced wine to drink,
the juice of my pomegranate.
His left hand is under my head,
and his right hand embraces me!

Don't think the brother/mother language too strange. I will explain the role of the mother as teacher in our next study. Now simply note that this short lyric moves us along in intimacy. Her first desire is that he would have always been with her, like a twin brother, and that like brother and sister they could kiss in public without anyone rolling their eyes. Her second desire is to bring him to the family home, and there to give him . . . well, more fruit juice (i.e., sexual delights).

In contrast to "the woman Folly" (Proverbs 9:13) who says "stolen water is sweet, and bread eaten in secret is pleasant" (Proverbs 9:17), here the woman Wisdom gives her beloved "spiced wine" and "the juice of my pomegranate" (Song 8:2) in her mother's house, hoping all the world knows. There is no shameful secrecy to pure passion. She wants to be alone for intimacy, but she wants everyone to know they are alone and intimate.

So, in the second half of this study I'm talking about pure passion, and I'm providing four P-lettered subpoints for you. I've given you two:

1. Pure passion is patient. Pure passion waits for the proper time and the proper person.
2. Pure passion is pleasurable. (That's what so much of this text is about.)

Here is the third:

3. Pure passion is a protection against impure passion.

Perhaps one of the most interesting discoveries I have made in studying themes related to the Song of Songs is how lust (impure passion) and love (pure passion) are set against each other. What I mean is that God's Word often places *love* next to *lust*, to give us a choice and an antidote. For example, in Romans 13:8–14,[53] before Paul writes about avoiding lust—"Let us walk properly as in the daytime, not in orgies . . . not in sexual immorality and sensuality" (v. 13), he speaks of love: "Owe no one anything, except to love each other" (v. 8). More specifically related to sexual love, we find that same mode of operation in Proverbs 5:15–20. In the context of avoiding adultery there is an exhortation to be intoxicated with one's wife (and watch for the imagery also used in the Song):

Drink water from your own cistern,
    flowing water from your own well.
Should your springs be scattered abroad,
    streams of water in the streets?
Let them be for yourself alone,
    and not for strangers with you.
Let your fountain be blessed,
    and rejoice in the wife of your youth,
    a lovely deer, a graceful doe.
Let her breasts fill you at all times with delight;
    be intoxicated always in her love.
Why should you be intoxicated, my son, with a forbidden woman
    and embrace the bosom of an adulteress?

In other words, as Paul House correctly notes, "Satisfaction with one's long-term love will negate succumbing to short-term surrender to temptation."[54] Similarly Barry Webb concludes, "To rejoice in the wife of one's youth, to be satisfied by her breasts and captivated by her love is to walk in the path of the wisdom that is grounded in the fear of Yahweh."[55]

For me, studying, teaching, and applying the Song's wisdom to my marriage has increased intimacy at every level. I have never been more happily married, and this increased intimacy decreases the draw of temptation. Pure passion is a protection against impure passion.

What a word of wisdom that is for today! Just think about what surrounds us on a daily basis. I often do sermon preparation in the mornings at Barnes and Noble. Each time I need to go to the bathroom I have to walk through the "Romance" section. Now, is the "Romance" section filled with commentaries on the Song of Songs or godly books on marriage and pure passion? Oh, no. Based on the flesh-filled covers (which are hard not to notice) and catchy titles (which, admittedly, sometimes catch my eye), I assume most involve extramarital liaisons.

That's just your average bookstore, where impure passion is promoted to pastors as they walk to the bathroom. If we think beyond that to the Internet or movies or television, we enter into another world of subtle and not so subtle godlessness.

In the early 1980s Harvard conducted a study on allusions to intercourse on television. They found that 70 percent of all allusions involved unmarried couples or prostitutes.[56] That was the 1980s, which were a great distance from the early 1960s and something like *The Dick Van Dyke Show* (1961–1966), where Rob and Laura (husband and wife) slept in separate beds! That is also a great distance from today where every sitcom and daytime drama features at least one "sex addict" (that's what I would call him if I were counseling him), a Don Juan or Casanova—the leading man who leads many easily-led women into bed. Think about it. When was the last time you saw a show or movie where the leading man was happily married, devoted to his wife, and the marriage bed was filled with pure passion? Tune in tonight? Coming to a theater near you? I doubt it.

I doubt it when one of our greatest film personalities, Woody Allen, when facing the media about his sexual relationship with the adopted daughter of his wife, shrugged his shoulders and said, "The heart wants what it wants." When someone that prominent makes that excuse, we are a long way from God's Word, wisdom, and ways.

1. Pure passion is patient.
2. Pure passion is pleasurable.
3. Pure passion is a protection against impure passion.

And finally,

4. Pure passion is a promotion of the Passion.

I don't know why you became a Christian. But I would imagine one common thread in our stories is that all of us found Jesus—his personality, character, claims, teachings, and miracles—to have a captivating beauty. In the words of Augustine (he'll redeem his theological reputation with this quote), Jesus is "the beauty of all things beautiful."[57]

When we Christians reflect that beauty by the way we think and act (or don't act) upon bodily passions, the world takes notice. That is, the single person who waits for marriage to express his or her passion promotes the gospel, as does the married couple who so passionately love each other. The world notices these things. The world notices the pure girl who won't. The world notices the Christian couple married for sixty years who still enjoy each other's friendship—the holding of hands, the tender surprising public kiss on the cheek. It's something strangely beautiful and alluring. Pure passion—held in check or rightly expressed—is a promotion of the Passion of Jesus Christ! I'll put it this boldly—it's the gospel in its most tangible/touchable/visible form.

The Battlefield

In *The Brothers Karamazov*, Dmitri says to Alyosha that "beauty is the battlefield where God and Satan contend with each other for the hearts of men."[58] Exactly. And so too is passion. God's Word teaches that *pure passion* is patient, pleasurable, a protection against impure passion, and a promotion of the Passion. And God's Word teaches that all of creation, especially the beauty of the human body, points us to the beauty of the Lord, our Creator, "the beauty of all things beautiful."

9

The Climax

THE SONG OF SOLOMON 8:5–7

Set me as a seal upon your heart,
as a seal upon your arm,
for love is strong as death,
jealousy is fierce as the grave.
Its flashes are flashes of fire,
the very flame of the LORD.

8:6

IN THE 1960S a young woman named Kim Grove was engaged to a young man named Roberto Casali. Before they were married, Kim would write little love notes and slip them into Roberto's fishing box, his back pocket, or whatever secret place she could find. Her notes were simple. Each one featured a drawing of this chubby, childlike couple—a man with dark black hair and a woman with blonde hair, both modestly undressed. And beneath each drawing was a short inscription, which always began "Love is. . . ."

Love is . . . the right word.
Love is . . . giving each other silly pet names.
Love is . . . someone who makes you weak in the knees.
Love is . . . counting every single freckle.
Love is . . . showing her the house where you spent your childhood.
Love is . . . making her queen.
Love is . . . keeping a light burning for him.
Love is . . . patching up a quarrel.

Love is . . . telling her she looks wonderful on a down day.
Love is . . . like wine, better as it matures.
Love is . . . when the passion slows down and the friendship speeds up.[1]

Roberto collected these notes and eventually showed them to the Tribune Media Services, who published the first comic in the *Los Angeles Times* on January 5, 1970. These comics became a worldwide success, featured in nearly every major newspaper for the last four decades. Their appeal was the mixture of simple art with universal themes. (You may have noted that what was quoted above is also reflective of themes found in the Song, which was written to a very different culture at a very different time).

Here in the Song, for the first and only time, we step back from the "story" and get the closest thing to *a definition of love* that the Song will give us.[2] This is why a number of scholars call 8:5–7 the climax of the Song of Songs.[3]

This short section reminds me of Job 28. In that passage there is an interruption in the heated dialogue between Job and his friends. Some think Job is speaking. I think it might be the author, who, similar to a Shakespearean aside, stops the characters and addresses the audience (i.e., readers) himself. The interruption to the drama is the question, "From where, then, does wisdom come?" (v. 20). The answer is: it will only be found with God (v. 23), and thus the proper disposition is, "the fear of the Lord, that is wisdom" (v. 28).

Here in the Song it is difficult to know who is speaking in this climactic "interruption," but it seems to me that each central character gives voice. The bride, groom, and daughters of Jerusalem turn to us and ask in essence, "What then is love?" And thankfully they provide the answer. They provide three simple pictures with three profound captions that teach us God's universal truths about marital love.

Love Is . . . Leaning on Your Husband

What is love? First, *love is leaning on your husband*. Look at verse 5a: "Who is that coming up from the wilderness, leaning on her beloved?" The "who" is the young bride, the "beloved" is her husband, and the speakers are the daughters of Jerusalem. The first five words in Hebrew are the same as in 3:6, which there refer to the grand coming of King Solomon: "What [or who] is that coming up from the wilderness . . . ?"[4] Here this ordinary man and woman return home in royal fashion, like a king and queen riding in their pure white, horse-drawn carriage. And the wilderness language—"coming up from the wilderness"—is, of course, reminiscent of coming up from Egypt through the desert into Canaan. As Bible readers we are supposed to pick up on the imagery. Their love has brought them home, to a kind of promised land, a land flowing with milk and honey and wine and fruit—mandrakes, pomegranates, and apples.

Finally we come to the simple picture. What do the daughters of Jerusalem see? They see this lovely couple coming home (that's the second half of the verse—his mother's home is now their home), and she is leaning on him. Love is leaning on your husband. Some think they are now an old couple returning home and reminiscing in their old age about old times. Others think they have returned from their honeymoon and are beginning their life together. I favor the second option, but I honestly like the ambiguity. We don't know if they are newlyweds or not so newly wed. We can safely say they are somewhere between their first weeks together and seventy-five years of marriage. What matters is not the time they have loved but the image of their love. She is leaning on him. We have seen pictures of him climbing her like a palm tree and of her drinking in his kisses like a sip of fine wine. But here the image is not erotic but affectionate. Leaning—if you can picture her with her head resting on the side of his chest—is a sign of affection (closeness, security), but it is also a sign of dependence.

You might think, as I did, of the lyrics to that old gospel song, "Leaning on the Everlasting Arms." The refrain goes like this:

Leaning, leaning,
Safe and secure from all alarms;
Leaning, leaning
Leaning on the everlasting arms.

Or you might think, as I also did, of the Last Supper and the apostle John leaning upon Jesus. John, the one "whom Jesus loved," was "*leaning* on Jesus' bosom" (John 13:23, KJV) or "breast" (John 13:25, KJV; 21:20, KJV). This is a remarkable picture because John has seen Jesus' power—how he can heal any sickness, calm the sea, walk on water, and raise the dead. He has also heard Jesus' authoritative teachings ("You have heard it said, but I say to you") and thundering judgments ("Woe to you scribes and Pharisees . . . brood of vipers"). Yet John still finds Jesus so loving and lovable that he leans upon him. What a sign of affection and dependence.

The way Christians are to lean upon Jesus is similar to the way a wife is to lean upon her husband. A wife does not lean upon her husband for everything, but she should lean upon him for loving leadership, which includes affection, protection, and provision. That's what it means to be a husband. That's what it means to love your wife as Christ loves the Church.

So, men, are you lovably leanable?

As a pastor, I have yet to hear any Christian wife complain about being married to someone who is respectable and easy to submit to because he lovingly leads like Jesus Christ. Paul said, "The husband *is* the head of the wife even as Christ is the head of the church" (Ephesians 5:23). Note the language—"is," not "ought to be." It's a statement of fact, not merely a suggestion. The husband is in "a position of *inescapable leadership*."[5] He either leads poorly by *not* serving, sacrificing, protecting, and providing, or he leads like Christ by doing these things. And the husband who leads like Christ will often find his wife's fair head leaning against his firm chest.

Before we leave this idea and image of the bride leaning against her groom, notice that the image here is likely nonsexual.[6] This is *surprising* because from the beginning of the Song ("Let him kiss me with the kisses of his mouth," 1:2), every scene or larger poetic unit has ended with sexual intimacy. But, here at the *climax* of the whole Song there is no climaxing, if you know what I mean. This is the opposite of the modern romantic movie in which all builds toward the bedroom scene (or *scenes* nowadays).[7] Here we get a picture of mature intimacy, one that teaches that the climax of love is not sex but relationship.[8] "This is my beloved . . . my friend" (5:16b). A love that involves, as C. S. Lewis wrote of his marriage, "mere ease and ordinariness. . . . No need to talk. No need to make love. No needs at all except perhaps to stir the fire"[9] and what he missed most when his wife died, "the tiny, heartbreaking commonplace."[10]

Love Is . . . Bigger Than Us Two

Love is leaning on your husband. That's the first idea and image of our text. The second is this: *love is bigger than us two*. Look at the second half of verse 5. The woman is speaking:

> Under the apple tree I awakened you.
> There your mother was in labor with you;
>   there she who bore you was in labor.

What is said here is this: where the first sparks of arousal flew into the air is now the place they return to settle and call home. This is his mother's house, the place where their love was born, the same place he was born.

We don't know if Mom is still alive or not. But we do know that this couple's love affair has always been a family affair[11] and that Mom matters in the matters of love. The bride's mother is mentioned at least three times (3:4; 6:9; 8:2; cf. 1:6; 3:11), and in 8:2 she is described as the bride's teacher—"she who used to teach me." But what did she teach? The wisdom of God's Word (cf. 2 Timothy 1:5)? Likely. But she also probably taught, in the language of Proverbs 30:19, "the way of a man with a virgin." That is, her mother taught her the art of lovemaking.[12] From the context it seems likely that this is the meaning of 8:2.

Now, that is a very foreign concept to us—a mother teaching her daughter about sexual intimacy. But think of it this way: who would you prefer to learn the art of lovemaking from—your mother, who cares deeply for you and has experience, or the girls at the college dorm or high school cafeteria who haven't been with one man long enough to know what really pleases a man? What wisdom do such fools have to offer you?

I know this is a strange topic, and I wouldn't be talking about it if their mothers weren't talked about in 8:2 and 8:5. But they are. And so here we are. And here's my word on the mother to mothers: Mothers, teach your daughters about these touchy topics that daily hang over their heads: What does losing one's virginity feel like, and being pregnant, and giving birth, and nursing babies? And when the time is right, teach them about more than the birds and the bees; teach them also about the milk under the tongue, the wine between the teeth, the lilies and the grazing stags. Teach them how to handle a young stag at the start of spring. Listen, if "the talk" sounds like a lecture on mechanical engineering, then you're not listening to how the Song does it. "The talk" (or "talks!") should be alive with life, joy, and holiness.

God's wisdom is far removed from today's world, where the widespread attitude is that parents are the last to be consulted in the matters of love and that what consenting adults do in the privacy of their own bedrooms is nobody's business. God's wisdom is far removed from two people making a private agreement ("Hey, let's move in together and give it a try"), which is separated from the family's approval, the church's blessing, and even state law. Do you want to see a solid community crumble? There is an easy way to do it: just make the only rule about love that love is no bigger than us two, that sexuality is a personal, private affair. That attitude (and action upon that attitude) is killing our country and every country and community where it is king.

In contrast to this, in our passage we find such relevant wisdom from God's Word. Love is bigger than us two.

Let me further illustrate. Have you ever noticed that as intimate as the bride and groom are in the Song, the daughters of Jerusalem seem to hover above every scene (e.g., 1:4b, 11; 5:1c, 9; 6:1, 10, 13; 8:5, 8–9; cf. 2:7; 3:5; 5:8, 16; 8:4). Why are they there? They are "there" for two reasons:

(1) as students—to learn about love, and especially the lesson that true love waits for marriage, and (2) as witnesses—to witness true love. They are often called bridesmaids, and perhaps that is how they function, as traditional bridesmaids. They are official witnesses. They represent society by saying, "Yes, we approve of this union." And perhaps they do more than that. Perhaps, when times get tough they are supposed to come beside the couple and say, "Hey, we saw you get married with our own eyes. So confess your sin to her" or "forgive him" or whatever the issue is. "Work through it and get over it because you are not getting out of it."

Love is bigger than us two. That's the picture of the second half of verse 5. In some ways the picture here reminds me of a photograph taken at the wedding of a couple in my church, Mary and Paul Adams. After the service, Paul and Mary were surrounded by all the witnesses to their wedding for one large photo. That should be the picture we have in mind when we think of the union of one man and one woman in holy matrimony. The man and woman do not stand alone.

The imagery in the second half of verse 5 is especially interesting. Many scholars take "the apple tree" to symbolize what we would call "the family tree,"[13] and symbolic value is placed there because of what follows—a remembrance of the groom's mother in labor and giving birth. Although there is no mention of children anywhere in the Song (and this is what makes it unique among the erotic love poetry of the ancient world, where fertility and the gods of fertility are always related to love), this is likely a reference to conception and offspring.[14] First comes love, then comes marriage, then comes the baby in the baby carriage. Or, sometimes in the Bible, first comes marriage, then comes love, and then comes baby in the baby carriage. In other words, there is a flow of history being talked about here. And this couple does not stand outside their family genealogies. They gladly carve their names into the family tree and look forward to adding their children's names, and grandchildren's, and great-grandchildren's.

Physicist turned Old Testament professor turned part-time poet Tom Gledhill puts the point poetically like this:

Underneath the fruit tree's bowers,
heavy, ripe with golden showers,
'neath the shades of family tree,
branches of maternal pedigree,
there I stirred your sleeping form,
where your mother brought new birth
in agony of ecstasy writhing.[15]

Love is bigger than us two. Love came before us, and love will continue after us. We find ourselves and our personal yet publicly inaugurated and ratified covenant love for each other within the context of our society and the family in which we are but one generation.

Love Is . . . Wearing Your Wedding Ring Always

1. Love is leaning on your husband.
2. Love is bigger than us two.
3. Love is wearing your wedding ring always.

I wear my wedding ring always . . . because it's stuck. It's stuck either because my finger has fattened (which I can't imagine) or because my $80 gold ring is shrinking (which is more likely). Either way, I wear my ring always and proudly and gladly. That's the image here. The image is that of *happy permanence*.[16] In verses 6, 7 the bride sings to her husband this request: "Set me as a seal upon your heart, as a seal upon your arm" (v. 6a).

In the ancient world a person's seal was "the guarantee of his identity,"[17] like a photo ID or a signature today. Such seals were often made of "precious metals [and] . . . with ornately carved inscriptions."[18] They were sometimes called "signet rings" (Haggai 2:23; cf. Genesis 41:42; Jeremiah 22:24).

> This is the property of Douglas Sean Michael O'Donnell
> Second son of Padraic of Connemara, descendant of Irish nobility.

A seal might say something like that. So the request here is that of mutual, lasting possession: "Set me as a seal upon your heart" (deeply and inwardly) and "upon your arm" (publicly and externally—like a wedding ring today).[19]

The *reasons* for this commitment follow. Look at verses 6b, 7a:

> [F]or love is strong as death,
>   jealousy is fierce as the grave.
> Its flashes are flashes of fire,
>   the very flame of the LORD.
> Many waters cannot quench love,
>   neither can floods drown it.

Two images are given here, and they are both images of permanence: (1) "death" and (2) "the very flame of the LORD." The first image in verse 6b is an example of a Hebrew poetic device known as synonymous parallelism. See below how "love" and "jealousy" are parallel, and then also "death" and "the grave," and how the second word makes the first word more engaging and concrete.[20]

> . . . love is strong as *death*,
> jealousy is fierce as *the grave.*

So when we say "love," we are talking "godly jealousy,"[21] the kind of single-minded loyalty a husband and wife should have toward each other. And when we reach for an image of how strong this concept of love is, death is the closest thing we can think of. And when we say "death," we are talking "the grave"—that place no one digs oneself out of (cf. Ecclesiastes 9:11, 12). That's how permanent love is.

"Death" is the first image. "The flame of the LORD" is the second.

> [Love's] flashes are flashes of fire,
> the very flame of the LORD.
> Many waters cannot quench love,
> neither can floods drown it.

Here there are two antithetical elements: fire and water. Now, when fire and water go up against each other, who wins? If there is enough water, water will always win.[22] But here the fire wins. Why? Because it's no ordinary fire! It's "the flame of divine love,"[23] as Roland Murphy calls it, or it's a "god-awful" flame,[24] as Tremper Longman says, or it's "his fire of fires,"[25] as Robert Browning put it. It's "the very flame of the Lord," so says Solomon.

This is the only mention of "the Lord" in the Song (the word "flame" is suffixed by *ya(h)*, likely an abbreviation of Yahweh),[26] and it's quite an awesome image given here, one that makes my mind travel to two images from two great God-events in Exodus. There is the burning bush, which symbolizes El Shaddai's covenant redemption ("I will be who I will be"—i.e., "I will keep my promises about offspring, land, etc.") and perhaps God's eternality ("I AM WHO I AM"); and then there is the closing of the Red Sea—the waters open for Israel and close upon Pharaoh and his army. Here in the Song the image (at least how I see it) is that love is like that *burning bush* at the bottom of the *Red Sea*. It's aflame when the waters open, and it's *still* burning (somehow) even when millions of gallons close down upon it. The fire and smoke rise through and above the waters. Now that's an image of preserving permanence! That's love.

Love is wearing your wedding ring *always*. Love is like death and God-fire. It has this permanence about it. And this is why "if a man offered for love all the wealth of his house, he would be utterly despised" (v. 7b). This pithy wisdom saying is more than the Old Testament's version of the Beatles' song, "Money Can't Buy Me Love." It *is* saying that to us. But it is also saying, "How foolish if anyone thinks he can put a price on love." Love is not for sale. Love is not only "much better . . . than gold" (Proverbs 16:16), it can't be compared to gold . . . or silver, diamonds, or any other material possession.

This is a jab at King Solomon who collected whatever his "eyes desired"—pools and places, wine and women, gardens and gold (see Ecclesiastes 2:1–10; Song 8:11, 12). And it is a jab at our *Indecent Proposal* culture, where love always has its price. Money has no bearing on love because money is temporary, but love is permanent.

The Apostle Paul reflects on love in the same way. In 1 Corinthians he gives a definition of love, which does not come from cute love letters he slipped into the back pews of the Corinthian church, but rather from a stinging rebuke to a rich, "super-spiritual" church that lacked love. In 1 Corinthians 13:4–7 he gave them what is now the most famous definition of love:

> Love is . . .
> patient
> kind
> not envious
> not boastful
> not arrogant
> not rude
> bears all things
> believes all things
> hopes all things
> endures all things

And then what does he say? He says that "Love never ends" (v. 8a). Love has permanence about it.

Let me give two implications to that idea. The first is this: married love is an exclusive, lifelong commitment. It's like a ring or "seal" placed upon the arm and the heart—that is, it's a public and private promise, an internal and external vow.

Today when couples make up their own wedding vows, too often they give an "exaggerated view of the importance of romantic love."[27]

> I promise to whisper in your ear "I love you" each night before bed.
> I promise never to lose that "loving feeling."

I promise to run my fingers through your hair.

Okay, they're not that bad. But you get the idea. Romance and compatibility are the key concepts. Although the Song is not against compatibility or romance, it knows that compatibility will be challenged and that romance will come and go and that sexual passion will slow down and often slowly pass away. But love remains—that seal on the heart and arm.

> I, Douglas, take you, Emily, to be my wedded wife, to have and to hold from this day forward, for better or for worse, for richer, for poorer, in sickness and in health, to love and to cherish, till death do us part.

What symbol do you give of your love? A ring!

> With this ring, I thee wed, in the name of the Father and the Son and the Holy Spirit. Amen.

Love is not fundamentally about compatibility or romance but is rather an exclusive, lifelong commitment.

The second implication involves the gospel—the life, the death, and especially the resurrection of Jesus Christ. There is a permanence to our covenant commitment to Christ, which is not only until death ("till death do us part") but overcomes death ("O death, where is your victory? O death, where is your sting?" [1 Corinthians 15:55]).

Here I'm talking about the hope of the resurrection—Jesus' resurrection and ours. Jesus said, "I am the resurrection and the life. Whoever believes in me, though he die, yet shall he live" (John 11:25; cf. 8:51, 52). I'm talking about Easter! I'm talking about being "sealed" by the Spirit "for the day of redemption" (Ephesians 4:30; cf. 2 Corinthians 1:22; 2 Timothy 2:19). I'm talking about Jesus—"the one who died—more than that, who was raised" (Romans 8:34), the inseparable love of Jesus Christ. I'm talking about a love that tribulation can't touch, trials can't terminate, persecution can't put an end to, famine can't finish, nakedness can't nullify, danger can't demolish, the sword can't sever (see Romans 8:35) . . . a love that even death cannot destroy (Romans 8:38)!

If someone at this point wants to stop reading and shout, "Hallelujah," go ahead. "Hallelujah!" indeed. Praise the Lord!

Look again at Song of Songs 8:6. Now roll away the stone from over it. Jesus Christ transcends it. In Jesus, love is not merely compared to death, it has conquered death! "O death, where is your victory?"

Early in his life G. K. Chesterton wrote to his future wife, Frances, "You say you want to talk to me about death: my views about death are bright, brisk and entertaining. . . . The transformation called Death may be something as beautiful and dazzling as the transformation called Love."[28] Precisely! In Jesus, love has conquered death, and thus death is the doorway to eternal life and eternal love, love as we have never experienced it before—free of sin and sickness, temptations and trials.

Taking the Word at Its Word

B. B. Warfield was one of the great minds in the history of the church. He was professor of theology at Princeton from 1887–1921 and was well-known for his writings on the inspiration and inerrancy of the Bible. But what is not as well known is how he cared for his wife. At age twenty-five Warfield married, and he and his wife, Annie, went to Germany for their honeymoon. There Annie was struck by lightning and was paralyzed for life. Warfield spent almost forty years caring for her. In fact, all those years he never left his home for more than a few hours at a time.[29]

That's touching. I get choked up every time I think about it. That's wearing your wedding ring always. But what was he thinking? What was this great mind thinking? Why would he do that? To give forty years of his life to a woman who couldn't kiss him, couldn't make love to him, couldn't have children to carry on his prestigious name?

Why?

One reason is honor. Warfield lived in more honorable times than ours, and he was an honorable man. He did his loving duty. I'm sure that was one reason. He was a man of honor. But I also think, knowing that Warfield took God's Word at its word, he was a man of hope and that he held out hope for the resurrection, when he will one day see his wife's body as bright as the sun, as beautiful as the moon—her deep blue eyes, her flowing black hair, her full-toothed smile, and her perfectly contoured spine, the work of a master craftsman.

He was a man of honor. He was a man of hope. He was a man of love—he understood the nature of marital love as depicted here in 8:5–7: love is leaning on your husband; love is bigger than us two; and love is wearing your wedding ring always, till death do us part . . . until death itself departs.

One short sleepe past, wee wake eternally,
And death shall be no more, death, thou shalt die.[30]

10

Virginity and Eschatology

THE SONG OF SOLOMON 8:8–14

Make haste, my beloved,
and be like a gazelle
or a young stag
on the mountains of spices.

8:14

A FEW MONTHS AGO a friend was over for dessert, and she was talking with Emily and me about having raised three daughters on her own during the sexual revolution of the 1960s and 1970s. She shared how she regularly pressed home to her girls the virtue and value of virginity and how they actually heeded their mother's teaching. As an example of their obedience, she told us about the night her oldest daughter, a senior in high school at the time, came home from a date and said, "Mom, I really like him. And he really likes me. And when I tell him I'm not going to bed with him, he will *really* like me."

This girl so valued virginity that she knew any young man who was truly interested in her would also value it. He would value it so much that her firm stance on chastity would make her all the more appealing. She knew that the *chaste* are often most *chased*.[1]

The Value of Virginity

As we come to the end of the Song of Songs, we start with a vignette on virginity. In its usual poetic-dramatic form our text teaches *why* someone should remain a virgin until marriage and *how* to go about doing so.

Look first at verses 8, 9. Here it is difficult to know who is speaking. From the word "we"—"we have a little sister"—we can surmise it is neither the bride nor the groom. That leaves us with the daughters of Jerusalem, whose voice we have just heard in 8:5, or the bride's brothers, who were introduced in 1:6 (and if this whole Song is written in a chiastic structure, to hear their voice here would fit perfectly). Either way the ambiguity may be intentional. The ambiguity brings in every possible older sibling—male and female. All who fit that description should resonate with what follows. Look at verse 8:

> We have a little sister,
>   and she has no breasts.
> What shall we do for our sister
>   on the day when she is spoken for?

This verse is to be taken literally. They have a little sister, and her chest has not yet developed (cf. Ezekiel 16:7). She's on the cusp of puberty. Thus, before she hits that age they ask themselves, "What shall we do for our sister on the day when she is spoken for?"—that is, the day when some young man asks for her hand in marriage. Then, using metaphorical language, these siblings take responsibility—from prepuberty to preproposal—for their sister's purity. Below I have emphasized the poetic parallels:

> If she is a *wall*,
>   we will *build on her* a battlement of <u>silver</u>,
> but if she is a *door*,
>   we will *enclose her with* boards of <u>cedar</u>. (v. 9)

Being a "wall" means staying a virgin. The imagery is obvious. To be a "wall" is to not let anyone in or through, to be impenetrable and impregnable (literally!). To be a "door," however, means to be easy to open or get through (or into). It symbolizes the loss of virginity, and perhaps promiscuity or even the potential of promiscuity. So the deal is this: if the older siblings see their little sister acting in any way like a swinging door—demonstrating any weakness of mind or body—they will board her up before it's too late ("enclose her with boards of cedar.") They will make her a cedar chastity belt.[2] But if she has kept herself pure under their protective watch, they "will build on her a battlement of silver"; that is, they will reward her virginity with their full blessing and support ("silver" perhaps referring to a generous dowry to be given to her husband).[3] They will honor, celebrate, and adorn her self-protection with military splendor. She has fought the good fight, and thus she shall be rewarded for her victory.

After this voice of sibling virginity vigilance (vv. 8, 9), another voice arises. Now the bride speaks, or should I say boasts. She boasts in her virginity: "I was a wall, and my breasts were like towers; then I was in his eyes as one who finds peace" (v. 10).

I'll return to the "peace" part in a moment. For now simply note that this opening note on virginity comes to its crescendo. "I was a wall," she sings! "I kept myself pure for my beloved." Then she adds, "I kept myself pure even though my chest was well-developed. Your little sister 'has no breasts' (v. 8), but when I was her age, I had large ones—'my breasts were like towers' (v. 10), and *still* these towers were untouched, and what's behind this wall remained inaccessible." That's what she boasts about. Now Scripture says we are to boast in nothing "except in the cross of our Lord Jesus Christ" (Galatians 6:14). But here a slight allowance is made for the least boasted about teenage activity today—keeping one's virginity. She boasts in it. And to that we add our "Amen," or "You go girl!"

That is how the final scene starts. Or to speak in musical terms, that's how the coda begins. It begins with a tune on the theme of virginity. At first hearing it may seem odd to end an erotic love song by singing about keeping one's virginity. It is odd only if we forget the primary purpose of the Song. In our first study I argued that the refrain—"I adjure you, O daughters of Jerusalem, that you not stir up or awaken love until it pleases" (2:7; 3:5; 8:4)—is the poet's way of saying, "Young ladies, save yourselves for marriage." When we remember this central wisdom admonition and its original audience (young single women), then this final thought on virginity fits perfectly. As I have argued elsewhere,[4] Proverbs is a book for boys. The phrase "my son" (my son, do this/don't do that) is used twenty-three times there. The Song of Songs, however, is a song for girls—"O daughters." "O daughters, wait." Virgins stay virgins until the time is right![5]

How One Waits

I want to explore further what our text teaches about virginity. If you look carefully, you will see that two highly relevant questions are tackled here: (1) how one waits; and (2) why one waits.

First, how one waits.

Before we answer that question, let me first clarify that although these verses are told from a woman's perspective, the Bible holds no double standard. A man's virginity is just as valued as a woman's. That is one of the remarkable things about the Bible. In the Old Testament you will find verses like, "How can a young man keep his way pure?" (Psalm 119:9a)—sexual purity is a priority. Similarly, in the New Testament you will find verses like, "[Treat] younger men as brothers, older women as mothers, younger women as sisters, in all purity" (1 Timothy 5:1b, 2), or "with absolute purity" (NIV)— purity of eyes, hands, and imagination (cf. Matthew 5:27–30). So there is no double standard for men and women in the Bible. Everyone is to remain a "wall" until the "door" of marriage is opened.

Now on to our first question: how does one wait? Our text speaks of what I'll call *Five-Point Protection*. The five points are:

1. Family
2. Peers
3. Community
4. Self
5. Knowledge

The first three are external social protections. Verses 8, 9 discuss *family protection*. Older siblings, and especially older brothers, are to protect younger siblings, especially younger sisters. So the father dusting off his shotgun when his daughter's date shows up is not so far removed from the sentiments of our text. His intentional action communicates: "You touch her and I'll shoot you. Do we have an understanding?" Now I am exaggerating the image here (and I don't advocate such subtle violent threats), but I exaggerate only to point out a great deficiency in our day. We have too many fathers who are out of the picture and too many big brothers who aren't protective of their younger siblings, which is a picture so contrary to a Biblical worldview.

Besides family protection there is also *peer protection*. We perhaps see this in verse 10 with the bride's boast. We certainly see this in the bride's refrain, which exhorts the virgins to stay virgins until the time is right. In the Song it is not the father, the mother, an older sibling, or some sage or religious leader who gives this admonition, but a peer, a girl of the same or similar age. The newlywed bride seeks to protect her peers.

Third, there is *community protection*. I touched on this idea in the last study with my point that *love is bigger than us two*. The laws of these girls' community (in Exodus, Leviticus, Numbers, and Deuteronomy) frown upon the loss of virginity before marriage.[6] In their culture such a loss was not tolerated.

In our culture if you want to stay a virgin but are not surrounded by good family, peer, or community protection, you need to adjust your situation by increasing one of these protections. What I mean is this: if your family could care less about your virginity, you need to double your church family and friends. You need to surround yourself with likeminded people who care about your purity and will help you protect it.

As I shared in an early chapter, I became a Christian at age nineteen shortly after my son, Sean, was born. Sean was born out of wedlock with a woman who was not and is not my wife. When I told my mom and dad, "My girlfriend is pregnant," my mom said, "I thought we taught you better." Now, I'm very grateful for my parents. They were good parents who taught me many things. But neither my mother nor my father ever talked about love, sex, marriage, or virginity. To be fair, they did send me to Catholic grade school and high school, where indeed the nuns tried to impress upon me, like a ruler pressed upon my knuckles, the value of virginity. And I think that's what my mother meant when she said, "I thought we taught you better." But you see, only a very righteous child (which I was not) will listen to the voice of his teachers alone. Most of us need the right message coming from school, home, friends, and church. Most of us need five-point protection. We need five-point protection because passion is pleasurable, and our bodies begin to tell us that before we are wise enough to know how to respond to it appropriately. And at that point we can either let our bodies or the Body of Christ define the boundaries.

Point four is *self* or *self-resolve*. You might have the best big brothers and the most overly protective older sisters, but if you don't resolve to stay pure yourself—"I was a wall," she boasts in verse 10—then a swinging door you shall be. It's default mode in our culture.

This girl knows she is not independent. She has always had a community, yet her attitude here has a certain independence to it. "Siblings and friends," she says, "thanks for your concern about me. But in this area of purity I have vowed to myself not to be open or easy. I will not put myself in potentially compromising places or relationships. I will always have a plan of escape if I find myself in the wrong place, at the wrong time, with the wrong person. But listen, I like boys. And I really like this boy. And he really likes me. But we have resolved to wait until marriage." That's what she says. Self-resolve. Do you have it? If you don't have it, you'd better get it soon.

Point five is *knowledge*. Here I'm talking about sex education. Now, the Song of Songs is not a textbook on sex per se, but it is a book of knowledge. It does talk about the human body, the pleasures of intimacy, and the purity that ought to surround such pleasures. It teaches us that topics such as the facts of life, the birds and the bees, or whatever you want to call it are godly topics. God does not blush over the word *breast*. You might, but he doesn't. So when children grow up in the church and never hear about such things from parents, godly siblings, pastors, youth workers, children's workers, if they never hear the word s-e-x in c-h-u-r-c-h, let me ask you, where will they hear it? What knowledge are they getting and from whom?

As I was growing up, although everyone "righteous" around me tiptoed around this touchy topic, the late night cable movie at my buddy Timmy's house didn't, and the *Playboy* magazine in my friend Ryan's closet didn't, and the chitchat of ten-year-olds on the playground didn't. There and then is where and how I gained my knowledge of such things. And I'm not alone, am I? Knowledge—the knowledge of the passion and purity of this book—needs to come from us adults to our children, and it needs to come before little Timmy next door and old "Hugh Hefner" down the road do the talking for us.

Five-point protection:

1. Family
2. Peers
3. Community
4. Self
5. Knowledge

How does a young man or woman keep his or her way pure? That's how according to Solomon's Song.

Why One Waits

Staying with this fifth point, I want to transition to imparting knowledge, teaching you from this text *why one waits* or stays a virgin until marriage. The answer? One waits because of the benefits or the blessings of *peace* and *freedom*.

First, we have the blessing of peace. Again and for the final time we return to verse 10: "I was a wall, and my breasts were like towers; then I was in his eyes as one who finds peace." Here she does one of those, "Let me give you the long story . . . short," and she actually does it in less than ten Hebrew words. Here she says, "I kept myself pure. Then we got married and made love. And then my beloved saw that I found peace."

The Hebrew word here is *shalôm*, which means "completeness, whole-ness, total well-being," or it can just mean "peace" as we think of the word. She has internal and external peace. And this word "peace" fits well the context of the earlier military metaphors—wall, towers, battlements of silver. Thus the story can be written this way: this king has come to conquer, and he does. The wall is penetrated, and the towers fall into his hands. His banner now flies over the city fortress. Ah, but his banner over her is love (2:4), true love, godly love, love that has waited, passion that is pure.[7] His victory over her virginity (ironically) brings peace—to her, to him, to them, to everyone around them. Peace!

Over the past two decades of Christian ministry, I have never had a young man or woman confess to me, "Pastor, I stayed a virgin. Then I got married and lost my virginity on my wedding night. And boy was I dumb. What was I thinking? Oh, I feel so guilty. I'm so not at peace about this foolish behavior of mine." I've never had that happen. But let me tell you, on a very serious note, that *half* the people I have counseled have confessed something like this: "I was so foolish. I feel so guilty. When it came to sex, I played by my own rules, and right now peace is far from my heart. What can I do to find peace?"

Now, of course, I lead them to the Prince of Peace and the peace our Lord Jesus has made through the cross. "God forgave me—God can forgive you." But forgiveness does not mean forgetfulness. We live with the consequences of our sin. We are perfectly forgiven, but not always perfectly at peace.

In my situation, at first I thought my impurity had no possible negative side effects. It only brought pleasure. But then, in time, it only brought pain, chaos, and disorder—war. It brought anything but peace—to me, to her, to her family, to our families, to our schools, to our coaches, to our teams, to our community, to everyone within range of our impurity.

I have a motto: holiness equals happiness. Well, let me tell you from Scripture and from experience that *purity equals peace*. Purity—doing passion God's way—leads to peace with self, spouse, family, and community.

So, why wait? Why wait for marriage? Two reasons are given here. The first is peace (*shalôm*), and the second is *freedom*. Peace and freedom. Unlike the word "peace," the word "freedom" is not in our text, but the idea is clearly conveyed in verses 11–14. First, we'll look at verses 11, 12:

> Solomon had a vineyard at Baal-hamon;
>   he let out [rented] the vineyard to keepers;
>   each one was to bring for its fruit a thousand pieces of silver [an
>   astronomical sum].[8]
> My vineyard, my very own, is before me;
>   you, O Solomon, may have the thousand,
>   and the keepers of the fruit two hundred [but big deal].

Here the contrast is between King Solomon's vineyard and the bride's vineyard. Solomon's vineyard might literally be a vineyard he owned a few miles south of Megiddo (several days journey north from Jerusalem),[9] and it was so large that he had to rent it out to tenant farmers. It was his vineyard only on paper. He owned it, but he never had the pleasure of tending it and then directly eating from the fruit of its vines.

Solomon's vineyard could also symbolize his harem (cf. 6:8–10), which was quite large. In Mark Twain's *The Adventures of Huckleberry Finn*, Huck says to Jim that Solomon "had about a million wives."[10] A slight exaggeration—Solomon only had 700 wives and 300 concubines. He had a thousand, not a million (but still large enough!).

Whether this "vineyard" in verse 11 is some vast land that Solomon owns or (more likely) "a very thinly veiled allusion to his harem,"[11] either way in verse 12 the bride compares his vineyard to hers. Pretending to address Solomon,[12] she says, and I'll slightly paraphrase this time:

> My vineyard, my very own, is right here before me; O Solomon, you might have power and money and a seemingly incredible love-life, but you know nothing of "my beloved is mine and I am his," of one man/one woman/one marriage.[13]

That's verse 12. Then in verses 13, 14 the bride and the beloved (not Solomon) speak directly to each other. He invites her to speak (v. 13), and she speaks. She invites him to intimacy (v. 14). Her "mountains" (i.e., breasts; see 2:17; 4:6) are his to climb; her vineyard (i.e., vagina) is his alone to explore and enjoy. The "wall," where no men were allowed through (v. 10), has now become a vineyard (v. 11; see 2:15; 7:9c; cf. 4:12—5 :1), a place of pleasure for only one man, her "beloved" (v. 14). "*My* vineyard, *my* very own, is for *me* alone to give to him alone."[14] "No need to travel seven days up north. Make haste, you swift, graceful, potent, and passionate animal (my stag!). Come *now* into this vineyard. Taste freely these spiced mountains."

Solomon, who seemingly has all the freedom in the world, has been enslaved by his own overindulgence. He has too much land and too many ladies for one man to handle. His vineyard is at Baal-hamon—which literally means "lord of wealth," or perhaps even "owner of a crowd,"[15] or "husband of a mob."[16] Here Solomon's polygamy, with its expenses and complications, is contrasted with our couple's monogamous love. Their love is so simple, so direct, so beautiful, so pure, and so free. Free to travel to each other. Free to eat of each other's fruit. Whenever. One man/one woman/one marriage—that's freedom!

Often today Christians are rightly criticized for having nothing more to say about sex than "don't"—don't look, don't touch, don't indulge, don't enjoy. I want us to be known for saying "do"—do look, do touch, do indulge, do enjoy sexual relations *within marriage*. I want us to be known for saying both "do" and "don't." But here in verses 8–10, it's "don't"—don't fool around before marriage because waiting for marriage (vv. 11–14) will bring with it peace and freedom.

Eschatology

We are almost to the end.

On Mondays when I first sit down with the text for the next Sunday's sermon, by the end of the morning I try to come up with a preaching outline and a title that well summarizes its content and hopefully sparks interest. And so, when working on the current passage, I first entitled this final sermon "Uncompromised Purity; Unquenchable Passion." Not bad.

But then I thought, "Sure, that's not bad; and sure, that's a fitting title, but anyone could come up with that." So I said to myself, "Think, Douglas, think." So I closed my Bible and I thought. On Monday, then Tuesday, then Wednesday, and also Thursday and Friday I thought about titles. (Let the reader understand—I'm joking.) And then it finally came to me, "Virginity and Eschatology." Not bad at all! It's a gift, it really is. My next task then was to find something about eschatology in this text (still joking). Thankfully I did (no joke).

Look at the final two verses again. He says to her, "O you who dwell in the gardens, with companions listening for your voice; let me hear it" (v. 13). And she says, "Make haste ["hasten towards me" is the sense],[17] my beloved, and be like a gazelle or a young stag on the mountains of spices." *The End.*

That's how the Song ends.

Now notice two things here. First, there is this theme of unquenchable passion. We don't know how long they've been married at this point, but the last line of the poem is, as I've said, another invitation to intimacy. (Will they ever give it a break?) We know this because she has given this same invitation twice earlier. So it's quite clear. Scholars agree. In verse 14, "She is calling on him to make love to her," as Duane Garrett frankly phrases it.[18]

Here there is unquenchable passion. No doubt. But there is more than that. There is eschatology. Yes, eschatology. The word *eschatology* comes from the Greek word *eschatos*, which means "last." Eschatology is the study of the last days or the end times. The last things.

When I read these final two verses of the Song, I find it interesting that this book doesn't end with actual consummation ("I went into my garden") or a declaration of mutual love ("Now and finally, my beloved is mine and I am his"), or even the refrain one last time ("Do not arouse or awaken love until it so desires"). But instead it ends, if you will, with arms stretched out to each other, two lovers wanting to touch but not yet touching.[19] We are left with longing, with the same kind of longing that opened the Song: "Let him kiss me" (1:2).

It is my contention and others' that this longing leaves us longing for more.[20] In other words, the Song intentionally ends abruptly and inconclusively because the Song is not done. Love is not done. God is not done with his great love song and story. The Song of Songs ends with this eschatological angst.[21] What's going to happen next? And canonically this longing leads us forward to read Isaiah. (Isn't that interesting placement?) And from Isaiah we journey through the prophets, the Gospels, the Epistles, ending with the book of Revelation! Yes, Revelation, the last book of the Bible, a book that ends as the Song ends (interesting as well).

In Revelation 19:7 we read, "Let us rejoice and exult and give [God Almighty] the glory, for the marriage of the Lamb [Jesus] has come, and his Bride [the Church] has made herself ready" by keeping herself "pure" (staying a virgin spiritually) (v. 8). And then, in Revelation 22:20, this is how the book ends, how the Bible ends: in the last chapter and verse of our Bibles, our Lord Jesus/the Bridegroom says, "Surely I am coming soon," and the Church/the bride says, "Come" (v. 17), "Amen. Come, Lord Jesus!" (22:20). Make haste! That's how the Bible ends. That's how the Song ends. (Interesting indeed!)

So *virginity and eschatology* is what we have here. And what do both topics have in common? Waiting. (Something we as a culture excel in! Yeah, right.) Waiting for marriage; waiting for the marriage of the Lamb. Today we, as the Church, the bride of Christ, join the bride of the Song of Songs and her final plea. As we eagerly await the return of Christ (see Hebrews 9:28), "the descendant of David, the bright morning star" (Revelation 22:16), we hold our hands out with eschatological angst, knowing that only in the return and absolute reign of King Jesus can "the yearning for love [that] fills the cosmos" be met, consummated in and through and for the glory of Christ.[22] The Apostle Paul puts it like this:

> For the grace of God has appeared, bringing salvation for all people, training us to renounce ungodliness and worldly passions, and to live self-controlled, upright, and godly lives in the present age, *waiting* for our blessed hope, the appearing of the glory of our great God and Savior Jesus Christ. (Titus 2:11–13)

And so we wait.

Soli Deo gloria!

Notes

Chapter One: Understandest Thou What Thou Readest?

1. For this idea of starting in Acts 8, see Matthew Henry, *Matthew Henry's Commentary on the Whole Bible*, 6 vols. (repr. McLean, VA: Macdonald, 1985), 3:1053.

2. Marvin H. Pope, *Song of Songs*, Anchor Bible (New York: Doubleday, 1977), p. 17.

3. Franz Delitzsch, *Proverbs, Ecclesiastes, Song of Solomon*, C. F. Keil and F. Delitzsch, *Commentary on the Old Testament*, 10 vols. (repr. Peabody, MA: Hendrickson, 2006), 6:497.

4. Pope, *Song of Songs*, p. 17.

5. Daniel J. Estes, "Song of Songs," in Daniel C. Fredericks and Daniel J. Estes, *Ecclesiastes and the Song of Songs*, Apollos Old Testament Commentary (Downers Grove, IL: InterVarsity, 2010), p. 267. Cf. Roland E. Murphy, "Canticle of Canticles," in *New Jerome Biblical Commentary*, eds. Raymond E. Brown, Joseph A. Fitzmyer, and Roland E. Murphy (Englewood Cliffs, NJ: Prentice-Hall, 1990), p. 507.

6. Christopher W. Mitchell, *The Song of Songs: A Theological Exposition of Sacred Scripture*, Concordia Commentary (St. Louis: Concordia, 2003), p. *xx*.

7. While I disagree with M. Bossuet's sevenfold division of the text (based on this tradition), I agree that it is probable that the Song originated or was eventually used during the seven-week wedding celebration. See C. Hassell Bullock, *An Introduction to the Old Testament Poetic Books* (Chicago: Moody, 1988), p. 255.

8. Tom Gledhill, *The Message of the Song of Songs*, The Bible Speaks Today (Downers Grove, IL: InterVarsity, 1994), p. 27. Estes notes: "The term *šîr* is often, but not exclusively, used for lyric songs and especially for love songs (cf. Isa. 5:1 and Ezek. 33:32). It could well refer to a wedding song, for music was typically employed in wedding celebrations (Jer. 7:34; 16:9; 25:10; 33:11; cf. Murphy, *ABD* 6:151)" ("Song of Songs," p. 302).

9. Duane Garrett organizes his commentary as a song, with soprano, tenor, and chorus ("Song of Songs," in Duane Garrett and Paul R. House, *Song of Songs/Lamentations*, Word Biblical Commentary [Nashville: Thomas Nelson, 2004], p. 32). On page 31, he summarizes: "I suggest that the Song of Songs is a unified work with chiastic structure and is composed of thirteen individual songs, or *cantos*, for presentation by a male and a female soloist with a chorus."

10. Estes notes that the Song is "the most thoroughly poetic book in the Bible" ("Song of Songs," p. 286).

11. On this sound, Richard S. Hess notes: "The four words of the title (v. 1) as well as the first two words of the poem (v. 2) all contain a *šîn*, creating a *sh* sound. Indeed, the first word of the book (and only that word in the opening two verses) begins with a *šîn*, signaling the importance of this sound. Further, the first three words each contain a *šîn* followed by a *rêš* (an *r* sound), repeating the *šîr/šer* sound. In poetry, the sound repetition is significant. The *šîr/šer* sound would emphasize the word for 'song' three times at the beginning of the book, because it sounds like

šîr (song)" (*Song of Songs*, Baker Commentary on the Old Testament Wisdom and Psalms [Grand Rapids, MI: Baker, 2005], p. 39).

12. Lord Byron, "She Walks in Beauty," in *Love Poems*, Everyman's Library Pocket Poets, ed. Peter Washington (New York: Knopf, 1995), p. 91. Of additional interest, this poem was the first of several English poems that Isaac Nathan set to synagogue tunes, published as *Hebrew Melodies* (1815).

13. This idea of comparing poetry to propositional prose came from Kathleen B. Nielson. With different examples, this is how she began her lecture "Loving and Teaching the Poetry of the Bible," Seminar at PCA General Assembly (Nashville), July 1, 2010.

14. In *Sermon 79:1*, Bernard of Clairvaux teaches, "But in this marriage song it is affections, not words, that are to be considered" (*On the Song of Songs I-IV*, trans. Irene Edmonds, Cistercian Fathers Series [Kalamazoo, MI: Cistercian, 1980], 4:138). Leland Ryken adds, "The Song of Solomon is affective, not analytic" (*Words of Delight: A Literary Introduction to the Bible*, 2nd ed. [Grand Rapids, MI: Baker, 1992], p. 289).

15. Roland E. Murphy states, "These touches alone suffice to indicate why the Song should not be described as a treatise on 'free love.' The cultural setting is one that encouraged strict standards of sexual morality and marital fidelity (e.g., Deut 22:13–29). What this poetry celebrates is not eroticism for its own sake, and certainly not ribaldry or promiscuous sex, but rather the desires of an individual woman and man to enjoy the bond of mutual possession (2:16; 6:3; 7:10[9])" (*The Song of Songs*, Hermeneia [Minneapolis: Fortress, 1990], p. 98). See also Brevard S. Childs, who writes, "The Song is wisdom's reflection on the joyful and mysterious nature of love between a man and a woman within the institution of marriage. . . . The writer simply assumes the Hebrew order of the family as a part of the given order of his society, and seeks to explore and unravel its mysteries from within" (*Introduction to the Old Testament as Scripture* [Philadelphia: Fortress, 1979], p. 575). Cf. Daniel Grossberg, "Two Kinds of Sexual Relationships in the Hebrew Bible," *Hebrew Studies* 35 (1994): pp. 1–25.

16. Steven C. Horine has argued persuasively that the Song, including 1:2–4, is set within a marriage relationship. "An Integrative Literary Approach to the Song of Songs," PhD dissertation, Westminster Theological Seminary, 1998.

17. David A. Hubbard, *Ecclesiastes, Song of Solomon*, The Communicator's Commentary (Dallas: Word, 1991), p. 273. Othmar Keel adds, "The happy experience of finding another person whom one admires and to whom one also feels profoundly related ('bone of my bones') is expressed in the love songs through the address 'sister' or 'brother'" (*Song of Songs*, trans. Frederick J. Gaiser, A Continental Commentary [Minneapolis: Fortress, 1994], p. 31).

18. Garrett's remarks are worth adding: "The Song achieves something that medieval Christian culture could not fathom and that modern and postmodern culture cannot artfully attain: a man and woman who maintain passionate desire for each other in the context of conventional morality" ("Song of Songs," p. 102).

19. Nicholas of Lyra, *The Postilla of Nicholas of Lyra on the Song of Songs*, trans. James George Kiecker, Reformation Texts With Translation (1350–1650), ed. Kenneth Hagen (Milwaukee: Marquette University Press, 1998), p. 29. Cf. John Calvin's remark about the heretic Castellio who thought the Song was about an immoral

affair: "He [i.e., Castellio] considers that it is a lascivious and obscene poem, in which Solomon has described his shameless love affairs" (*Ioannis Calvini Opera quae supersunt omnia* [*Corpus Reformatorum* xxxix, 1873], p. 675).

20. Theodoret of Cyrus, *Commentary on the Song of Songs*, Preface, in *Ancient Christian Commentary on Scripture IX*, ed. J. Robert Wright (Downers Grove, IL: InterVarsity, 2005), p. 290.

21. Quoted without reference in George L. Klein, ed., *Reclaiming the Prophetic Mantle* (Nashville: Broadman, 1992), p. 119. For hundreds of more examples of allegories, see Richard A. Norris Jr., trans. and ed., *The Song of Songs: Interpreted by Early Christian and Medieval Commentators*, The Church's Bible, gen. ed. Robert Louis Wilken (Grand Rapids, MI: Eerdmans, 2003).

22. See Martin Luther, "Lecture on the Song of Solomon: A Brief but Altogether Lucid Commentary of the Song of Songs," trans. Ian Siggins, *Luther's Works*, 56 vols. (St. Louis: Concordia, 1972), 15:264. Roland Murphy adds a helpful reminder: "Despite the pretense of exegetical precision, exaggeration and uncontrolled fantasy seem to be flaws endemic to allegorical exposition" (*The Song of Songs*, p. 93).

23. On this issue, here are two helpful comments:

The two Greek terms, *eros*, "carnal love," and *agape*, "caritas, spiritual love," reflect a dichotomy that has entered into classical Christian theology. The classical Hebrew outlook, on the contrary, finds it proper to apply the same root, *'ahabah*, to all aspects of love. The ideal relationship of man to God, "You shall love the Lord your God" (Deut. 6:5), the love of one's fellow man, "You shall love your neighbor as yourself" (Lev. 19:18), "You shall love him (the stranger) as yourself" (Lev. 19:34), and the love of man and woman, "How fair and how pleasant you are, O love, with its delights!" (Song of Songs 7:7)—all are expressed in the Bible by the same Hebrew word. (Robert Gordis, *The Song of Songs and Lamentations*, rev. ed. [New York: Ktav, 1974], p. *x*.)

[The Song] portrays the love between the Lord and his people as *desire*. With his immensely influential *Agape and Eros*, Anders Nygren persuaded three generations of theologians and exegetes that self-giving love, *agape*, and desire, *eros*, are two incompatible sorts of love, and that only the former characterizes the relation between the biblical God and his people; no allegory plausibly solicited by the Song can agree. (Robert W. Jenson, *Song of Songs*, Interpretation (Louisville: John Knox, 2005), p. 12.)

24. John Updike puts it well: "Carnal passion has its natural place in the annals of Israel; Judaism recognized that the body is the person, a recognition extended in the strenuous Christian doctrine of the bodily resurrection. A world-picture must include everything that is the case, and the love frenzy of the young . . . completes, along with the cynicism of Ecclesiastes, the despair of Lamentation[s], the problematic of Job, and the plagues and war-fury of Numbers, the picture. We might even say that, in this era of irrepressible sexual awareness, we trust the Bible a bit more because it contains, in all its shameless, helpless force, The Song of Solomon" ("Fore-

word," in Lawrence Boadt, ed., *The Song of Solomon: Love Poetry of the Spirit* [New York: St. Martin's, 1999], p. 10).

25. Pope writes: "The quest for the supposed lost key has been futile, for the door to the understanding of the Song was not locked, nor even shut, but has been wide open to any who dared to see and enter. The barrier has been a psychological aversion to the obvious, somewhat like the Emperor's New Clothes. The trouble has been that interpreters who dared acknowledge the plain sense of the Song were assailed as enemies of truth and decency. The allegorical charade thus persisted for centuries with only sporadic protests" (*Song of Songs,* p. 17).

26. Estes, "The Song of Songs," p. 289.

27. I reference a line from the seventh book of Elizabeth Barrett Browning, *Aurora Leigh: A Poem in Nine Books* (New York: Thomas Y. Crowell & Co., 1883), p. 265.

28. According to UBS 4 there are no quotations or allusions to the Song of Songs in the New Testament (Barbara Aland et al., eds., *The Greek New Testament,* 4th rev. ed. [Stuttgart: Deutsche Bibelgesellschaft, 1993], pp. 887–901). Conversely, Ernst Wilhelm Hengstenberg claims, "The New Testament is pervaded by references to the Song of Songs. . . . Proportionally no book of the Old Testament is so frequently referred to, implicitly or explicitly" ("Prolegomena to the Song of Solomon," in *Commentary on Ecclesiastes with Other Treatises,* trans. D. W. Simon [Edinburgh: T&T Clark, 1860], p. 297).

29. Iain Provan, *Ecclesiastes/Song of Songs,* NIV Application Commentary (Grand Rapids, MI: Zondervan, 2001), p. 254.

30. Mitchell, *The Song of Songs,* p. 7.

31. C. Hassell Bullock's summary reflects well my view of authorship: "It is our opinion that 1:1–29:27 is Solomonic in authorship, although some allowance may be made for editorializing in the process of compilation and final edition of the book" (*An Introduction to the Old Testament Poetic Books,* p. 159).

32. The book title, Ecclesiastes, is the Greco-Latin form of the Hebrew *qōhelet.* It might be that Ecclesiastes is a "royal autobiography," that is, "[t]he person who calls himself Qoheleth [the Preacher] pretends to be Solomon in order to argue that if Solomon cannot find satisfaction and meaning in life in these areas, no one can" (Tremper Longman III, *The Book of Ecclesiastes,* New International Commentary on the Old Testament [Grand Rapids, MI: Eerdmans, 1998], p. 7). Yet, from looking at what the text itself says about the author (see 1:1, 2, 12, 16; 2:1–12, 15, 17, 20; 4:13; 7:25–29; 8:2–5; 10:16, 17, 20; 12:9, 10)—especially calling him "the son of David" and "king in Jerusalem" (1:1), and then describing his wisdom (1:12–18; 2:12; cf. 7:25), wealth (2:1–11), and literary achievements (12:9, 10; cf. Proverbs 1:1)—I find no reason we shouldn't call the author of Ecclesiastes "Solomon." Moreover, as Longman points out, "the verb *qahal,* on which the name Qoheleth is formed, occurs a number of times in 1 Kings 8, which is Solomon's speech at the dedication of the Temple" (*Ecclesiastes,* Cornerstone Biblical Commentary [Wheaton: Tyndale, 2006], p. 253).

33. See Ernest C. Lucas, *Exploring the Old Testament: A Guide to the Psalms and Wisdom Literature* (Downers Grove, IL: InterVarsity, 2003), p. 175.

34. "In the entire Rabbinic literature, we find no one contesting Solomon's authorship of the Song of Songs, understanding the title: 'The song of songs, which is

Solomon's' literally." Rabbi A. J. Rosenberg, "The Midrashic Approach to the Song of Songs," A. Cohen, ed., *The Five Megilloth* (New York: Soncino, 1984), p. 11.

35. Mitchell argues that the phrase "which is Solomon's" is "more naturally understood as *lamed auctoris*, introducing the author of the text" (*The Song of Songs*, p. 549). Note also what Longman says: "The superscription is like the title page of a modern book in that it provides information about the genre, *author*, and occasionally the subject matter and date of a book (e.g., Isa. 1:1; Jer. 1:1–3; Nah. 1:1). Superscriptions are found in other wisdom contexts as well (Prov. 1:1; Eccles. 1:1), where, interestingly, Solomon is either mentioned or implied" (Tremper Longman III, *Song of Songs*, New International Commentary of the Old Testament [Grand Rapids, MI: Eerdmans, 2001], p. 87, emphasis mine).

36. In favor of Solomonic authorship, see Gleason L. Archer, *A Survey of Old Testament Introduction* (Chicago: Moody, 1964), p. 474; Lloyd G. Carr, *The Song of Solomon*, Tyndale Old Testament Commentary (Downers Grove, IL: InterVarsity, 1984), p. 19; John G. Snaith, *Song of Songs*, New Century Bible Commentary (Grand Rapids, MI: Eerdmans, 1993), p. 5.

37. On the superlative, Pope comments, "The construct connection of the same noun in the singular and plural, 'song of (all) the songs.' As with 'slave of slaves' (Gen 9:25), 'king of kings' (Dan 2:37; Ezra 7:12), 'prince of princes' (Num 3:32), 'God of gods' (Deut 10:17), 'heaven of heavens' (1 Kings 8:27), 'beauty of beauties' (Jer 3:19), 'vanity of vanities' (Eccles 1:2 and *passim*), 'ornament of ornaments' (Ezek 16:7, applied to the development of the breasts and pubic hair of a female) always indicates some sort of superlative sense" (*Song of Songs*, p. 294).

38. Contra Origen's view (and others) that the Song is the apex of all revelation or the best of all the songs in Scripture.

39. See Rosenberg, "The Midrashic Approach to the Song of Songs," p. 13.

40. Bruce K. Waltke views the three references to Solomon in the Song (1:5; 3:6, 7; 8:11, 12) as "all negative" (*An Old Testament Theology: An Exegetical, Canonical, and Thematic Approach* [Grand Rapids, MI: Zondervan, 2007], p. 164). While these references are arguably all negative, I view only the last as certainly negative.

41. *NLT Study Bible* (Carol Stream, IL: Tyndale, 2008), p. 1085.

42. Paul R. House is helpful here: "[T]he fact that Solomon himself did not always heed its teachings does not mute its value or render it invalid" (*Old Testament Theology* [Downers Grove, IL: InterVarsity, 1998], p. 469).

43. Note that the character of Solomon is not talked about as a historical but a present person. The Song is written as if he were still alive.

44. With all that said, nevertheless, I agree with Longman: "Fortunately, little is at stake in terms of authorship" (*Song of Songs*, p. 7).

45. Duane A. Garrett notes: "Wisdom in the Bible is meant to teach the reader how to live in the world. For this reason politics, personal morality, economics, social behavior, and many other areas of life all come under its teaching. And certainly courtship, sensual love, and marriage cannot be excluded since these areas are among the most basic universals of human experience. The Song of Songs celebrates love, but it also teaches love; in this respect it must be counted as wisdom literature" (*Proverbs, Ecclesiastes, Song of Songs*, New American Commentary [Nashville: Broadman, 1993], pp. 366, 367). Cf. Katharine J. Dell, "Does the Song of Songs

Have Any Connection to Wisdom?" in Anselm C. Hagedorn, ed., *Perspectives on the Song of Songs*, Beihefte zür Zeitschrift fur die alttestamentliche Wissenschaft 346 (Berlin: de Gruyter, 2005), pp. 8–26.

46. Longman writes that the "simplest theory" is that the "daughters of Jerusalem," "daughters of Zion," and the "young women" (i.e., virgins) reference the same group (*Song of Songs*, p. 94).

47. William Sanford LaSor et al., *Old Testament Survey: The Message, Form, and Background of the Old Testament*, 2nd ed. (Grand Rapids, MI: Eerdmans, 1996), p. 514.

48. Pope, *Song of Songs*, p. 318.

49. Hess writes, "Certainly, the maidens in the Song are unmarried women who are, or shortly will be, sexually mature" (*Song of Songs*, p. 51).

50. Hubbard, *Ecclesiastes, Song of Solomon*, p. 344; cf. Keel, *Song of Songs*, p. 278.

51. What is the appropriate age to talk to your children about sex? Here the Bible implies preteen or early teen is best. James Dobson agrees. He thinks age ten is an appropriate time for boys to learn about sex. See *Bringing Up Boys: Practical Advice and Encouragement for Those Shaping the Next Generation of Men* (Wheaton: Tyndale, 2001), p. 89.

52. Garrett writes: "The man and woman of Song of Songs are young. Their bodies are perfect: beautiful eyes, black hair, golden skin, and not a tooth missing (Song 4:2). The young man leaps on the hills like a gazelle (Song 2:9). The young woman's cheeks have the blush of youth (Song 6:7). They are new to love and to sexuality. It is a glorious, wonderful, and fleeting time—like the springtime that the Song itself describes (Songs 2:10–13)" ("Song of Songs," p. 104).

53. The term "poetic drama" I borrow from Waltke, *An Old Testament Theology*, p. 164. I acknowledge that while the Song is not a drama, it holds some dramatic features—characters and a "loose temporal progression" or a "collage or kaleidoscope of scenes that suggests a story," as Daniel Estes phrases it ("The Song of Songs," pp. 291, 292).

Chapter Two: Better Than Wine

1. Richard S. Hess, *Song of Songs*, Baker Commentary on the Old Testament Wisdom and Psalms (Grand Rapids, MI: Baker, 2005), p. 52.

2. Ariel Bloch and Chana Bloch, *The Song of Songs: A New Translation* (Berkeley, CA: University of California, 1995).

3. Hess, *Song of Songs*, p. 50.

4. Gary Brady, *Heavenly Love: The Song of Songs Simply Explained*, Welwyn Commentary Series (Darlington, UK: Evangelical, 2006), p. 28.

5. Richard A. Norris Jr., trans. and ed., *The Song of Songs: Interpreted by Early Christian and Medieval Commentators*, The Church's Bible, gen. ed. Robert Louis Wilken (Grand Rapids, MI: Eerdmans, 2003), p. 24.

6. Charles Simeon, "Canticles," *Expository Outlines on the Whole Bible*, 21 vols. (repr. Grand Rapids, MI: Zondervan, 1956), 7:421.

7. Adam Clarke, *The Holy Bible, containing the Old and New Testaments: The text printed from the most correct copies of the present authorized translation, in-*

cluding the marginal readings and parallel texts with a commentary and critical notes, Vol. 3 (New York: Azor Hoyt, Printer, 1828), p. 610.

8. Bernard, quoted in Tremper Longman III, *Song of Songs*, New International Commentary on the Old Testament (Grand Rapids, MI: Eerdmans, 2001), p. 89.

9. Milton, quoted in T. J. Meek, H. T. Kerr, and H. T. Kerr Jr., *The Song of Songs*, The Interpreter's Bible (New York and Nashville: Abingdon, 1956), p. 99.

10. As Longman notes, "The characters of the Song are not specific. That is, the woman is not a particular woman but stands for all women. The same may be said for the man. These characters are developed intentionally in a nonspecific way since they are not reporting about a particular couple. These poems invite later readers to place themselves in the position of the woman and the man. In this way, the Song is similar to the book of Psalms, where the reader is implicitly encouraged to put him- or herself in the place of the first person speaker" (*Song of Songs*, p. 91).

11. Athalya Brenner shows that the woman's voice constitutes 53 percent of the text, the man's 34 percent, the chorus 6 percent, and headings and dubious cases 7 percent. *The Israelite Woman: Social Role and Literary Type in Biblical Narrative* (Sheffield, UK: JSOT, 1985), pp. 46–50.

12. David A. Hubbard, *Ecclesiastes, Song of Solomon*, The Communicator's Commentary (Dallas: Word, 1991), p. 275.

13. Tom Gledhill, *The Message of the Song of Songs*, The Bible Speaks Today (Downers Grove, IL: InterVarsity, 1994), p. 94.

14. Duane Garrett says, "Of course, the man's kisses may reach other parts of the woman's body as well, and the language suggests that Song of Songs will explore their sexual relationship" ("Song of Songs," in Duane Garrett and Paul R. House, *Song of Songs/Lamentations*, Word Biblical Commentary [Nashville: Thomas Nelson, 2004], p. 129).

15. Michael V. Fox states that a kiss with the mouth was "the most intimate and sensual kiss" (*The Song of Songs and the Ancient Egyptian Love Song* [Madison, WI: University of Wisconsin Press, 1985], p. 97).

16. Unlike Proverbs, in which we have warnings about wine (Proverbs 23:29–35; 31:4, 5), here in the Song wine is always viewed positively (Song 1:2, 4; 2:4 [margin]; 4:10; 5:1; 7:9; 8:2).

17. Cairo Love Songs, group A, no. 20G. W. K. Simpson, trans., *The Literature of Ancient Egypt: An Anthology of Stories, Instructions, and Poetry*, ed. W. K. Simpson (New Haven, CT: Yale University Press, 1973), p. 311.

18. Pablo Neruda, "Drunk as Drunk," in *Love Poems*, Everyman's Library Pocket Poets, ed. Peter Washington (New York: Knopf, 1995), p. 109.

19. See also the Jewish sage Ben Sira of Jerusalem (early second century B.C.): "What is life to one who is without wine?" (Sirach 31:27); "Wine and music gladden the heart, but the love of [lovers] is better than either" (40:20).

20. Many commentators, even those who are not purely allegorists, see Yahweh's drawing power in verse 4. While it is true that the same verb is used of the drawing/dragging strength of divine love in the Old Testament (see Hosea 11:4; Jeremiah 31:2), note that the subject of this verse is the bride, not the groom. She asks to be drawn away, which is slightly different from God, who without provocation tenderly beckons his people to follow.

21. For example, John G. Snaith lists Deuteronomy 32:15; Psalm 23:1–3, 4, 5; Jeremiah 22:24; Micah 7:19 (*Song of Songs*, New Century Bible Commentary [Grand Rapids, MI: Eerdmans, 1993], p. 14).

22. While "shepherd" is used as a metaphor for "king" in the Bible, only two of the sixteen uses of the word "shepherd" from Genesis through Ecclesiastes reference royalty. In 2 Samuel 5:2 (which is the same as 1 Chronicles 11:2) "shepherd" is paralleled with "prince."

23. Gledhill, *The Message of the Song of Songs*, p. 96.

24. Othmar Keel, *Song of Songs*, trans. Frederick J. Gaiser, A Continental Commentary (Minneapolis: Fortress, 1994), p. 45.

25. I agree with Longman when he writes, "It is verses like these that render attempts to build a narrative out of the Song, climaxing (poetically and sexually) at the end of the fourth chapter, so wrong-minded" (*Song of Songs*, p. 93).

26. For an excellent treatment on this theme, see Barry Danylak, *Redeeming Singleness: How the Storyline of Scripture Affirms the Single Life* (Wheaton, IL: Crossway, 2010).

27. For a good illustration of what to look for in a future husband, see Elisabeth Elliot's description of Jim Elliot in *Passion and Purity: Learning to Bring Your Love Life under Christ's Control* (Grand Rapids, MI: Revell, 1984), pp. 32–34.

28. Brady, *Heavenly Love*, p. 33.

29. Ibid.

30. Ibid.

31. Steve Scafidi, "Prayer for a Marriage," *Sparks from a Nine-Pound Hammer* (Baton Rouge: Louisiana State University Press, 2001), p. 55.

32. C. J. Mahaney, *Sex, Romance, and the Glory of God: What Every Christian Husband Needs to Know* (Wheaton, IL: Crossway, 2004), p. 27.

33. Ibid., p. 28.

34. See especially ibid., pp. 37–46.

35. John Piper, *When I Don't Desire God: How to Fight for Joy* (Wheaton, IL: Crossway, 2004), p. 9.

36. The lyrics to this hymn are worth quoting in full:

Compared with Christ, in all beside
No comeliness I see;
The one thing needful, dearest Lord,
Is to be one with thee.

The sense of thy expiring love
Into my soul convey;
Thyself bestow, for thee alone,
My all in all, I pray.

Loved of God, for him again
With love intense I'd burn;
Chosen of thee ere time began,
I choose thee in return.

37. Keith Gordon Green, "My Eyes Are Dry," *The Ministry Years, Vol. 1* (Sparrow Records, 1998), emphasis mine.

Chapter Three: The Metaphors and Metamorphosis of Loving Words

1. The New English Bible (NEB) gives the sense, "Do not look down on me."
2. Duane Garrett comments, "She never hints that she is of non-Israelite extraction. The Song nowhere addresses the matter of racial tension or implies that an interracial relationship is at the center of the story" ("Song of Songs," in Duane Garrett and Paul R. House, *Song of Songs/Lamentations*, Word Biblical Commentary [Nashville: Thomas Nelson, 2004], p. 133). Lloyd G. Carr adds, "The girl is usually identified as a country girl from Shunem, a small agricultural village in Lower Galilee ('Return, O Shulammite' 6:13)" (*The Song of Solomon*, Tyndale Old Testament Commentary [Downers Grove, IL: InterVarsity, 1984], p. 47).
3. Theodore of Mopsuestia was the first to suggest this: "[Solomon] took Pharaoh's daughter as his wife. But . . . she was dark, as all the Egyptian and Ethiopian women are. . . . The Hebrews and their beautiful wives, and the other princesses as well, ridiculed her on account of her unseemliness, her small height and her dark complexion" (*Paraphrase on the Commentary of Theodore of Mopsuestia*, in *Ancient Christian Commentary on Scripture IX*, ed. J. Robert Wright [Downers Grove, IL: InterVarsity, 2005], p. 299).
4. See, for example, Manuel Jinbachian, "The Genre of Love Poetry in the Song of Songs and the Pre-Islamic Arabian Odes," *The Bible Translator* 48 (1997): p. 126.
5. In Sonnet 127, Shakespeare summarizes the sense:

In the old age black was not counted fair,
Or if it were it bore not beauty's name;
But now black is beauty's successive heir,
And beauty slandered with a bastard shame.

6. Tremper Longman III, *Song of Songs*, New International Commentary on the Old Testament (Grand Rapids, MI: Eerdmans, 2001), p. 98.
7. The antithetical parallelism is clear:

Very dark/like tents of Kedar (negative darkness)
Lovely/like the curtains of Solomon (positive darkness)

8. I agree with Garrett: "[I]t is best to translate the word as 'lotus' rather than as 'lily.' Even so, one should bear in mind that the lotus is in fact a variety of lily and that the Israelites may not have carefully distinguished the two" ("Song of Songs," p. 148).
9. Paige Patterson observes, "The lily was especially prominent as a decorative carving in the pillars of the temple and on the molten sea furnishing of the temple (1 Kings 7:19, 22, and 26). This flower was especially associated with nuptial occasions and perhaps even gave its name to wedding festivities" (*Song of Solomon*, Everyman's Bible Commentary [Chicago: Moody, 1986], p. 45).
10. I borrowed the last two lines from Longman's clear interpretation (*Song of Songs*, p. 111).

11. I take this voice to come from "the daughters of Jerusalem." Note that this is the only time they talk in this poem. Also note they are mentioned twice—at the very beginning (1:5) and end of this inclusio (2:7), which again emphasizes that they are the target audience, focusing on what they are to learn about love. Put differently, they are in the inclusio because they are to apply what is between the beginning and the end!

12. The wearing of jewelry was an issue of contention in the early church (e.g., Tertullian, "On the Apparel of Women," *Anti-Nicene Fathers*, Vol. 4 [Peabody, MA: Hendrickson, 1994], pp. 14–25). The Song of Songs gives a necessary corrective, balancing the Bible's caution (e.g., Isaiah 3:16–24; 1 Timothy 2:9, 10; 1 Peter 3:3–5) with its celebration (e.g. Genesis 24:22; Psalm 45:12, 13; Proverbs 25:12; 31:22; Ezekiel 16:10–14). As beautiful as a woman's body can be, it is not wrong to enhance such beauty with externals—jewelry, makeup, perfumes, etc., so long as internal beauty is not neglected or underestimated.

13. Garrett, "Song of Songs," p. 144.

14. See the chariots of Tutankhamen, in J. B. Pritchard, ed. *Ancient Near East in Pictures Relating to the Old Testament*, 3rd ed. (Princeton: Princeton University Press, 1969), p. 60; see also Figure 13 in Othmar Keel, *Song of Songs*, trans. Frederick J. Gaiser, A Continental Commentary (Minneapolis: Fortress, 1994), p. 57.

15. Garrett, "Song of Songs," p. 145.

16. D. H. Lawrence's "Green" can be found in *Love Poems*, Everyman's Library Pocket Poets, ed. Peter Washington (New York: Knopf, 1995), p. 118.

The dawn was apple-green,
The sky was green wine held up in the sun,
The moon was a golden petal between.

She opened her eyes, and green
They shone, clear like flowers undone
For the first time, now for the first time seen.

17. On the human eyes, see Tom Gledhill, *The Message of the Song of Songs*, The Bible Speaks Today (Downers Grove, IL: InterVarsity, 1994), p. 120.

18. Ibid., p. 120.

19. Ibid., 119. Cf. Keel, *Song of Songs*, p. 69.

20. Gledhill, *The Message of the Song of* Songs, p. 119.

21. This reflects what Ernest C. Lucas calls a "responsible" attitude to love (*Exploring the Old Testament: A Guide to the Psalms and Wisdom Literature*, Old Testament, Vol. 3 [Downers Grove, IL: InterVarsity, 2003], p. 198).

22. Gary Brady, *Heavenly Love: The Song of Songs Simply Explained*, Welwyn Commentary Series (Darlington, UK: Evangelical, 2006), p. 59.

23. Brady quotes this *Police* song in ibid., p. 148.

24. Gledhill, *The Message of the Song of Songs*, p. 121.

25. Marvin H. Pope notes, "Delitzsch . . . conceded flatly, in a footnote, that in Hebrew 'house of wine' means the house in which wine is drunk. . . . The most likely sense is that of a wine cellar, a place where wine is stored and drunk" (*Song of Songs*, Anchor Bible [New York: Doubleday, 1977], p. 374).

26. Gledhill writes, "Since, as we have already seen, wine is associated in the Song with the idea of kissing, it seems better to interpret the house of wine metaphorically as his mouth, into which he invites her to enter, to enjoy their deep kissing" (*The Message of the Song of Songs*, p. 125).

27. This is the first use of this term of endearment, used thirty-one times of him in the Song.

28. The two images of 1:13, 14, along with the image of the apple tree in 2:3, complement each other. Her beloved is like a lush desert oasis—filled with sweet perfumes, natural beauty, and fresh fruit.

29. Dennis F. Kinlaw says, "Love's consummation is classic in its chasteness" ("Song of Songs," in *Expositor's Bible Commentary*, Vol. 5 [Grand Rapids, MI: Zondervan, 1991], p. 1230).

30. Throughout the Song the scenes change from rural to domestic, domestic to rural, or rural to domestic and back to rural. In 1:12—2:6, however, the motifs are mixed. The couple is on a "couch" (1:16; cf. 1:12) inside a "house" (1:16; 2:4), and yet the outside imagery remains—trees, blossoms, and vineyards. Perhaps it is all metaphorical.

31. John G. Snaith comments, "The climactic use of this word is missed if we do not realize that the word for 'our couch' denotes in Am. 6:4 particularly stylish and magnificent couches used for feasting; so the couch here in Ca. 1:16 is not any old bed!" (*Song of Songs*, New Century Bible Commentary [Grand Rapids, MI: Eerdmans, 1993], p. 25).

32. Commentating on Genesis 2:21–25, Matthew Henry quaintly observes, "The woman was made of a rib, out of the side of Adam; not made out of his head to rule over him, nor out of his feet to be trampled upon by him, but out of his side to be equal with him, under his arm to be protected, and near his head to be beloved" (*Matthew Henry's Commentary on the Whole Bible*, 6 vols. [repr. McLean, VA: MacDonald, 1985], 1:20).

33. Kinlaw writes, "It is pastoral; so their metaphors are drawn from nature. Notice the extensive references to animals, birds, trees, flowers, and mountains. The site of their lovemaking is among the cedars and firs, in all of their greenery. It hints of a return to Eden (Gen 2:18–25), with its simplicity, naïveté, equality, and purity. It is as if this were the original couple" ("Song of Songs," p. 1221).

34. In order to dismiss the God of Christianity as a wrathful God, people today will often say, "I believe in a God of love." But the irony is that the whole concept of a God of love is uniquely Christian. In his book *The Reason for God*, Tim Keller shares about the times he was a panelist on a monthly radio program that featured Christians and Muslims discussing various religious themes. He writes,

When we covered the topic of God's love, it was striking how different our conceptions were. I was told repeatedly by Muslim speakers that God was indeed loving in the sense of being merciful and kind to us. But when Christians spoke of the Lord as our spouse, of knowing God intimately and personally, and of having powerful effusions of his love poured into our hearts by the Holy Spirit, our Muslim friends balked. They told us that it was disrespectful, in their view, to speak of anyone knowing God personally. (*The Reason for God: Belief in an Age of Skepticism* [New York: Dutton, 2008], p. 82)

35. Henry, *Matthew Henry's Commentary on the Whole Bible*, 3:1057.
36. Gregory of Nyssa, *Commentary on the Song of Songs*, trans. Casimir Mc-Cambley (Brookline, MA: Hellenic College Press, 1987), p. 49. Compare this verse from Isaac Watts, "Christ the King at His Table":

Though in ourselves deformed we are,
and black as Kedar's tents appear,
yet, when we put thy beauties on,
fair as the courts of Solomon.

Brady also notes, "Preaching on Song of Songs 1:5–6, Richard Sibbes taught that God's people are imperfect on earth (outwardly and inwardly). God allows this in order to draw us from earth, humble us and increase our patience. We must confess our blackness to him and long for heaven, not being discouraged but seeing our glory" (*Heavenly Love*, p. 56).
37. Samuel J. Stone, *Lyra Fidelium: Twelve Hymns of the Twelve Articles of the Apostles' Creed* (London: Messrs. Parker and Co., 1866).
38. Charles Wesley, *Psalms and Hymns*, 1738.
39. Samuel Crossman, "My Song Is Love Unknown," *The Young Man's Meditation* (1664).
40. See Brady, *Heavenly Love*, p. 76.

Chapter Four: The Voices of Spring
1. Robert Gordis suggests "this may be the most beautiful expression of love in the spring to be found anywhere in literature" (*The Song of Songs and Lamentations*, rev. ed. [New York: Ktav, 1954], p. 52). There are many excellent examples of Renaissance poems that feature the theme of arousing love in springtime. The most famous would be Christopher Marlowe's "The Passionate Shepherd To His Love." The Marlowe poem, which in part is printed below, can be found in Pamela Norris, ed., *Come Live with Me and Be My Love: A Pageant of Renaissance Poetry and Painting* (New York: Bulfinch, 1993), p. 65.

Come live with me and be my love
and we will all the pleasures prove,
that valleys, groves, or hills, or fields,
or woods and steepy mountains yield.

Another later example is George Meredith's "Love in the Valley." The section I cite came from *Marriage Poems*, Everyman's Library Pocket Poets, ed. John Hollander (New York: Knopf, 1997), p. 29.

Then come merry April with all thy birds and beauties!
With thy crescent brows and thy flowery, showery glee;
With thy budding leafage and fresh green pastures;

And may thy lustrous crescent grow a honeymoon for me!

Come merry month of the cuckoo and the violet!
Come weeping Loveliness in all thy blue delight!
Lo! the nest is ready, let me not languish longer!
Bring her to my arms on the first May night.

2. For an excellent short summary, see Christopher Ash, *Marriage: Sex in the Service of God* (Vancouver: Regent College, 2003), pp. 195–197.

3. On 1 Corinthians 7:1–7, Roy E. Ciampa and Brian S. Rosner write, "While a property ethic applied to sexuality was common in the ancient world, including the OT . . . the distinctive reciprocity of Paul's comments (the husband's body belongs to the wife and vice versa) recalls the notes of mutual belonging in the Song of Solomon (2:16a; 6:3; cf. 7:10)" ("1 Corinthians," in G. K Beale and D. A. Carson, eds. *Commentary on the New Testament Use of the Old Testament* [Grand Rapids, MI: Baker, 2007], p. 714).

4. See also Ezekiel 34:30 and Revelation 21:3.

5. Tremper Longman III nicely summarizes: "*Winter* is gone and spring has arrived. Springtime is the universal time for love: warmer weather, the fragrance of flowers—a time to be outside, a time for the removal of clothes and intimacy" (*Song of Songs*, New International Commentary on the Old Testament [Grand Rapids, MI: Eerdmans, 2001], p. 121).

6. R. E. Murphy, "Cant 2:8–17—A Unified Poem?" in *Melange bibliques et orientaux en l'honneur de M. Mathias Delcor*, ed. A. Caquot, S. Legasse, and M. Tardieu (Kevelaer: Butzon und Bercker, 1985), pp. 305–310.

7. Although Duane Garrett views this only as an invitation ("the couple has already consummated their relationship with sexual intercourse"), he nevertheless concedes that it "signals her willingness to give him her love and her body" ("Song of Songs," in Duane Garrett and Paul R. House, *Song of Songs/Lamentations*, Word Biblical Commentary [Nashville: Thomas Nelson, 2004], p. 163).

8. Daniel J. Estes takes this view, seeing "her scented breasts" as "the mountains on which . . . her gazelle can frolic" ("Song of Songs," in Daniel C. Fredericks and Daniel J. Estes, *Ecclesiastes and the Song of Songs*, Apollos Old Testament Commentary [Downers Grove, IL: InterVarsity, 2010], p. 322).

9. Longman writes, "We might also point to 5:13, where the man's lips are said to be like perfumed lilies, and suggest that there the reference is to the woman's lips on which he feeds" (*Song of Songs*, p. 125). Christopher W. Mitchell speaks of this likely double entendre in this way: "[S]ince the beloved herself is a lily . . . and various aspects of her are described with lilies (4:5; 7:3 [ET 7:2]), the designation that . . . [her beloved] is 'he who browses among the lilies' (2:16; 6:3) may signify his devoted attention to her and intimacy with her. That implication is consistent with the verse that follows (2:17), where the Shulammite encourages him to be like a gazelle or hart upon mountains that may represent herself" (*The Song of Songs: A Theological Exposition of Sacred Scripture*, Concordia Commentary [St. Louis: Concordia, 2003], p. 719). On page 721 he adds, "Hence many commentators perceive 2:17 to be an invitation by the Shulammite for . . . her husband and lover, to enjoy intimacy with herself." Mitchell lists Marvin H. Pope, *Song of Songs*, Anchor Bible (New

York: Doubleday, 1977), pp. 409, 410; Roland E. Murphy, *The Song of Songs*, Hermeneia (Minneapolis: Fortress, 1990), pp. 139, 142; John F. Brug, *Commentary on Song of Songs* (Milwaukee: Northwestern, 1995), p. 40.

10. Most commentators agree that "foxes" are viewed negatively, as they are throughout Scripture (e.g., Luke 13:32) and ancient literature (e.g., Aristotle, *History of Animals*, 448b.1; Plato, *Republic*, 365c).

11. Robert Davidson, who in the end goes with the most common view that foxes symbolize "young men . . . on the prowl" (cf. Murphy, *The Song of Songs*, p. 141), at first comes closest to my view: "The only major puzzle in the poem is verse 15 with its references to the little foxes which spoil or destroy the vineyards. Just as foxes raid hen farms today, so they used to cause havoc in the vineyards in ancient times. A Greek poem says:

A plague on the foxes, bushy tailed vermin that creep
To plunder the vines in the evening when Micon's asleep.

"The girl may thus be pleading that nothing should be allowed to destroy the love that is blossoming between them. There may, however, be a more explicitly sexual meaning, with the little foxes representing all other eager young men, and the vineyard representing the girl's sexuality. She may be teasing her lover, playfully suggesting that he better watch out since there are others vying with him for her favors" (*Ecclesiastes and the Song of Solomon*, Daily Study Bible Series [Philadelphia: Westminster, 1986], p. 118).

12. It could be that the woman is referring to the flying fox, since that species eats fruit. See Oded Borowski, *Agriculture in Iron Age Israel* (Winona Lake, IN: Eisenbrauns, 1987), pp. 156, 157. Another suggestion focuses on the foxes' burrowing, for that activity "endangers both the vines and the walls" (Othmar Keel, *Song of Songs*, trans. Frederick J. Gaiser, A Continental Commentary [Minneapolis: Fortress, 1994], p. 108).

13. I'll add another possible application here: the Bible is sensitive to life situations. For example, a man need not give military service during the first year of marriage (Deuteronomy 24:5); and sexual relations should naturally resume after a woman's monthly menstrual period (see Leviticus 15:24), and a few weeks (at least two) after giving birth (Leviticus 12:5).

14. Estes, "Song of Songs," p. 323.

15. Martin Luther raises and answers a valid question: "Why does he swear by creatures, when that seems to be prohibited in Matt. 5:34–37, where Christ prohibits swearing by heaven or by one's head, etc.?" For his interesting answer, see "Lecture on the Song of Solomon: A Brief but Altogether Lucid Commentary of the Song of Songs," trans. Ian Siggins, *Luther's Works*, 56 vols. (St. Louis: Concordia, 1972), 15:216, 217.

16. Estes summarizes: "Gordis (1974: 28) argues plausibly that the language is a close imitation of the names 'the God of hosts' and 'God Almighty', and he demonstrates that traces of this background can be construed in the LXX and the Midrash. Several recent commentators, including Fox (1985: 110), Murphy (1990:137), Snaith (1993: 33–34), Grossberg (2005: 231) and R. M. Davidson (2007: 622–623), have accepted this approach to the understanding of the oath. LaCocque (1998: 63–64)

reasons, 'No one in the Israelite audience of the poem could have missed such transparent allusions. The formulation could not be construed as a slip of the tongue or a mere poetic substitute for the customary religious content of an oath; besides, the occasion was neither casual nor perfunctory'" ("Song of Songs," p. 321). Cf. Tom Gledhill, *The Message of the Song of Songs*, The Bible Speaks Today (Downers Grove, IL: InterVarsity, 1994), p. 128.

17. Estes notes: "The oath formula implies swearing by Yahweh, because swearing by other gods was tantamount to idolatry (Schneider, *TDNT* 5:459; Pope, *IDB* 3:576). This construction represents a strong statement, in this case prohibiting the arousal of sexual passion" ("Song of Songs," p. 321).

18. I agree with Mitchell: "The Song itself contains an implicit Gospel message of forgiveness for those who have been sexually immoral and have repented and ceased their immorality with the help of the church" (*The Song of Songs*, p. 9).

Chapter Five: Greater Than Solomon

1. Edna St. Vincent Millay, "The Betrothal," in *Marriage Poems*, Everyman's Library Pocket Poets, ed. John Hollander (New York: Knopf, 1997), p. 35.

2. Roland E. Murphy comments: "The rhythm and sound of the lines is very attractive: the repetition of q/k, b, and s in v. 1" (*The Song of Songs*, Hermeneia [Minneapolis: Fortress, 1990], p. 146).

3. Providing a helpful Wisdom Literature context to Song of Solomon 3:2, Duane Garrett writes, "Her act of looking for a man in the streets and plazas of the city is comparable to the behavior of both Lady Wisdom and the prostitute in Prov. 1:20–21; 7:10–13; 8:1–4. In each case, the 'woman' in question is hunting for a man in order to entice him. This is of itself neither good nor evil; the character and purposes of the woman in question give the action its moral quality. The woman of the Song does not seek to instruct the man (as does Lady Wisdom) or to drag him down to Sheol (as does the prostitute); she seeks the true lover and companion for her heart" ("Song of Songs," in Duane Garrett and Paul R. House, *Song of Songs/Lamentations*, Word Biblical Commentary [Nashville: Thomas Nelson, 2004], p. 171).

4. Daniel J. Estes, "Song of Songs," in Daniel C. Fredericks and Daniel J. Estes, *Ecclesiastes and the Song of Songs*, Apollos Old Testament Commentary (Downers Grove, IL: InterVarsity, 2010), p. 336.

5. Note how often her "mother" is talked about (1:6; 3:4; 6:9; 8:2; cf. his mother, 8:5). Of the minor characters, she is a "major" one.

6. Estes, "Song of Songs," p. 335.

7. As Jill M. Munro notes, "[H]er mother's house (3:4; 8:2) is also the place of security *par excellence*" ("Spikenard and Saffron: The Imagery of the Song of Songs," *Journal for the Study of the Old Testament*, 203 [Sheffield, UK: Sheffield Academic Press, 1995], p. 70).

8. Tremper Longman summarizes: "In any case, the central motive of the poem is quite clear: she is pining for her absent lover and she pursues him until she finds him and brings him back to a place of intimacy where they can experience union. Thus again, we get a pattern that we have seen and will see repeated numerous times in the Song: absence and longing lead to search and discovery, which results in intimacy and joy" (*Song of Songs*, New International Commentary on the Old Testament [Grand Rapids, MI: Eerdmans, 2001], p. 129).

9. Tom Gledhill phrases it this way: "This moment of relief, ending in the climax of consummation, is closed by the adjuration to the daughters of Jerusalem not to awaken love until it pleases" (*The Message of the Song of Songs*, The Bible Speaks Today [Downers Grove, IL: InterVarsity, 1994], p. 145).

10. Did her mother (and father) die and she inherit the house? Or was this couple living with her widowed mother (similar perhaps to Peter's situation in Matthew 8:14)? We don't know.

11. "To be in the service of Venus makes one bold, for 'she never dwells in cowardly hearts' (according to *"Estuans intrinsecus,"* a poem of the medieval *Carmina Burana* [songs of the Benediktbeuern monastery])." Othmar Keel, *Song of Songs*, trans. Frederick J. Gaiser, A Continental Commentary (Minneapolis: Fortress, 1994), p. 124.

12. From Justin Taylor, "Why Ross Douthat Is My Favorite Movie Reviewer," *Justin Taylor* (blog), *The Gospel Coalition*, September 16, 2010, http://thegospelco alition.org/blogs/justintaylor/2010/09/16/why-ross-douthat-is-my-favorite-moviereviewer/.

13. Garrett, "Song of Songs," p. 171.

14. I agree with Murphy (thus contra Estes, Garrett, et al.) that "only the king (Solomon) is the object of attention" (*The Song of Songs*, p. 152), and thus verses 6–10 are not about a bridal procession (she is not mentioned here).

15. Christian D. Ginsburg describes this litter: "Palanquins were and are still used in the East by great personages. They are like a couch, sufficiently long for the rider to recline, covered with a canopy resting on pillars at the four corners, hung round with curtains to exclude the sun; they have a door, sometimes of lattice-work, on each side. They are borne by four or more men, by means of strong poles, like those of our sedan-chairs; and in traveling great distances, there are always several sets of men to relieve each other" (*The Song of Songs and Coheleth* [New York: Ktav, 1970], p.152).

16. Of interest, David A. Hubbard writes: "'*Silver*,' '*gold*,' and '*purple*' cloth, probably of wool, all add to the picture of opulent beauty. The cloth was dyed with liquid pressed from the Mediterranean shellfish called *murex*. A student of mine once calculated the number of shellfish required for the dyers to collect one ounce of the fluid—over ten thousand" (*Ecclesiastes, Song of Solomon*, The Communicator's Commentary [Dallas: Word, 1991], p. 301).

17. It may be the crown is simply a laurel wedding garland or wreath and not a crown of state. But I think a gold or silver crown fits better with the idea of opulence being expressed here.

18. Richard S. Hess, *Song of Songs*, Baker Commentary on the Old Testament Wisdom and Psalms (Grand Rapids, MI: Baker, 2005), p. 122.

19. Because poetry sometimes parallels "Zion" with "Jerusalem" (2 Kings 19:21; Isaiah 2:3; 37:22; etc.), here "Zion" seems to be used as a synecdoche for "Jerusalem."

20. Keel, *Song of Songs*, p. 136.

21. *Merriam-Webster's Collegiate Dictionary*, 11th ed. (Springfield, MA: Merriam-Webster, 2009), p. 485.

22. Longman comments: "The Solomon/royal fiction is being exploited here, not because of Solomon's reputation in the area of love per se (where he has a dubi-

ous reputation!), but rather because of his incredible wealth. In other words, this poem expresses the woman's poetic imagination as she reflects upon the wonders of love and, in the case of this poem at least, marriage" (*Song of Songs*, p. 133).

23. Ibid., p. 136. I agree with Tom Gledhill "that the role of Solomon in the Song is minimal" (*The Message of the Song of Songs*, p. 150).

24. Garrett, "Song of Songs," p. 181.

25. Throughout Christian history, Solomon has been viewed in both positive and negative light. Camille R. La Bossiere and Jerry A. Gladson provide two famous examples: "In Dante's Paradiso, the voice of St Thomas Aquinas introduces Solomon as the brightest of the twelve lights of philosophy (10.109–14), then argues for him as the model of kingly prudence (13.94–108). The fate of Solomon is the subject of speculation in Piers Plowman. In the 'C' text, Conscience uses the case of Solomon to argue that God's blessings can be withdrawn if the recipient proves unworthy (C.4.326–34) and concludes that Solomon is now in hell (see also B.12.226–7 4)" (In Lawrence Boadt, ed., *The Song of Solomon: Love Poetry of the Spirit* [New York: St. Martin's, 1999], p. 43). Here in the Song, the Piers Plowman view is more in view.

26. On Hippolytus, see Jocelyn McWhirter, *The Bridegroom Messiah and the People of God: Marriage in the Fourth Gospel* (Cambridge: Cambridge University Press, 2006), p. 2. See also Jack R. Lundbom, "Mary Magdalene and Song of Songs 3:1–4," *Interpretation*, 49 (1995): pp. 172–175; Ann Roberts Winsor, *A King Is Bound in the Tresses: Allusions to the Song of Songs in the Fourth Gospel*, Studies in Biblical Literature, Vol. 6 (New York: Peter Lang, 1999). Winsor finds thirteen words in John 12:3; 20:1, 11–18 that correspond with about sixty verbal and thematic parallels in the Song.

27. Throughout Scripture God's people are exhorted to seek God. For example, "You will seek me [the Lord] and find me, when you seek me with all your heart" (Jeremiah 29:13), and "But from there [the promised land] you will seek the LORD your God and you will find him, if you search after him with all your heart and with all your soul" (Deuteronomy 4:29; cf. 1 Chronicles 28:9; Psalm 27:8; Proverbs 8:17; Isaiah 55:6). With that in mind, what Jesus said to Zacchaeus (after Zacchaeus seemingly sought and found Jesus) is all the more unexpected.

28. Mark Dever, *The Message of the Old Testament: Promises Made* (Wheaton, IL: Crossway, 2006), p. 555.

29. See Hubbard, *Ecclesiastes, Song of Solomon*, pp. 267–269.

30. I am reminded of the first line of C. Hassell Bullock's endorsement for my book *The Beginning and End of Wisdom:* "I have long thought that the wisdom literature of the Old Testament is a good grid on which to introduce our unbelieving and troubled world to the gospel—it is so down-to-earth and practical."

31. Saint Augustine, *Confessions*, trans. R. S. Pine-Coffin (New York: Penguin, 1961), 8.12.

Chapter Six: A Love Feast in the Beautiful Garden

1. Malcolm Muggeridge, quoted in Ian Hunter, *Malcolm Muggeridge: A Life* (New York: HarperCollins, 1980), pp. 40, 41.

2. Malcolm Muggeridge, *Christ in the Media* (Grand Rapids, MI: Eerdmans, 1977), p. 46.

3. Mike Mason, *The Mystery of Marriage: Meditations on the Miracle* (Sisters, OR: Multnomah, 1985), p. 141.

4. See Gary Brady, *Heavenly Love: The Song of Songs Simply Explained*, Welwyn Commentary Series (Darlington, UK: Evangelical Press, 2006), p. 138.

5. Tremper Longman explains: "*Wasf* is an Arabic term, which simply means description, and its application to biblical scholarship originated with the research of J. G. Wetzstein in the nineteenth century. Wetzstein was not a biblical scholar, but rather a German diplomat living in Syria at this time. As he attended local weddings, he noted similarities between the customs and songs of the day and what he read in the Song of Songs. In correspondence with the eminent biblical scholar Franz Delitzsch, he talked about songs where the groom and the bride would describe one another's physical beauty as a prelude to lovemaking. Delitzsch published excerpts of his personal correspondence with Wetzstein in an appendix in his commentary. Since this time, other more ancient analogies to these descriptive songs have been discovered and described, but they have nonetheless retained the name *wasf* in the literature" (*Song of Songs*, New International Commentary on the Old Testament [Grand Rapids, MI: Eerdmans, 2001], p. 140).

6. Longman answers the question, "Why Gilead?" saying, "Perhaps because it is a beautiful part of that world. Gilead refers to the region in the central Transjordan that surrounds the Jabbok River. It was a distant and awe-inspiring site. The goats, black, stream down, likely to give the impression of lush, flowing hair that captures the man's attention" (Ibid., p. 144).

7. Richard S. Hess, *Song of Songs*, Baker Commentary on the Old Testament Wisdom and Psalms (Grand Rapids, MI: Baker, 2005), p. 129.

8. Brady, *Heavenly Love*, p. 142.

9. Compare Longman, *Song of Songs*, p. 146.

10. Longman again is helpful: "The *fawn* is a youthful deer, and so perhaps the breasts of a young, recently matured woman are being described. The emphasis on the *twin* nature of her breasts seems to point out the obvious, but perhaps he is struck by their symmetrical nature. Most interesting, and less often commented upon, is the posture of the animals of the imagery. They are grazing among the *lilies*. Are we to picture them from the rear then? That is, as they stick their heads into the sweet smell of the flowers, their rounded rumps with their small tails may remind the poet of breasts with their protruding nipples. Perhaps we carry the image too far, but then again there are no formulas for knowing when to stop" (Ibid., p. 147).

11. I agree with the note in the *New Geneva Study Bible*: "The lovers have been together through the night" ([Nashville: Thomas Nelson, 1995], p. 1008).

12. From Andrew Marvell, "To His Coy Mistress," in *Love Poems*, Everyman's Library Pocket Poets, ed. Peter Washington (New York: Knopf, 1995), p. 36.

13. See *Wittenberg Door* (December 1977/January 1978). This issue gives a humorous literal drawing of the bride.

14. Tom Gledhill, *The Message of the Song of Songs*, The Bible Speaks Today (Downers Grove, IL: InterVarsity, 1994), p. 154.

15. See page 190 of Richard N. Soulen, "The *Wasfs* of the Song of Songs and Hermeneutic," *Journal of Biblical Literature*, 86 (1967): pp. 183–190.

16. Mason, *The Mystery of Marriage*, p. 137.

17. Phillip D. Jensen and Tony Payne, *Pure Sex* (Sydney, Australia: Matthias, 2003), p. 28.

18. Gledhill, *The Message of the Song of Songs*, p. 147. Duane Garrett has a different line count, but proposes the same results—this poem is at the center: "By my line count, there are four hundred lines of poetry in the Song, and 4:16 begins at line 200. Thus, although no proposed chiasmus 'works' perfectly, it is worth noting that near the center of the poem a dramatic sexual union occurs between the man and the woman and that numerous elements are repeated on either side of the event in chiastic sequence" ("Song of Songs," in Duane Garrett and Paul R. House, *Song of Songs/Lamentations*, Word Biblical Commentary [Nashville: Thomas Nelson, 2004], p. 31). Othmar Keel notes, "These songs form a high point in the Song, marked not only by their content but also structurally by their central location in the collection" (*Song of Songs*, trans. Frederick J. Gaiser, A Continental Commentary [Minneapolis: Fortress, 1994], p. 184).

19. Gledhill, *The Message of the Song of Songs*, p. 147.

20. Lloyd G. Carr, *The Song of Solomon*, Tyndale Old Testament Commentary (Downers Grove, IL: InterVarsity, 1984), p. 106.

21. Garrett, "Song of Songs," p. 202.

22. Normally affixes are so common that the English word "my" wouldn't be categorized as a "key" word. Yet, with that morphological commonness acknowledged, I believe my point on "my" still stands: The poet uses this affix intentionally, and at the key point (the final verse) to summarize the theme of this poem.

23. Again there is modesty both in the sex talk (4:1–16) and the sex act (5:1). It is all virtuously veiled. On this theme of modesty, Estes writes, "Out of sight of the reader, the couple between 4:16 and 5:1 enjoys sexual intercourse" (Daniel J. Estes, "Song of Songs," in Daniel C. Fredericks and Daniel J. Estes, *Ecclesiastes and the Song of Songs*, Apollos Old Testament Commentary [Downers Grove, IL: InterVarsity, 2010], p. 361). Leland Ryken adds, "We might note in passing that the symbolic mode of the Song of Solomon, in which sexual consummation, for example, is pictured as claiming a sensuous garden, has built into it a certain reserve that keeps the poem far from pornography" (*Words of Delight: A Literary Introduction to the Bible*, 2nd ed. [Grand Rapids, MI: Baker, 1992], p. 287). Also Gledhill: "The language which is used to describe the act of sexual union ranges across a very broad spectrum. It varies from the coarse and vulgar use of four letter words, through the vast variety of current slang, the cool and clinical descriptions of the medical manual, the beauty of poetic metaphor and simile. . . . We have seen that the biblical metaphors are somewhat restrained (knowing, entering, coming into the garden, eating honey and the honeycomb, drinking wine and milk, gathering myrrh and spice) and we are drawn comfortably into their orbit without too much visual stimulation. . . . Chaucer's raunchy bumpkin who 'pricketh harde and deepe' is at the other end of the spectrum" (*The Message of the Song of Songs*, p. 175).

24. C. S. Lewis writes, "Solomon calls his bride Sister. Could a woman be a complete wife unless, for a moment, in one particular mood, a man felt almost inclined to call her Brother?" (*A Grief Observed* [New York: HarperOne, 1989], p. 61).

25. On 4:12 Keel comments, "One of the most beautiful things and one of the greatest pleasures known to the ancient Near East was a garden—a carefully enclosed and heavily watered plot of ground planted with fragrant plants, blooming

bushes, and trees filled with choicest fruits. The inner court of every house had some kind of garden. A few herbs for the kitchen, a grape vine, or a fig tree usually had to suffice. To sit under these trees in peace and to enjoy their fruits without disturbance was the highest form of happiness (1 Kings 4:25 [5:5]; Mic. 4:4)" (*Song of Songs*, p. 169).

26. "It is an orchard—the Hebrew here uses the Persian loan word *pardes* from which comes our word paradise (cf. Eccles. 2:5)." Robert Davidson, *Ecclesiastes and the Song of Solomon*, Daily Study Bible Series (Philadelphia: Westminster, 1986), p. 131.

27. Cf. Deuteronomy 32:13, 14; Job 20:17; Isaiah 7:15. Paul R. House summarizes it well: "Song of Solomon 1:2–5 :1 does not duplicate this original oneness, but it comes very close to doing so" (*Old Testament Theology* [Downers Grove, IL: InterVarsity, 1998], p. 467).

28. Keel says, "Eating and drinking are metaphors for the lovers' erotic pleasures, but that metaphor does not exhaust the meaning of these terms. Eating and drinking imply appropriation in the fullest sense (Jer. 15:16; Ezek. 2:8; 3:1ff.; 23:33–34). The object of a person's love becomes part of that person" (*Song of Songs*, p. 183).

29. On 4:16ab, Keel comments: "On the one hand, the refreshing north wind, which appears also in an Egyptian love song already cited (pp. 172ff.), augments the cool shadows of the garden (cf. 2:3). On the other hand, the warm south wind stimulates the slumber-inducing fragrances of the garden. As in Isa. 43:6, 'north' and 'south' form a merism (expressing a totality through opposing poles or contrasting parts), which leads into the series of merisms in 5:1. Merisms are typical of hymns (cf. 'heaven,' 'earth,' and 'sea' in Ps. 96:11; 'young' and 'old' in Ps. 148:12); there is something exuberant and expressive in their urge toward completeness, their yearning for totality" (Ibid., p. 181).

30. Contra the ESV, I take the bride to be the speaker here.

31. C. S. Lewis, *The Four Loves*, Harcourt Brace Modern Classic (New York: Harcourt Brace & Company, 1988), p. 56.

32. Ibid., p. 110.

33. Estes summarizes the scholarship: "The final line of the verse seems to be uttered by a voice different from that of the couple, although Keel (1994: 184) argues unconvincingly that this is Solomon urging his companions to enjoy the wedding feast. Various suggestions for the identity of the speaker have been offered (cf. Trible 1978: 163), including the wedding guests (G. L. Carr 1984: 129; Gouder 1986: 39) and the daughters of Jerusalem (Hubbard 1991: 311; Exum 2005c: 182–183). It may well be, however, that this undesignated speaker is God himself (cf. R. M. Davidson 2003: 61–62) expressing his pleasure in their lovemaking and encouraging them to enjoy fully their newfound sexual intimacy within marriage. If this is indeed the case, then God is giving . . . [this couple] his 'sanction to enjoy fully the sexual feast that they have just sampled for the first time, just as he gave his approval to Adam and Eve to eat fully from the fruit of the Garden of Eden (Gen. 2:16)' (Estes 2005: 421)" ("Song of Songs," p. 362).

34. Ed and Gaye Wheat summarize their book in a way that is also fitting to summarize this point: "The message, in brief, is this: You have God's permission to

enjoy sex within your marriage" (*Intended for Pleasure*, 3rd ed. [Grand Rapids, MI: Revell, 2005], p. 14).

35. David A. Hubbard, *Ecclesiastes, Song of Solomon*, The Communicator's Commentary (Dallas: Word, 1991), p. 311.

36. On page 745, G. Schwab nicely summarizes, "One's view of sex has in it a theology, a view of God" ("Book of Song of Songs 1," in *Dictionary of the Old Testament: Wisdom, Poetry and Writings*, ed. Tremper Longman III and Peter Enns [Downers Grove, IL: InterVarsity, 2008], pp. 737–750).

37. Dan B. Allender and Tremper Longman III, *Intimate Allies: Rediscovering God's Design for Marriage and Becoming Soul Mates for Life* (Wheaton, IL: Tyndale, 1995), p. 213.

38. The botanical description is not of a realistic garden but is intended to bring together a wide variety of flora with their smells and colors to describe a paradisiacal existence (cf. Jenson, *Song of Songs*, p. 50; Gledhill, *The Message of the Song of Songs*, p. 164; Keel, *Song of Songs*, p. 180). Roland E. Murphy notes: "This garden is unreal, in the sense that no garden in the ancient Near East would have nourished such a wide variety of plants and trees. Gerleman rightly calls it a 'utopian, fantasy-garden,' that contains the precious aromatic plants of the ancient world [from Gillis Gerleman, "Ruth, Das Hohelied," *Biblischer Kommentar, Altes Testament*, ed. Martin Noth et al. (Neukirchen-Vluyn: Neukircherner, 1965)]. One suspects that the terms are chosen for sound and exotic qualities, rather than for botanical reasons" (*The Song of Songs*, Hermeneia [Minneapolis: Fortress, 1990], p. 160).

39. On the Song of Songs as an extended commentary on Genesis 2, Daniel Lys writes, "Le Cantique n'est rien d'autre qu'un commentaire de Gen. 2" ("The Song [of Songs] is nothing other than a commentary on Genesis 2"), *Le Plus Beau Chant de al Creation: Commentarie du Cantique des Cantiques*, Lectio Divina 51 (Paris: Cerf., 1968), p. 52. See also Francis Landy, "The Song of Songs and the Garden of Eden," *Journal for the Study of the Old Testament*, 98 (1979): pp. 513–528. On an interesting but overall unconvincing study on the theme "The Garden Temple," see Edmee Kingsmill, *The Song of Songs and the Eros of God: A Study in Biblical Intertextuality* (Oxford: Oxford University Press, 2009), pp. 155–178.

40. Carr, *The Song of Solomon*, p. 56. For more on this imagery, Longman writes, "In the Song of Songs we read about the man and the woman in the garden. They are naked, and feel no shame. Specific poems that support this statement include 1:15–17; 2:1–7, 8–17; 4:10—5:1; 6:1–3; 6:11–12; 7:7–11 (English 7:6–10); 7:12–14 (English 7:11–13). One cannot help but hear echoes of the Garden of Eden while reading these poems. The implication of a canonical reading of the Song is that the book speaks of the healing of intimacy. Not that that healing is fully accomplished. On the one hand, the Song celebrates their union and proclaims that intimacy happens in this world. On the other hand, the cautionary poems show that lapses occur in even the best relationships. The redemption of our intimate human relationships, indeed like the redemption of our relationships with God, is an already—not yet phenomenon" (*Song of Songs*, p. 65).

41. Augustine, quoted in Jenson, *Song of Songs*, p. 52.

42. C. S. Lewis said it this way: "One thing, however, marriage has done for me. I can never again believe that religion is manufactured out of our unconscious, starved desires and is a substitute for sex. For those few years H. and I feasted on

love; every mode of it—solemn and merry, romantic and realistic, sometimes as dramatic as a thunderstorm, sometimes as comfortable and unemphatic as putting on your soft slippers. No cranny of heart or body remained unsatisfied. If God were a substitute for love we ought to have lost all interest in Him. Who'd bother about substitutes when he has the thing itself? But that isn't what happens. We both knew we wanted something besides one another—quite a different kind of something, a quite different kind of want" (*A Grief Observed*, pp. 19, 20).

43. C. S. Lewis, *Screwtape Proposes a Toast* (London: Collins, 1971), pp. 97, 98.

44. Muggeridge, *Christ in the Media*, p. 46.

Chapter Seven: A Reprieve and Return to Eden

1. David A. Hubbard, *Ecclesiastes, Song of Solomon*, The Communicator's Commentary (Dallas: Word, 1991), p. 313.

2. Barry G. Webb, *Five Festal Garments: Christian Reflections on the Song of Songs, Ruth, Lamentations, Ecclesiastes, and Esther*, New Studies in Biblical Theology (Downers Grove, IL: InterVarsity, 2000), p. 30.

3. Tom Gledhill, *The Message of the Song of Songs*, The Bible Speaks Today (Downers Grove, IL: InterVarsity, 1994), p. 183.

4. From act 1, scene 1 of William Shakespeare, *A Midsummer Night's Dream*. Lysander says this line to Hermia.

5. As Othmar Keel notes: "Finally, it is possible that squeezing his hand through the hole says something about the purpose of the nocturnal visit. 'Hand' is occasionally used in the OT (Isa. 57:8, 10) and in Ugaritic . . . as a euphemism for 'phallus.' The 'hole' could then be understood as a symbol for the vagina. Thus this gesture would silently express the lover's desire. But whether this gesture is a sexual pantomime or merely a helpless hand pushed through the hole in the door in an attempt to open the bolt, the result is a strong stirring of the woman's emotions as she watches (in darkness?) from inside. The word translated 'inmost being' literally means the abdominal organs, e.g., the intestines (cf. 2 Sam. 20:10), or more often the female (Isa. 49:1; Ps. 71:6; Ruth 1:11) or male (Gen. 15:4; 2 Sam. 16:11; 7:12) reproductive organs" (*Song of Songs*, trans. Frederick J. Gaiser, A Continental Commentary [Minneapolis: Fortress, 1994], p. 192). See also Lloyd G. Carr, *The Song of Solomon*, Tyndale Old Testament Commentary (Downers Grove, IL: InterVarsity, 1984), pp. 133–135. Yet Gledhill's caution is worth heeding: "The verses which have been interpreted in this way are 5:4–5 (literal translations) ' . . . he thrusts forth his hand through the hole', 'I arose to open for my lover', 'My hands dropped flowing myrrh upon the bolt.' References to holes, opening doors and bolts, carry their literal primary meaning here. Any sexual meaning exists purely in the mind of the reader, as the secondary meaning is too distanced from the actuality of the narrative description. In other words, the phrases are not being used metaphorically as in the example of 'the mountains of Bether' where there is a clear meaningful transfer of ideas from the context as a whole. If we start looking for references to intercourse and private parts everywhere, we lose track of the main theme of the Song and begin to sink into a quagmire of eroticism" (*The Message of the Song of Songs*, p. 180).

6. Robert Davidson notes: "If we translate as the Jerusalem Bible does, 'I trembled to the core to my being', then that trembling or thrill has a strongly sexual element in it. By the time she gets up, heavily perfumed—she had probably been

expecting her lover—and reaches the door, he is gone (v. 5). She has overplayed her hand. She is left standing, disappointed. 'My soul failed me when he spoke' (v. 6) is not a very happy rendering of a phrase which could mean either 'I wanted to hear his voice' (GNB) or even 'I nearly died when I found he had gone'" (*Ecclesiastes and the Song of Solomon*, Daily Study Bible Series [Philadelphia: Westminster, 1986], p. 135).

7. I borrow from Keel, who writes, "As was customary, she had undressed completely for sleeping (1 Sam. 19:24; cf. Neh. 4:23 [17]). The [garment] mentioned here is a close-fitting, ankle-length, shirt-like undergarment. In warm weather it could also be worn by itself, as shown by the portrayal of Judean women on an Assyrian relief (fig. 116; cf. 2 Sam. 13:18–19). The outer garment, needed in cold weather, was also used as a blanket (cf. Exod. 22:25–26; Deut. 24:13). The same relief shows that people usually went barefoot (less often they wore sandals; cf. Cant. 7:1 [2]). Before preparing for an evening at home or going to bed, one washed one's feet (Gen. 24:32; 2 Sam. 11:8). The woman has made her detailed preparations (perhaps accompanied by a sense of longing and waiting?), has gone to bed, and is already half asleep. The Hebrew word translated 'What?' is an extraordinary form of the interrogative particle, otherwise occurring only in Esth. 8:6 (also twice); it expresses astonishment and indignation. The lover (arriving late?) has apparently all too easily taken for granted that she would once again get dressed and dirty her feet. Many exegetes are puzzled by the woman's reaction. They think they need allegory, mythology, or depth psychology to explain her behavior. But what she does is hardly out of the ordinary" (*Song of Songs*, p. 189).

8. Daniel J. Estes summarizes various scholars' views: "The myrrh on the door bolt has prompted several different interpretations. Glickman (1976: 63) suggests that Solomon leaves some myrrh at the door as a sort of affectionate reminder to indicate that he has been there to see her (cf. also Murphy 1990: 171). On the other hand, Bloch and Bloch (1995: 181–182; cf. Gordis 1974: 90) link the 'liquid myrrh' *(môr'ōbēr)* with the oil of myrrh in Esth. 2:12, thus arguing that Shulammith is prepared for lovemaking with Solomon and that her words in 5:3 were flirtatious coquetry that Solomon misinterpreted. A straightforward reading of the verse could well indicate that as Shulammith belatedly rises to open the door to admit Solomon, she first anoints her hands with myrrh" ("Song of Songs," in Daniel C. Fredericks and Daniel J. Estes, *Ecclesiastes and the Song of Songs*, Apollos Old Testament Commentary [Downers Grove, IL: InterVarsity, 2010], p. 368). On page 369 Estes adds: "While the myrrh is 'passing along' *('br)* her fingers, Solomon is 'passing by' *('br)*, indicating that this opportunity for lovemaking has been lost."

9. I borrowed the card illustration from Davidson, *Ecclesiastes and the Song of Solomon*, p. 135.

10. Marvin Pope suggests this represents "a bit of coy pretense intended to tease the eager male" (*Song of Songs*, Anchor Bible [New York: Doubleday, 1977], p. 515).

11. Keel explains the possible background to the watchmen's behavior: "The guards would treat a woman wandering the streets at night as a roving adulteress (Prov. 7:11–12) or as a prostitute. According to a Middle Assyrian law book from the twelfth century B.C.: 'A prostitute dare not veil herself; her head remains uncovered. Anyone seeing a veiled prostitute should arrest her, gather witnesses, and

bring her to the entrance of the palace. Her jewelry may not be taken, but the one who arrests her receives her clothing. She should be given 50 blows with a club and have asphalt poured over her head.' This mentality might have spread into Israel under the influence of Assyrian domination. But even if Israel's practice were less brutal, the Assyrian background helps explain the rough treatment of the woman" (*Song of Songs*, p. 195).

12. According to Gledhill, "It is unlikely that there was any formal judicial act here. In her struggle to free herself, her flimsy garments were torn from her, leaving her battered, *bruised*, shivering and half naked. This is a picture of her defenselessness, without her clothing as a covering, without her lover as a protection" (*The Message of the Song of Songs*, p. 178).

13. For this chiastic diagram, see Keel, *Song of Songs*, p. 206.

14. Ibid.

15. Tremper Longman III, *Song of Songs*, New International Commentary on the Old Testament (Grand Rapids, MI: Eerdmans, 2001), p. 173.

16. See Roland E. Murphy, *The Song of Songs*, Hermeneia (Minneapolis: Fortress, 1990), p. 169.

17. Duane Garrett, "Song of Songs," in Duane Garrett and Paul R. House, *Song of Songs/Lamentations*, Word Biblical Commentary (Nashville: Thomas Nelson, 2004), p. 220.

18. On the idea of it being a beard, Longman writes: "Next comes the woman's description of the man's *cheeks* and *lips*. Or is the first half of the verse really speaking of the man's beard? I think this likely, especially considering the fact that as far as we can tell men in all periods of Israel's history wore beards. Indeed, there were laws that prohibited clipping beards (Lev. 19:27; 21:5), and to shave was embarrassing (2 Sam. 10:4; Isa. 15:2). The description of the cheeks as growing a bed of spices also seems to fit with the view that this half verse is really about a beard (which, after all, also grows). Interestingly, though, the emphasis that the poet places on the beard has nothing really to do with its looks, but rather its smell. The man's beard is a veritable garden of spices" (*Song of Songs*, p. 172).

19. Longman comments: "In the ancient Near East and elsewhere in the Bible (Prov. 5:15–20), these are highly erotic images. The images of fountain and garden probably are to be visualized together since a garden would need a water supply. The focus may well be on the ultimate place in the act of lovemaking, the woman's vagina. Two of the images are in the present verse, garden and fountain. She is not a garden or fountain open to every passer-by; she is rather a *locked* garden, a *sealed* fountain. These images describe her inaccessibility. However, as we will see soon, she will open up her treasures to the man who will enter her garden ('enter' often has the overtones of sexual intercourse). With the image of sealing and locking, we would be hard pressed to miss the idea of virginity (at least up to now)" (Ibid., p. 155).

20. Gledhill nicely describes: "She is a luscious extensive garden, with a dazzling variety of flora and fauna. . . . This is the garden into which the lovers enter. She is the garden into which her beloved comes, and yet they are both enfolded in it. She envelops him in her embrace, and creates a new world for him, a new dimension, in which he lives and moves and has his being. It is all too easy to develop the garden imagery into an asymmetrical metaphor, in which the man 'enters' his garden and eats its fruit. Our Song itself lends credence to this. The physical asymmetry of the

act of sexual union, a biological and anatomical inevitability, also underscores this aspect. But the emotional, psychological and mental reciprocity is something that is a mutual two-way interaction. Her garden waters the man, gives him succor and wholeness. She is equally a shade to him, as he is to her (2:3). They taste the sweetness of each other's fruit" (*The Message of the Song of Songs*, pp. 186, 188).

21. I surmise that "he grazes" refers to sexual intimacy due to (a) the overall context—every poem thus far has ended this way, and (b) the immediate context—the intimate physical descriptions he gives of her body in the next poem (see 6:4—8:4, especially 7:1–3, 7–9 with 10).

22. An excellent poem on our text's theme is Stephen Dunn, "After the Argument," which ends with the line "their sex was a knot." I found this poem in Garrison Keillor, ed. *Good Poems* (New York: Viking, 2002), pp. 131, 132.

23. Hubbard, *Ecclesiastes, Song of Solomon*, p. 313.

24. The reference is to Jonathan Edwards. See Elisabeth D. Dodds, *Marriage to a Difficult Man: The Uncommon Union of Jonathan and Sarah Edwards* (Laurel, MS: Audubon, 2005).

25. This is Estes's clever turn of phrase (see "Song of Songs," p. 370).

26. See Robert W. Jenson, *Song of Songs*, Interpretation (Louisville: John Knox, 2005), p. 62.

27. Keel observes: "After arriving late and waking his beloved from her half-sleep with his passionate urgency, the man responds to her hesitation by trying to get in on his own; when that attempt does not work, the inconstant lover changes his mind and leaves. This poem has been titled 'Punished Coyness' (Rudolph) or 'Love's Sorrow through Rejection' (Schneider), but this view is biased from the man's perspective, thinking the woman should always be at his beck and call without delay. One could just as well entitle the poem 'The Inconsiderate Lover' or 'Love's Sorrow through Impatience'; this view would also be biased, ascribing fault to the man, just as the other titles did to the woman. But the poem is not about determining guilt; it is about a recurrent and painful experience of people in love: their feelings do not always match. When she opens the door, he has changed his mind and left. The word used here in Hebrew . . . is rare; it means 'turn aside,' 'be inconstant,' 'vacillate' (Jer. 31:22). The related Arabic word *chamiqa* means 'be foolish'" (*Song of Songs*, p. 194).

28. I follow Glickman's thought on this section, especially verses 2, 3. S. Craig Glickman, *A Song for Lovers* (Downers Grove, IL: InterVarsity, 1976), pp. 60–65, 182–185.

29. "This is really *her* book" (Carr, *The Song of Solomon*, p. 130).

30. Hubbard, *Ecclesiastes, Song of Solomon*, p. 316.

31. At night prostitutes roamed the city streets and public squares to entice men (see Proverbs 7:12; Ezekiel 16:24).

32. Estes, "Song of Songs," p. 379.

33. Estes further notes: "A similar careless attitude is in view in Matt. 25:1–12, when Jesus contrasts the five wise virgins with the five foolish virgins, who were not prepared for the arrival of the bridegroom for the wedding feast" (Ibid., p. 370).

34. Gledhill, *The Message of the Song of Songs*, p. 184.

35. Estes, "Song of Songs," p. 376.

36. Amelia and Greg Clarke, *One Flesh: A Practical Guide to Honeymoon Sex and Beyond* (Kingsford, Australia: Matthias, 2001), p. 45.

37. Gary Brady writes of John Owen's interpretation, "In applying this verse to Christ John Owen uses the word 'lovely' eleven times over. He speaks of how lovely Christ is with regard to his person, birth, life, death, resurrection and ascension, glory and majesty, grace and consolations, tender care, power and wisdom, ordinances, vengeance and pardon. 'What shall I say?' he concludes. 'He is altogether lovely'" (*Heavenly Love: The Song of Songs Simply Explained*, Welwyn Commentary Series [Darlington, UK: Evangelical, 2006], p. 184).

38. This phrase is borrowed from C. S. Lewis, *The Four Loves*, Harcourt Brace Modern Classic (New York: Harcourt Brace & Company, 1988), p. 105.

39. John Bunyan once exhorted husbands to be "such a believing husband to your believing wife that she may say, 'God has not only given me a husband, but such a husband as preaches to me every day the way of Christ to His church'"; quoted in Douglas Wilson, *Reforming Marriage* (Moscow, ID: Canon Press, 1995), p. 10.

40. Allender and Longman summarize: "Marriage is not merely a convenience to overcome loneliness or an expedient arrangement to propagate the race. First and foremost, marriage is a mirror of the divine-human relationship. Every marriage is meant to represent God: his perfect relationship with himself—Father, Son, and Holy Spirit—as well as his relationship with his people. But as the Bible recounts the divine-human relationship, we see that it is not a pretty picture. God's people have affairs with other gods; they abandon him, their first love. The Bible uses marriage imagery—love, bride, Bridegroom, redemption, sacrifice, and even prostitution, adultery, and divorce—to describe God's relationship to his people. And the Bible, though not a how-to book of marital skills and principles, is nevertheless the guiding story of what God intended for our marriages, what went wrong, and how we can restore that intimacy. The Bible reveals to us the marriage story that is to shape our marriages" (*Intimate Allies*, p. xviii).

Chapter Eight: How Beautiful!

1. Calvin did not "touch" in the sense of writing any detailed commentary. In the *Institutes*, for example, he only quoted the Song three times (see *Institutes of the Christian Religion*, Library of Christian Classics, ed. John T. McNeill, trans. Ford Lewis Battles [Philadelphia: Westminster, 1960], 1.11.14, 3:16.4, 3.20.9). The first reference is merely a quote from a member at the Council of Nicea; the second two are Calvin's one-line Christological allegories.

2. Matthew Henry died before completing the New Testament. He only wrote on the Gospels and Acts. After his death, thirteen other ministers completed Romans through Revelation based in part on notes taken by Henry's congregants.

3. Charles Spurgeon, *Commenting and Commentaries* (New York: Sheldon & Company, 1876), p. 14.

4. Matthew Henry, *Matthew Henry's Commentary on the Whole Bible*, 6 vols. (repr. McLean, VA: MacDonald, 1985), 3:1053.

5. See Ann E. Matter, *The Voice of My Beloved: The Song of Songs in Western Medieval Christianity* (Philadelphia: University of Pennsylvania Press, 1990), p. 3. The opening words of Denys Turner's excellent overview is telling: "I have compiled this volume in part to document and in part to explain a curious fact of western Christian history. Male celibates, monks and priests, have for centuries described, expressed and celebrated their love of God in the language of sex.

They did this in many genres of writing, occasionally in poetry, more often in set treatises of love, but most prolifically and characteristically in a thousand years of commentarial tradition on the Song of Songs" (*Eros and Allegory: Medieval Exegesis of the Song of Songs*, Cistercian Studies Series 156 [Kalamazoo, MI: Cistercian, 1995], p. 17).

6. See J. P. Migne, ed. *Patrologia Latina* (Paris: J. P. Migne, 1844–1864), pp. 109–111, cited in Endel Kallas, "Martin Luther as Expositor of the Song of Songs," *Lutheran Quarterly*, 2:3 (Autumn 1988): p. 323. See also Max Engammare, *Qu'il Me Baise Des Baisers De Sa Bouche: Le Cantique des Cantiques à La Renaissance* (Geneve: Droz, 1993), pp. 483, 484.

7. Engammare, *Qu'il Me Baise*, p. 483.

8. The authorized glosses of the 1611 English Bible were representative of the interpretations of the sixteenth- and seventeenth-century British Church. Chapter 1 of the Song, we are officially informed, is about "The Churches love unto Christ," the end of chapter 3 of "The Church glorying in Christ," and chapter 8 of "The love of the Church to Christ." Even the English Puritans, who adhered almost exclusively to the literal-historical sense of Scripture and opposed adamantly the authority of tradition in Biblical exegesis, were as overtly allegorical, traditional, and mystical in their interpretation of the Song as any medieval monk. Their abundant literature is dramatic testimony to this irony. From the London printing presses the writings of John Cotton (1584–1652), Thomas Brightman (1562–1607), John Robotham (fl. 1654), Samuel Smith (1588–1665), William Gearing (fl. 1667), John Brayne (fl. 1647), Edward Leigh (1602–1671), John Collinges (1623–1690), John Mayer (1583–1664), John Lloyd (1664–1682), Thomas Wilson (1563–1622), Arthur Hildersham (1563–1632), Thomas Ager (fl. 1660), John Trapp (1601–1669), Nathanael Homes (1599–1678), and many others saturated the popular market with meditations, commentaries, and paraphrases on "the faithful soul's inflamed desire of Christ" (to borrow from the note on 1:2 in the Geneva Bible).

9. Martin Luther was one of very few exceptions. He attempted to stray from this tradition. However, in my reading of his short commentary on the Song, his advertised "new path" followed many of the same roads of medieval exegesis. Beginning in 1530, Luther gave the first of his twenty-four classroom lectures on his "Brief but Altogether Lucid Commentary on the Song of Songs." Disenchanted with the allegory of the church fathers, mystified by the speculations of the schoolmen, and displeased with all rabbinic solutions, Luther sought to bring the Song to a safe middle ground. Advocating the *simplicem sensus* of the literal text, he offered the church perhaps the most complex clarification of Solomon's Song. Attending to the literary genre and historical context, he turned this love song into a "figurative narrative" about "the greatest of all human works, namely, government." This, Luther assured his students, is the "simplest sense and the real character of this book." Confident of the original author's intent, he demonstrated through his verse by verse exposition how Solomon "prays for the preservation and extension of this his kingdom . . . and encourages the inhabitants and citizens of his realm to be of good cheer in their trials and adversities." Politics, not sex or beatific visions, was the meat of Luther's interpretive scheme.

10. Henry, *Matthew Henry's Commentary on the Whole Bible*, 3:1092.

11. On the sexual attitudes in early Christianity, see Peter Brown, *The Body and Society: Men, Women, and Sexual Renunciation in Early Christianity* (New York: Columbia University Press, 1988).

12. See William Keith Chambers Guthrie, *Orpheus and Greek Religion: A Study of the Orphic Movement* (Princeton, NJ: Princeton University Press, 1952), pp. 217, 218.

13. I borrow from some of C. S. Lewis's language here. However, I don't fully agree with Lewis's more positive view of Francis's remarks. Lewis writes, "Man has held three views of his body. First there is that of those ascetic Pagans who called it the prison or the 'tomb' of the soul, and of Christians like Fisher to whom it was a 'sack of dung,' food for worms, filthy, shameful, a source of nothing but temptation to bad men and humiliation to good ones. Then there are the Neo-Pagans (they seldom know Greek), the nudists and the sufferers from Dark Gods, to whom the body is glorious. But thirdly we have the view which St. Francis expressed by calling his body 'Brother Ass.' All three may be—I am not sure—defensible; but give me St. Francis for my money. Ass is exquisitely right because no one in his senses can either revere or hate a donkey. It is a useful, sturdy, lazy, obstinate, patient, lovable and infuriating beast; deserving now the stick and now a carrot; both pathetically and absurdly beautiful. So the body. . . ." (*The Four Loves*, Harcourt Brace Modern Classic [New York: Harcourt Brace & Company, 1988], p. 100).

14. Quoted in Tom Gledhill, *The Message of the Song of Songs*, The Bible Speaks Today (Downers Grove, IL: InterVarsity, 1994), p. 30.

15. Bertrand Russell, *Why I Am Not a Christian* (London: Unwin, 1957), p. 29.

16. On this point, see Dennis F. Kinlaw, "Song of Songs," in *Expositor's Bible Commentary*, Vol. 5 (Grand Rapids, MI: Zondervan, 1991), p. 1205.

17. Although he writes of the medieval church, C. S. Lewis's critique is applicable to earlier Christianity: "But according to the medieval view passionate love itself was wicked, and did not cease to be wicked if the object of it were your wife. If a man had once yielded to this emotion he had no choice between 'guilty' and 'innocent' love before him: he had only the choice, either of repentance, or else of different forms of guilt" (*The Allegory of Love: A Study in Medieval Tradition* [Oxford: Oxford University Press, 1936], p. 14).

18. Duane Garrett summarizes: "For Augustine . . . the higher level of holiness was found in celibacy. The end result, intellectually codified for centuries in the Western church and ultimately institutionalized in the Catholic Church, was a two-tiered spirituality in which marriage is legitimate, to some degree even wondrous, but forever held back in a lower level of spirituality by that most carnal of activities, sex. To be close to God, one had to be continent" ("Song of Songs," in Duane Garrett and Paul R. House, *Song of Songs/Lamentations*, Word Biblical Commentary [Nashville: Thomas Nelson, 2004], p. 101). In Augustine's own words: "Therefore the good of marriage is indeed ever a good: but in the people of God it was at one time an act of obedience unto the law; now it is a remedy for weakness, but in certain a solace of human nature. Forsooth to be engaged in the begetting of children, not after the fashion of dogs by promiscuous use of females, but by honest order of marriage, is not an affection such as we are to blame in a man; yet this affection itself the Christian mind having thoughts of heavenly things, in a more praiseworthy manner

surpasses and overcomes" ("On the Good of Widowhood," *Nicene and Post-Nicene Fathers*, Vol. 3 [Peabody, MA: Hendrickson, 1995], p. 445).

19. For example, see John 1:14; 2:21; Romans 8:23; 12:1; 1 Corinthians 6:20; 7:28a, 39; 15:42ff.; 2 Corinthians 5:1–10; Philippians 1:20; 3:20, 21; Colossians 2:9; Hebrews 10:10, 19–22.

20. I have argued elsewhere (*The Beginning and End of Wisdom: Preaching Christ from the First and Last Chapters of Proverbs, Ecclesiastes, and Job* [Wheaton, IL: Crossway, 2011], pp. 114–117) that the book of Job prepares us for Christ by getting us to think on the seeming paradox of a righteous man's sufferings and the justice of God. In a similar manner, by giving God's stamp of approval on the physical, perhaps the Song of Songs prepares us for the incarnation—that God uses the human body (his only Son's own flesh!) to redeem humans.

21. See Bruce K. Waltke, *An Old Testament Theology: An Exegetical, Canonical, and Thematic Approach* (Grand Rapids, MI: Zondervan, 2007), p. 163.

22. See Garrett, "Song of Songs," p. 101.

23. E.g., David was captured by Bathsheba's beauty—"the woman was *very beautiful*" to behold (2 Samuel 11:2).

24. David is described as being "handsome" and having "beautiful eyes" (1 Samuel 16:12). Marvin H. Pope adds: "Human beauty, and especially that of woman, is not infrequently noticed in the Old Testament, as a matter of general interest and as having special relevance to the context; cf. Gen 6:2, 12:11, 14, 24:16; 29:17; Deut 21:11; Judg 15:2; II Sam 11:2, 13:1, 14:27; I Kings 1:3f; Esther 1:11, 2:7; Job 42:1; Ps 45:12 [11E]" (*Song of Songs*, Anchor Bible [New York: Doubleday, 1977], p. 55).

25. See Douglas Wilson, *Reforming Marriage* (Moscow, ID: Canon, 1995), pp. 55–57.

26. Leland Ryken, *Words of Delight: A Literary Introduction to the Bible*, 2nd ed. (Grand Rapids, MI: Baker, 1992), p. 285.

27. This is the highest occurrence of the word in the Old Testament.

28. Garrett, "Song of Songs," p. 250.

29. Ryken, *Words of Delight*, p. 284.

30. Garrett, "Song of Songs," p. 242.

31. Daniel J. Estes, "Song of Songs," in Daniel C. Fredericks and Daniel J. Estes, *Ecclesiastes and the Song of Songs*, Apollos Old Testament Commentary (Downers Grove, IL: InterVarsity, 2010), p. 395.

32. On this word, Lloyd G. Carr comments: "This is the only place in the Old Testament this word appears. It is variously rendered as a proper name 'Shulamith' (so Delitzsch), or as in JB as the name of the place from which the girl comes (*cf.* Introduction, p. 47). Neither view is entirely satisfactory, nor has won general acceptance" (*The Song of Solomon*, Tyndale Old Testament Commentary [Downers Grove, IL: InterVarsity, 1984], p. 154).

33. What young Claudio said of Hero, his beloved, in Shakespeare's *Much Ado About Nothing* (act 1, scene 1), is what our hero says of his bride.

34. From Shakespeare's *Romeo and Juliet*, act 2, scene 2.

35. For helpful commentary on the city of Tirzah, see Tremper Longman III, *Song of Songs*, New International Commentary on the Old Testament (Grand Rapids, MI: Eerdmans, 2001), p. 179.

36. Leone, quoted in Gledhill, *The Message of the Song of Songs*, p. 158.

37. Iain Provan, *Ecclesiastes/Song of Songs*, NIV Application Commentary (Grand Rapids, MI: Zondervan, 2001), p. 290.

38. Richard S. Hess, *Song of Songs*, Baker Commentary on the Old Testament Wisdom and Psalms (Grand Rapids, MI: Baker, 2005), p. 158.

39. Jonathan Edwards wrote, "There is very great delight the Christian enjoys in the sight he has of the glory and excellency of God. How many arts and contrivances have men to delight the eye of the body. Men take delight in the beholding of great cities, splendid buildings and stately palaces. And what delight is often taken in the beholding of a beautiful face. May we not well conclude that great delights may also be taken in pleasing the eye of the mind in seeing the most beautiful, the most glorious, the most wonderful Being in the world?" ("The Pleasantness of Religion," in *Sermons and Discourses, 1723–1729, The Works of Jonathan Edwards*, Vol. 14, ed. Kenneth P. Minkema [New Haven, CT: Yale University Press, 1997], pp. 108, 109).

40. Albert Cook notes that the term in 7:6 is "heavily weighted toward physical lovemaking" (*The Root of the Thing: A Study of Job and the Song of Songs* [Bloomington, IN: Indiana University Press, 1968], p. 110).

41. On 7:9, Garrett comments: "In light of the height that these trees could attain, as well as the primitive nature of any climbing equipment that the ancient orchard farmer might have possessed, going up a date palm to get the fruit would have been no small task. This does not mean that making love to the woman requires some heroic show of strength on his part; it only means that desire to enjoy her pleasure is equal to the desire and determination one would need in order to scale the date palm for its fruit" ("Song of Songs," p. 244).

42. David A. Hubbard comments that this verse expresses the man's "desire for intercourse with the same passion and intensity as *'I will go my way to the mountain of myrrh'* (4:6)" (*Ecclesiastes, Song of Solomon*, The Communicator's Commentary [Dallas: Word, 1991], p. 334). On that same page, see his discussion for other possible erotic images.

43. Carr, *The Song of Solomon*, p. 151.

44. See Roland Murphy, "Toward a Commentary on the Song of Songs," *Catholic Biblical Quarterly*, 39 (1977): pp. 491ff.

45. Ariel Bloch and Chana Bloch, *The Song of Songs: A New Translation* (Berkeley, CA: University of California, 1995), p. 107.

46. Paul R. House writes, "It is also appropriate to comment that the marital love depicted here and elsewhere in the canon is heterosexual in nature. Leviticus 18:22 and 20:13 show that the Old Testament is well aware of homosexual sexuality. Its denial there and the rest of the canon's emphasis on male-female marital bonds point to the conclusion that heterosexual marriage is the only type sanctioned in the Old Testament. Paul's statements in Romans 1:18–32 also agree with this conclusion" (*Old Testament Theology* [Downers Grove, IL: InterVarsity, 1998], p. 468).

47. The word translated "desire" in 6:12 is *nephesh*, "soul" or "being"; 7:10 has *t'shuqah*, which actually means "desire."

48. Garrett, "Song of Songs," p. 246.

49. Othmar Keel titles this section in his commentary, "Lifting the Curse" (*Song of Songs*, trans. Frederick J. Gaiser, A Continental Commentary [Minneapolis: For-

tress, 1994], p. 251). Garrett adds, "In the Song, the ideal of love and marriage is represented almost as though the fall had never happened" ("Song of Songs," p. 246).

50. In the "Afterword" to Bloch and Bloch's translation and commentary, Robert Alter writes, "The graceful aspect of the original [Hebrew] needs to be stressed, for metaphoric representation, certainly as it is deployed here, is artful mediation: if the poet frankly imagines the body, male and female, as an alluring map of erogenous zones, the figurative language of the poem again and again translates that bodily reality into fresh springs, flowering gardens, highlands over which lithe animals bound, spices and wine, cunningly wrought artifacts, resplendent towers and citadels and gleaming pools. In more explicit erotic literature, the body in the act of love often seems to displace the rest of the world. In the Song, by contrast, the world is constantly embraced in the very process of imagining the body. The natural landscape, the cycle of the seasons, the beauty of animal and floral realm, the profusion of goods afforded through trade, the inventive skill of the artisan, the grandeur of cities, are all joyfully affirmed as love is affirmed" (*The Song of Songs*, p. 130).

51. It is likely that Keel's reading is right, that the "new as well as old" choice fruits refer to "erotic pleasures—both those as yet unknown, coming as a surprise, and those that are old and proved" (*Song of Songs*, p. 260).

52. Concerning 7:12, Garrett comments, "Her invitation to him to go to the fields is probably a double entendre. No doubt lovers did literally go out into the fields to enjoy their love in privacy. The level of privacy one could find out in the fields, in contrast to the close quarters in the confines of cities and villages, to say nothing of houses with extended families, is evident in the rape legislation of Deut. 22:23–27. At the same time, the fields, like the gardens, vineyard, and meadows of the Song of Songs, symbolize the pleasures of love" ("Song of Songs," p. 246).

53. Compare 1 Corinthians 7, 13; Ephesians 5; 1 Thessalonians 4:3–9.

54. House, *Old Testament Theology*, p. 467.

55. Barry G. Webb, *Five Festal Garments: Christian Reflections on the Song of Songs, Ruth, Lamentations, Ecclesiastes, and Esther*, New Studies in Biblical Theology (Downers Grove, IL: InterVarsity, 2000), p. 32.

56. For this study and other observations, see Steve Gallagher's section, "Effects of Television," in *At the Altar of Sexual Idolatry* (Dry Ridge, KY: Pure Life Ministries, 2007), pp. 165, 166. Cf. "Viewing Sensuality," in R. Kent Hughes, *Set Apart: Calling a Worldly Church to a Godly Life* (Wheaton, IL: Crossway, 2003), pp. 51–62.

57. To be accurate, Augustine said this in reference to God the Father: "My Father, supremely good, beauty of all things beautiful" (*The Confessions of St. Augustine*, trans. John K. Ryan [New York: Image, 1960], 3.6). Similarly Gregory of Nyssa put it this way: "Hope always draws the soul from the beauty which is seen to what is beyond, always kindles the desire for the hidden through what is constantly perceived. Therefore the ardent lover of beauty, although receiving what is always visible as an image of what he desires, yet longs to be filled with the very stamp of the archetype. And the bold request which goes up the mountains of desire asks this: to enjoy the Beauty not in mirrors and reflections, but face to face." Gregory, quoted in Patrick Sherry, *Spirit and Beauty: An Introduction to Theological Aesthetics*, 2nd ed. (London: SCM, 2002), p. 56.

58. Fyodor Dostoyevsky, *The Brothers Karamazov* (New York: Macmillan, 1922), p. 110.

Chapter Nine: The Climax

1. All of these examples are taken from Kim Casali, *Love Is . . . in Bloom* (New York: Abrams Image, 2007).

2. Michael Sadgrove rightly comments that "this is the only place in the Song where any attempt is made to probe the meaning of the love that is its theme; everywhere else it is simply described" ("The Song of Songs as Wisdom Literature," *Studia Biblica* [Sheffield, UK: JSOT, 1978], p. 245).

3. E.g., Roland E. Murphy, *The Song of Songs*, Hermeneia (Minneapolis: Fortress, 1990), p. 196; Tom Gledhill, *The Message of the Song of Songs*, The Bible Speaks Today (Downers Grove, IL: InterVarsity, 1994), p. 226; Daniel J. Estes, "Song of Songs," in Daniel C. Fredericks and Daniel J. Estes, *Ecclesiastes and the Song of Songs*, Apollos Old Testament Commentary (Downers Grove, IL: InterVarsity, 2010), p. 407.

4. In 3:6 it is translated "what" instead of "who" because the "what" refers to Solomon's carriage.

5. Douglas Wilson, *Reforming Marriage* (Moscow, ID: Canon, 1995), p. 24.

6. I say "likely" because this phrase is surrounded by "arousal" language (vv. 4b, 5b). What type of "leaning" is she doing? Something erotic? I think this is unlikely but not impossible.

7. See Estes, "Song of Songs," p. 296.

8. Barry G. Webb, *Five Festal Garments: Christian Reflections on the Song of Songs, Ruth, Lamentations, Ecclesiastes, and Esther*, New Studies in Biblical Theology (Downers Grove, IL: InterVarsity, 2000), p. 23.

9. C. S. Lewis, *The Four Loves*, Harcourt Brace Modern Classic (New York: Harcourt Brace & Company, 1988), p. 35.

10. C. S. Lewis, *A Grief Observed* (New York: HarperOne, 1989), p. 37.

11. On the importance of the family in ancient Israel, see Gledhill, *The Message of the Song of Songs*, p. 223; Dennis F. Kinlaw, "Song of Songs," in *Expositor's Bible Commentary*, Vol. 5 (Grand Rapids, MI: Zondervan, 1991), p. 1225.

12. See Estes, "Song of Songs," p. 404.

13. On the significance of "the apple tree," Duane Garrett comments: "It may be that the appearance of the apple tree is significant. A peculiarity of many apple trees is that they appear gnarled and twisted and, especially in winter, have more of an aged look than do many other trees. Nevertheless, they produce luscious fruit that, with its reddish coloration, full and rounded shape, and juicy flesh, seems to be the very image of youth. The branches of the tree fork in many directions; there is nothing linear about an apple tree (in contrast, for example, to the date palm). All of this suggests that the apple tree symbolizes not merely sexuality but sexuality as it continues from generation to generation. The old give birth to the young, and the 'family tree' continues to spread and grow though the years" ("Song of Songs," in Duane Garrett and Paul R. House, *Song of Songs/Lamentations*, Word Biblical Commentary [Nashville: Thomas Nelson, 2004], p. 253).

14. Richard S. Hess, *Song of Songs*, Baker Commentary on the Old Testament Wisdom and Psalms (Grand Rapids, MI: Baker, 2005), p. 237.

15. Gledhill, *The Message of the Song of Songs*, p. 223.

16. On this theme Paul R. House writes: "Permanence is inherent in the canon's statements about marriage. Only death separates Sarah from Abraham (Gen 23:2), Jacob from Rachel (Gen 35:19) or Ezekiel from his wife (Ezek 24:15–18). Even the key divorce text in the Pentateuch, Deuteronomy 24:1–4, treats the dissolution of marriage as a last resort that must be regulated lest the land be defiled. Malachi 2:14–16 states flatly that God hates divorce resulting from treacherous treatment of spouses. Proverbs 5:15–23 at the least implies that the joy one takes in the spouse of one's youth is to last a lifetime, or as long as both lives last" (*Old Testament Theology* [Downers Grove, IL: InterVarsity, 1998], p. 468).

17. Robert W. Jenson, *Song of Songs*, Interpretation (Louisville: John Knox, 2005), p. 90.

18. Gledhill, *The Message of the Song of Songs*, p. 227.

19. We find a similar balance in Deuteronomy 11:13, 18: "And if you will indeed obey my commandments that I command you today, to love the LORD your God, and to serve him with all *your heart* and with all your soul . . . you shall therefore lay up these words of mine in your heart and in your soul, and you shall *bind them as a sign* on your hand, and they shall be as frontlets between your eyes."

20. Synonymous parallelisms are "very seldom precisely synonymous"; that is, the second line "does not simply repeat what has been said, but enriches it, deepens it, transforms it by adding fresh nuances and bringing in new elements," which in turn "renders it more concrete and vivid and telling." James Muilenburg, quoted in Sidney Greidanus, *The Modern Preacher and the Ancient Text: Interpreting and Preaching Biblical Literature* (Grand Rapids, MI: Eerdmans, 1988), p. 62. Robert Alter calls this "focusing" (*Art of Biblical Poetry* [New York: Basic, 1987], pp. 2–26, 62–84). Others also call it "climactic" parallelism. Norman Gottwald labels these three terms as "repeated, contrasted, and advanced" (*Interpreter's Dictionary of the Bible*, Vol. 3 [Nashville: Abingdon, 1976], p. 839).

21. On this theme of jealousy, see K. Erik Thoennes, *Godly Jealousy: A Theology of Intolerant Love* (Fearn, Ross-shire: Mentor, 2005). On jealousy in the Song, see Barry G. Webb, "The Song of Songs: A Love Poem and as Holy Scripture," *Reformed Theological Review*, 49 (1990): p. 98. Also two good summaries are below:

Although there are those who are paranoid about infidelity, neurotically dependent, or wrongly jealous (exemplified in literature by Othello), exclusivity is not of itself corrupt or oppressive. It is wrong, indeed perverse, for the lover to be indifferent to the presence of rivals. Also, jealousy in this context need not refer to the paranoid suspicion that one's lover is faithless. If the jealousy of Yahweh over Israel is the model, the term refers to a proper possessiveness in the setting of a wholesome relationship. (Garrett, "Song of Songs," p. 256)

"Jealousy" (the Hebrew word means "to be inflamed" or "to have violent affection of the mind either for or against someone or something") may be attributed to God (Ex. 20:5), who is sometimes moved with hot indignation when robbed of His honor (Deut. 4:24). Therefore, the concept before us is not that of a carnal and baseless jealousy but of a righteous concern and protective care that is the inevitable posterity of genuine love. (Paige Patterson, *Song of Solomon*, Everyman's Bible Commentary [Chicago: Moody, 1986], p. 116)

22. Perhaps Estes is right: "The expression 'many waters' *(mayim rabbîm)* is often used in the Ug. literature to speak of Yam, the rival of Baal, and in the OT refers to the powers of chaos only Yahweh can control (Gen. 1:2; Ps. 93:4; Isa. 51:10; cf. May 1955: 18; Keel 1994: 276). If this phrase does indeed indicate the forces of chaos, then implicitly Yahweh is presented here as the protector of love, for only he is sufficient to thwart that foe" ("Song of Songs," p. 409).

23. Murphy writes, "Human love has or resembles the flame of divine love; both can be compared in intensity (and perhaps even in origin, in the sense of 1 John 4:7?)" (*The Song of Songs*, p. 197).

24. Tremper Longman III, *Song of Songs*, New International Commentary on the Old Testament (Grand Rapids, MI: Eerdmans, 2001), p. 213.

25. From Robert Browning, "Any Wife to Any Husband":

It would not be because my eye grew dim
Thou couldst not find the love there, thanks to Him
Who never is dishonored in the spark
He gave us from *his fire of fires*, and bade
Remember whence it sprang, nor be afraid
While that burns on, though all the rest grow dark.

26. On page 24 of *Five Festal Garments* Webb explains:

Finally, it can hardly be without significance that it is at this point that we have the only, if veiled, reference in the book of God. Love is the 'flame of Yah' (*šalhebetyáh*). It could be that the abbreviated divine name Yah (=Yahweh) on the end of this word is used simply to indicate a superlative, and it is so taken by the NIV, 'a mighty flame'. But the context speaks against this. 'Yah' is used here in close conjunction with 'jealousy' (*qin'â*) and 'fire' (*'ēš*), both of which are closely associated with Yahweh in Israelite tradition. Furthermore, it is most fitting that there should be an allusion to Yahweh when the poem moves transparency into wisdom mode, since the very first principle of Old Testament wisdom is the fear of Yahweh. More particularly, what is being suggested is that the love depicted here, and hence in the Song as a whole, has its ultimate source in Yahweh, and indeed partakes of his very nature. In keeping with the allusive character of the Song, however, this powerful point is made with exquisite indirectness rather than being forced crudely upon us. The Song is not as secular as at first it appears.

27. Gledhill, *The Message of the Song of Songs*, p. 222.

28. From Peter Washington, ed., *Love Letters*, Everyman's Library Pocket Poets (New York: Knopf, 1996), p. 162.

29. See Roger Nicole, "B. B. Warfield and the Calvinist Revival," in John D. Woodbridge, ed., *Great Leaders of the Christian Church* (Chicago: Moody, 1988), p. 344.

30. This is the last line of John Donne, "Holy Sonnet X." Taken from John Donne, *The Complete English Poems*, Everyman's Library (New York: Knopf, 1991), p. 441.

Chapter Ten: Virginity and Eschatology

1. For the story behind the chaste-chased terminology, see Gary Brady, *Heavenly Love: The Song of Songs Simply Explained*, Welwyn Commentary Series (Darlington, UK: Evangelical, 2006), p. 240.

2. Note that they use wood, not silver or any other expensive material.

3. So argues David A. Hubbard, *Ecclesiastes, Song of Solomon*, The Communicator's Commentary (Dallas: Word, 1991), pp. 344, 345.

4. See Douglas Sean O'Donnell, *The Beginning and End of Wisdom: Preaching Christ from the First and Last Chapters of Proverbs, Ecclesiastes, and Job* (Wheaton, IL: Crossway, 2011), pp. 48–51.

5. In his helpful essay "Preaching Poetry," George L. Klein summarizes five lessons from the Song of Songs. He includes: *"Sexual enjoyment should be reserved for marriage."* But then he adds the disclaimer: "This is not the major theme of the Song, and it would be a mistake to over-moralize here" (*Reclaiming the Prophetic Mantle*, ed. George L. Klein [Nashville: Broadman, 1992], p. 121). I disagree. If the refrain is foundationally moral, then it is not overmoralizing to touch on the theme of the Song's refrain.

6. For example, see Deuteronomy 22:13–21.

7. I am indebted to Duane Garrett for seeing this juxtaposition of imagery ("Song of Songs," in Duane Garrett and Paul R. House, *Song of Songs/Lamentations*, Word Biblical Commentary [Nashville: Thomas Nelson, 2004], p. 263).

8. See Othmar Keel, *Song of Songs*, trans. Frederick J. Gaiser, A Continental Commentary (Minneapolis: Fortress, 1994), p. 282.

9. Hubbard notes: "Solomon's vineyards are several days' journey to the north, if Ibleam (also called Belemoth or Khirbet Balama), a town a few miles south of Megiddo, is the correct site of '*Baal Hamon*,' otherwise unmentioned in the Bible. But the lover's '*vineyard*' is right there before him, available and eager and committed" (*Ecclesiastes, Song of Solomon*, p. 346).

10. Mark Twain, *The Adventures of Huckleberry Finn* (New York: Harper & Brothers, 1899), p. 107.

11. Garrett, "Song of Songs," p. 261.

12. I agree (again!) with Tom Gledhill: "The appearance of *Solomon* here in the Song is a literary device; he is not one of the participating actors in the poem, but appears as a character foil to the girl. He is being 'set up' as a bad example, as the archetypal lecherous plutocrat who thinks that his money has the power to obtain anything he wants. This interpretation hinges on the nature of the girl's words in verse 12, *the thousand shekels are for you, O Solomon*. The view taken here is that they are negative in tone, *i.e.* she is telling *Solomon*, and all those similar types of men he represents, that money is powerless to buy love and allegiance. She can have nothing to do with such commerce; she cannot be bribed, seduced or hired. Her message is identical to that of 8:7, 'If one were to give all the wealth of his house

for love, it would be utterly scorned'" (*The Message of the Song of Songs*, The Bible Speaks Today [Downers Grove, IL: InterVarsity, 1994], p. 238).

13. "Paradoxically, the more women Solomon has, the less deeply personal and fulfilling can be his relationship with any one of them." Barry G. Webb, *Five Festal Garments: Christian Reflections on the Song of Songs, Ruth, Lamentations, Ecclesiastes, and Esther*, New Studies in Biblical Theology (Downers Grove, IL: InterVarsity, 2000), p. 27.

14. Keel, *Song of Songs*, p. 282.

15. Gledhill, *The Message of the Song of Songs*, p. 239.

16. Garrett, "Song of Songs," p. 261.

17. See Christopher W. Mitchell, *The Song of Songs: A Theological Exposition of Sacred Scripture*, Concordia Commentary (St. Louis: Concordia, 2003), p. 1278.

18. Garrett, "Song of Songs," p. 265.

19. William J. Dumbrell is one of many scholars who notes this: "The sequences—lover separated, expression of desire, lovers united—are used throughout the book as the pattern of all the cycles, except the last" (*The Faith of Israel: A Theological Survey of the Old Testament,* 2nd ed. [Grand Rapids, MI: Baker, 2002], p. 279).

20. Martin Luther put it this way: "This canticle [ends by] look[ing] forward to the spiritual kingdom of Christ." Martin Luther, "Lecture on the Song of Solomon: A Brief but Altogether Lucid Commentary of the Song of Songs," trans. Ian Siggins, *Luther's Works*, 56 vols. (St. Louis: Concordia, 1972), 15:259.

21. Tremper Longman III similarly notes: "It honestly seems an odd way to end a poem; we might expect that the conclusion would bring complete and unbreakable intimacy. Perhaps, however, this better expresses love in the real world. We yearn and hope and occasionally get glimpses of a deep and satisfying relationship, but complete union is reserved not for this world but for the eschaton" (*Song of Songs*, New International Commentary on the Old Testament [Grand Rapids, MI: Eerdmans, 2001], p. 220).

22. Concerning 1:2–4 John Updike writes that the urgency of the opening cry "anticipates that last utterance of the New Testament, in Revelation: 'Surely I come quickly. Amen. Even so, come, Lord Jesus.' The yearning for love fills the cosmos." From John Updike's "Foreword" in Lawrence Boadt, ed., *The Song of Solomon: Love Poetry of the Spirit* (New York: St. Martin's, 1999), p. 9.

Scripture Index

General Index

Index of Sermon Illustrations

Christ-figure but simply as a talking lion, and in the same way knowing the story of Jesus opens up the true meaning of the Song, 22

Filmmaker Sam Goldwyn said, "for a successful film you need to start with an earthquake and then work up to the climax!" and the Song is an earthquake of eros, 28

Temptation
Paul House: "Satisfaction with one's long-term love will negate succumbing to short-term surrender to temptation," 107

Virginity
Well-taught daughter tells her mother, "Mom, I really like him. And he really likes me. And when I tell him I'm not going to bed with him, he will really like me," 123

The Word of God
David Suchet, star of the British TV series *Poirot*, reads Romans 8 in a Gideon Bible in a hotel room and comes to know Christ, 73–74

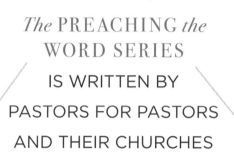